The Abundant Life

Daily Devotions through the Year

Dianne Krenz

CPH
SAINT LOUIS

Copyright © 1998 Concordia Publishing House
3558 S. Jefferson Avenue, St. Louis, MO 63118-3968
Manufactured in the United States of America

Library of Congress Cataloging-in-Publication Data

Krenz, Dianne, 1942-
    The abundant life : daily devotions through the year / Dianne Krenz.
        p.   cm.
    ISBN 0-570-05322-6
    1. Meditations. 2. Lutheran Church—Prayer-books and devotions—English. 3. Devotional calendars. I. Title.
BV4811.K74   1988
242'.2—dc21   98-13253
                                                                    CIP

2   3   4   5   6   7   8   9   10   07   06   05   04   03   02   01   00   99   98

The Abundant Life

I came that they may have life, and have it abundantly. John 10:10 RSV

To live abundantly takes on new meaning when one becomes a Christian. While living His life on earth, our Lord was interested in helping people reach their full potential. His loving eyes always saw in each life not only the sordid details of what that person was but also what the person could be. This is still true for us today.

In one of the few verses of Scripture describing Jesus' childhood, Luke tells us that Jesus increased in wisdom and in stature and in favor with God and man. The abundant life that Jesus wants us to have encompasses all of these aspects of life.

The Christian's abundant life is a fourfold experience of being alive physically, spiritually, mentally, and socially. We have been given bodies and minds to help us to be alive and to live abundantly in our relationship with God and our fellow human beings. All these aspects of life for the Christian are interrelated, joining together to make a full, overflowing aliveness that can best be described as the abundant life. Jesus is the way, the truth, and the life. He came that we might have life and have it in abundance. He laid down His life on the cross to give us life in the fullest sense—purposeful life here and everlasting life in heaven.

Lord, show us how to live abundantly to Your honor and glory; in Jesus' name. Amen.

Harold Midtbo

1 John 4:7–21

Unspeakable Love!

I have loved thee with an everlasting love; therefore with lov-ing-kindness have I drawn thee. *Jeremiah 31:3 KJV*

God is the absolute center of all that exists. All nature and all created things revolve around Him. He is also the center of all His people, who form a wide circle around Him. His purpose is to draw them to Himself, their center, in eternal life.

"I have loved thee with an everlasting love" means that God loved us and planned our salvation even before the world was created, when we were but thoughts in the creative mind of God. Amazing condescension! Unspeakable love!

"With loving-kindness have I drawn thee" tells us that His love was first expressed in the kindness of our creation and con-tinued care. But it is most beautifully expressed in the kindness of our salvation. What loving-kindness this is: "God so loved the world that He gave His one and only Son, that whoever believes in Him shall not perish but have eternal life" (John 3:16). Wonderful love, indeed!

Looking beyond His cross to His throne, Jesus promised: "But I, when I am lifted up from the earth, will draw all men to Myself" (John 12:32). He drew us through Baptism and by His Word. He continues to draw us through the preaching and teaching of His pure Gospel message. At the last He will draw us to Himself in heaven and give us a crown of life.

Drawn to Your cross, O Lord, may we walk in Your footsteps here and enjoy the warmth of Your loving-kindness in heaven; through Jesus Christ, our Lord. Amen.

Carl H. Harman

Joshua 1:1–9

Prepared for an Adventure

Do not be discouraged, for the LORD your God will be with you wherever you go. *Joshua 1:9*

Exploring the unknown can be an adventure. To be asked to lead a nation of many thousands was a great challenge for Joshua. God set a great adventure before him when He chose Joshua to lead the people of Israel from the wilderness into the land of Canaan.

At first Joshua wondered whether he could handle the job. So God encouraged this servant who would succeed Moses: "Be strong and courageous. Do not be terrified; do not be discouraged, for the LORD your God will be with you wherever you go." The days ahead would be filled with anxiety and uncertainty. The task was tremendous, yet God assured Joshua, as He assures us: "The LORD your God will be with you wherever you go."

Putting our trust in the Lord, we can go on our way unafraid. He promises strength when strength is needed. He gives courage when courage is needed. He confirms our faith in Jesus, our Savior. His power and His presence in His Word and sacraments support us as we face the unborn tomorrow of opportunity and challenge. We don't know what God may require of us in our future. But whatever He requires, we will be able to perform because He will be with us always.

Speak a word of encouragement to us, Lord Jesus, as we face the uncharted waters of our future. Amen.

Henry C. Lubben

Ecclesiastes 3:1–14

Time: A Gift from God

But seek first His kingdom and His righteousness, and all these things will be given to you as well. *Matthew 6:33*

One of the gifts God has given us is time. Time is something that passes inevitably. We can fritter it away, muttering about how time flies, or we can see today as a day of new possibilities, using our time to give God His rightful place in our thinking, doing, and all of living. The life we have is our allotted time. We are to use it to "seek first His kingdom and His righteousness." Faith in Christ drives out anxiety about our daily needs and replaces worry with confidence that "all these things will be given" to us.

Time is the stuff life is made of. Yet we often fail to see time as a precious gift from God. It often becomes "my time"—time that we use, abuse, fill, or waste. We suffocate it with worry or let it fly by, filled only with fantasy about what we could do.

God's Word tells us there is a time for every purpose under heaven. A Christian's purpose is to make the most of each day, seeking opportunities to serve our living God.

Lord God, give me the wisdom to spend my time in worthwhile things; in Jesus' name. Amen.

William Wagner

Matthew 5:38–48

Conformity

Do not conform any longer to the pattern of this world.
Romans 12:2

Are you a conformist or a nonconformist? Most of us are accused of conforming to the ways and ideas of the people with whom we associate. As human beings we do not like to be different. Conformity is not always bad. Nonconformity just to be different can indicate complete self-centeredness and can be obnoxious. On the other hand, conformity can at times be sinful. We dare not go along with the crowd when it is doing something wrong. We can't sin to be one of the group.

God does not want us to be foolishly different or isolated from other people, but He does expect us to refuse to conform to what is against His will. The sinful world will constantly tempt us to forget God and go along with evil. Phillips translates Romans 12:2 like this: "Don't let the world around you squeeze you into its own mould." We need courage to stand firm and say "No!" to what we know is wrong in God's sight.

Where can we get this strength? Phillips continues: "But let God remake you so that your whole attitude of mind is changed. Thus you will prove in practice that the will of God [is] good." We need to be filled with the strength of God's Spirit. Sustained by His Word and remembering His mercy in Christ, we will find the power to resist conforming to this world.

Heavenly Father, empower us through Your Word and Sacrament so we may courageously live as Your people; for the sake of Jesus Christ, our Lord. Amen.

Oswald C. J. Hoffmann

Exodus 33:7–11

Loyal Friend

The LORD would speak to Moses face to face, as a man speaks with his friend. *Exodus 33:11*

How many friends have I had through the years? Really loyal friends are few. Keeping friends is difficult. How blessed is the one who has true friends!

A loyal and trusted confidant, Joshua must have been a great comfort to Moses. He could lend a sympathetic ear as Moses unburdened his heart under the pressures of his office. Joshua was a kindred soul with whom Moses could share the privileged moments of communion with God.

We should value highly God's gift of good friends. Luther numbered "good friends" among the temporal blessings a gracious Lord bestows on us. Good friends reduce our sorrows and multiply our joys by sharing both with us.

God Himself was the best friend Moses ever had. God spoke with him face to face. He chose Moses to represent Him before Israel. He supplied Moses with fitness and the courage to work at a monumental task. Above all, God loved and forgave Moses, the sinner.

God also befriends us. "Greater love has no one than this, that he lay down his life for his friends" (John 15:13). God revealed His great love to us in giving His Son, Jesus, who in love for us endured utter friendlessness on the cross so we might enjoy God's peace and friendship eternally.

Jesus, friend of sinners, bind us together in friendship with You and with one another. Amen.

Norbert W. Meyer

Genesis 1:26–28

"Off to Work I Go"

A man can do nothing better than to eat and drink and find satisfaction in his work. *Ecclesiastes 2:24*

Somehow Sunday has become separated from the rest of the week. We enter our churches, hear the powerful Word of God, receive the true body and true blood of our Lord in Holy Communion, and then wander out into the world, somehow feeling that the next six days are unimportant to God or not part of our following Him. Nothing could be further from the truth!

Our weekday role is an opportunity to serve God. God ordained work. He placed Adam and Eve into the Garden of Eden. They were not to be idle but were to be the caretakers of His creation.

The place you spend your week is the place where you are to be God's child, serving in the name of the Lord Jesus Christ. If at times you do not enjoy your work, then perhaps you have forgotten for whom you really work and need to be reminded of what St. Paul said: "Whatever you do, work at it with all your heart, as working for the Lord and not for men" (Colossians 3:23).

What a blessing work is! It is our opportunity to serve God as His children, restored to Him through the death and resurrection of Jesus Christ, whose work is the salvation of the world.

Father, may I always labor in the service of Jesus Christ, Your Son and my Lord. Amen.

Bruce W. Biesenthal

John 1:6–9

His Witnesses

You will receive power when the Holy Spirit comes on you; and you will be My witnesses in Jerusalem, and in all Judea and Samaria, and to the ends of the earth. *Acts 1:8*

Have you ever asked yourself, "Why am I here?" Many people today are asking that question. The search for an answer leads many to a Pandora's box of philosophies and religions. But there is only one answer that is true: We have been placed here to praise God and to be witnesses of Jesus Christ. There is no greater calling in life than to share the love of God with people. We are not an accident of evolution; we are individuals brought into being by our triune God that we might love Him and praise Him forever.

While we are here on earth, our primary purpose, according to God's plan for our lives, is to remind people of sin and to reveal the love and forgiveness of God for all people in Jesus Christ. We bring eternal comfort into the lives of others when we proclaim that Christ died to pay for their sins so they might be with Him in paradise someday. Our life in Christ is not an aimless drift into oblivion but a fulfillment of the purpose for which Christ has called us to be His own.

Lord Jesus, by the power of Your Spirit, help us tell others of Your love by both our words and our actions. Amen.

William R. A. Ney

1 Peter 1:3–9

Every Sunday—Glory

One thing I ask of the LORD … that I may dwell in the house of the LORD all the days of my life, to gaze upon the beauty of the Lord. *Psalm 27:4*

When the Romans built a wall across northern England, they placed a tower at intervals of every mile. These towers provided elevated points where sentinels could stand and watch. When God built the battlements of the Christian life, He placed at every seventh day a day that is thrust above life's common level for the safeguarding of our souls. On that day we behold the Lord's beauty.

Why do we go to church? Whatever our answer, the motive ought to be to see the beauty of the Lord. There should be more than custom, sentiment, routine, or any human factor to turn the steps of men, women, and children toward the church on the Lord's day. There ought to be the deep, unspoken hope that we will have contact with God and see His beauty.

No one can live by bread alone. We need God. When the morning of the Lord's Day brings us to the place of worship, we ought to say, as did the Greeks to Philip (John 12:21): "Sir, we would see Jesus." We ought to say this because one day we shall actually see Him face to face. So we desire to see Him now by faith. Through His Word and sacraments, He communes with us.

God the Father, maker of heaven and earth, open our hearts to the Word that reveals to us the glory of Your Son. Amen.

Arnold G. Kuntz

1 John 4:1–6

Faith Is Not Feelings

Jesus told the synagogue ruler, "Don't be afraid; just believe."
Mark 5:36

Sometimes we mistake feelings for faith and a change in feelings for loss of faith. Faith is not feelings. Feelings or emotions change with every moment's experiences. Faith endures the ups and downs of life with the conviction that God is still faithful and can be trusted. It is easy to confuse faith and feelings, but feelings are more fickle than faith. Fine weather, a compliment, an encouraging bit of news—all of these can make us feel good, but they are not what faith is made of. Faith is trust in Jesus Christ. It is a matter of conviction even when feelings about other things change.

Perhaps we are too much influenced by TV and movies and the way our entertainment culture plays with our emotions. Perhaps our retained childishness leads us to consider everything that "feels good" to be truly good. Perhaps our deceptive sinful nature tests our convictions on the basis of how we feel rather than on what God has done for us in Jesus Christ on the cross. Our Lord Jesus Christ did not "feel" good about His death while in Gethsemane, but He trusted His Father's good and gracious will and was faithful to His mission on earth. We can trust Him no matter how we feel.

Lord, help me see beyond feelings so I can trust You regardless of how I feel; in Jesus' name. Amen.

Richard C. Eyer

Ephesians 1:17–21

The Gift of Mind and Memory

I remember the days of long ago, I meditate on all Your works. *Psalm 143:5*

Would you like to see a walking, talking miracle? Look in your mirror. What you see is a person who cannot only walk and talk but can also think and learn and remember and reason and do many other remarkable things—all because God has given you a most amazing gift: your mind.

"It boggles your mind," we say when reading about those high-tech super computers that can process millions of bits of data, store them, and retrieve them in mere fractions of seconds. We easily overlook that our own mind out boggles any electronics that science can produce. The way our mind can recapture our past surpasses wonder, as when a snatch of music or a glimpse of a photo can carry us back to another place and time and special people. How faith-reviving when memory takes us back to times and occasions when God's presence was felt and His abiding love was impressed upon us!

When memory turns into a cruel tormentor with thoughts of guilt and remorse over past sins, how wonderful to have the Spirit remind us, "The blood of Jesus, His Son, purifies us from all sin" (1 John 1:7). "Therefore, there is now no condemnation for those who are in Christ Jesus" (Romans 8:1).

Thank You for Your gifts of mind and memory, dear Lord. By Your Holy Spirit continue to use them for upbuilding our faith and life; for Jesus' sake. Amen.

Albert W. Galen

2 Corinthians 10:12–18

Christian First, Athlete Second

May I never boast except in the cross of our Lord Jesus Christ. *Galatians 6:14*

Can we, like the apostle Paul, be more proud of our God-given Christian faith than any of our accomplishments? A top professional football player once gave a beautiful testimony of his Christian faith: "I like to think of myself as a Christian, who just happens to be a football player." How easily we invert the order! We are known first by our profession, our job, or our achievements in this or that field, and, oh, yes, we happen to be Christians too.

The apostle Paul and the football player were proud of their Savior first and foremost. Their own achievements were only incidental. It was the cross of Christ, symbolizing His sacrificial death for their sins and assuring them of eternal life, that gave them cause for rejoicing. Not of themselves, but of Him did they boast.

This is a worthy goal for all of us—to be known and seen first of all as followers of Christ, then as persons who were enabled to accomplish less important things as well. The cross of Christ is our proudest achievement, which we ourselves did not achieve! Salvation is a gift of God through Christ, who died for us on the cross. Of Him we boast.

Heavenly Father, let the cross of Christ be so precious to us that we boast of nothing else; for Jesus' sake. Amen.

Norbert V. Becker

John 3:16–21

Smart Love

This is my prayer: that your love may abound more and more in knowledge and depth of insight. *Philippians 1:9*

Intelligent love, or "smart love," flows out of the knowledge of God's love for us sinners. The next step is to work earnestly at knowing the person who is loved. That's what Paul means when he says we should love with "knowledge and depth of insight."

So often we think that if we love someone we will automatically do the right thing for that person. It just isn't so. Thousands of marriages and families are in shambles because the people involved didn't get to know more deeply those whom they love.

"Smart love" grows out of an experience of the love of God in our own lives, and it then depends on truly getting to know the persons we love. Knowing when to say something and when to be quiet—that's part of intelligent love. So is knowing when to do something and when not to do it or when to pull away entirely for a while and pray for someone you love.

We look to Jesus, the author and finisher of our faith and its fruits, to strengthen, enrich, and guide our love with His gift of wisdom.

Lord, give us strength and depth of insight to perform the duties of love You expect from us; in Jesus' name we pray. Amen.

Frederick C. Hinz

Working

Whatever you do, work at it with all your heart, as working for the Lord, not for men. *Colossians 3:23*

For many people work is drudgery. Their feelings about work are mostly negative and their attitudes toward those for whom they work are anything but positive. For such St. Paul has good advice. When you work, give it your all. And think of work as service done for God, not others. That's bound to improve your view of work.

Christians work to give God glory. That's a revolutionary notion. It puts a positive twist on the "labor of our hands." If such an attitude were translated into labor-management relations, things might improve decidedly. Both managers and laborers might be more concerned with what they put into their work as opposed to what they get out of it.

In Paul's day, working conditions for the common laborer were worse, if anything, than they are today. Workers in Colosse must have been astounded by Paul's advice. But if they thought it through, or better, tried it Paul's way, putting their whole heart into their labor and thinking of it as something done for and dedicated to their God, they soon discovered what a difference such an attitude makes.

Work always as if you are working for the Lord.

Dear Lord, brighten my daily work by receiving it as a tribute to Your love and goodness; for Jesus' sake. Amen.

Leland Stevens

Acts 1:1–11

Be a Missionary!

You will receive power when the Holy Spirit comes on you; and you will be my witnesses in Jerusalem, and in all Judea and Samaria, and to the ends of the earth. *Acts 1:8*

Picture in your mind a large pond. Now also picture a rock in your hand. Throw the rock into the middle of the pond, and watch what happens. Circular waves radiate from the point of impact. Now read again Acts 1:8. The world is the pond, and Jesus Himself is the rock. From Him, the disciples spread the Gospel in ever-widening circles throughout the world.

The Holy Spirit gave power to the disciples to preach the Good News of Jesus Christ, crucified for the sin of all and risen as victorious Lord. The Spirit empowers all Christians through God's Word and the sacraments of Baptism and Holy Communion to be Christ's witnesses. Every heart without Christ is a mission field. Every heart with Christ is a missionary.

We are called to be our Lord's heralds and to share the good news of God's love with our world. Our hearts are like Jerusalem, the starting place. Once the impact of the Gospel touches our hearts, God's love and power radiate through our words and actions to our surrounding world.

The Holy Spirit gives us the ability to believe and to proclaim the message of Christ. You are a missionary for Jesus!

Lord Jesus, by the Spirit's power we believe and share Your Word. Open our eyes to all opportunities to glorify You. Amen.

A. Leroy Gerner

Psalm 122

A House of Prayer

I will pray with my spirit, but I will also pray with my mind; I will sing with my spirit, but I will also sing with my mind. *1 Corinthians 14:15*

Today we meet God in the quiet of His house. There we bow our heads and pray. We unite our voices with those of fellow Christians in singing hymns. But there is more than greets the eye and the ear. There our hearts reach out to the heart of God.

Ours, however, is not a groping toward some vague unseen presence whom we call the Supreme Being or great architect of the universe. We pray and sing with an understanding born of the Word of God. We worship God the Father, who has made us, God the Son, who has redeemed us through His precious blood, and God the Holy Spirit, who has called us by the Gospel and enlightened us with His gifts. We pray to the triune God, who is not a prisoner within the laws of nature but "able to do immeasurably more than all we ask or imagine" (Ephesians 3:20).

In His presence burdens are lifted from our shoulders—burdens of sin, worry, and fear. Peace comes into our hearts, His peace that passes all understanding. He in His own wise and loving way fulfills His promises to all who call on His name. With prayerful spirit and mind we listen as He speaks to us through His ambassador, our pastor.

Heavenly Father, we come into Your presence with awe and thanksgiving. Help us hear Your voice and the salvation story with great joy; through Jesus Christ, our Lord. Amen.

Charles A. Behnke

Mark 1:35–39

Dealing with Stress

I can do everything through Him who gives me strength.
Philippians 4:13

Everyone experiences tension or pressure. At least two-thirds of all medical visits are for stress-related illnesses. The best way to manage stress is to nourish faith in our loving God. In His love God did not spare His own Son but gave Him up for us all. This is proof that He really cares for us.

God is almighty. He can enable us to meet every situation. When we believe this from the depths of our being and make it a habit to turn to Him for strength and direction, we are better prepared for any crisis or degree of stress.

As we let God's principles guide us, we learn to give thanks in all circumstances and to put the best construction on what others say and do. It is better to show forgiving love and understanding about a broken window, burned toast, or a dented fender than to explode with anger.

Let us develop a strong relationship with family, friends, and neighbors. God uses them to give support. We can relieve stress by taking control of our time. We may leave a little earlier to be on time for an appointment. If we expect a long wait, we may take along some inspirational reading. Practicing our faith and using common sense help us deal with stress.

Lord God, source of all strength, we can do all things in You; in Jesus' name. Amen.

Herbert M. Kern

Ephesians 5:15–20

Live Now

Be very careful, then, how you live—not as unwise but as wise, making the most of every opportunity. *Ephesians 5:15–16*

Sometimes people say, "I have an hour to kill." Time is not an enemy to destroy. It's a gift to treasure and use. Time is among our most precious earthly possessions. What good are money, job, or family if we have no time? The apostle encourages us to make "the most of every opportunity."

Jesus teaches us to be selective. His public career lasted not much more than 1,000 days. He did not teach and heal all the time. He slept and rested like others. Yet when His earthly life was over, He prayed to His Father, "I have brought You glory on earth by completing the work You gave Me to do" (John 17:4). Jesus was concerned about doing His Father's will to live and die and rise again as the deliverer from sin and its eternal effects, mainly death.

Let us, like Jesus, concentrate on doing our Father's will. Let us plan our time and organize our activities to make time for God and take time for people. Let us make wise use of little moments of time that are otherwise wasted.

On Judgment Day we will be asked to give an account of our life to the Lord. May He say to each of us, "Well done, good and faithful servant!" (Matthew 25:21).

Eternal God, help us use today to the full, bringing glory to You; in Jesus' name. Amen.

Herbert M. Kern

Acts 17:24–28

The Maker's Guide

This God is our God for ever and ever; He will be our guide even to the end. *Psalm 48:14*

You buy an item and bring it home. But first it needs to be assembled. You can fumble around with screwdriver and wrench, trying to get all the pieces together properly. Or you can follow the manufacturer's directions.

Isn't that the way it is with so much of life? Sensible people get directions before doing things. They follow guidelines prepared by people who already know the way. They learn from others' information and insight.

How much more important it is for us to follow the guidelines for life itself! The best directions we have come from our maker, God Himself. Through His Word, God gives us this command: "Love the Lord your God with all your heart and with all your soul and with all your strength" (Deuteronomy 6:5); "Love your neighbor as yourself" (Luke 10:27). Jesus' life is an example for us to imitate. And when we fail to meet His standard, we are forgiven for Jesus' sake.

When we are faced with a particular situation, we can ask, "What did Jesus do?" We can also pray, "Lord, guide me. Show me what You want me to do. Help me make wise use of my time, money, and talent." God directs. Let us be willing to follow.

Lord Jesus, You died in our place that we may live in Your presence forever. Give us courage to follow Your guidelines for living this life. Amen.

Herbert and Alma Kern

Romans 7:7–25

Forgiving and Forgetting

You will again have compassion on us; You will tread our sins underfoot and hurl all our iniquities into the depths of the sea. *Micah 7:19*

"Forgive and forget" are nice words and sound advice, though a lot easier said than done. At times we seem to be able to muster enough love to say, "I forgive you." The forgetting, however, may be just about impossible. When a certain word is said, our memory goes into "instant recall." We want to get even by extracting as much pain as the other person has caused us.

Then we look at the other side of the coin. All of us say and do things we later regret. All of us hurt those we love the most, then assume we do not have to seek forgiveness because, after all, they should understand. We say we love the Lord Jesus, but we ignore His teaching. We say we love God, but we do not obey His Word. We pray to Him, but we shudder for fear that He will not approve of what He sees us doing.

Yet God does not give up on us. He reconciles us to Himself by washing us in the blood of His Son. He daily renews His promise to tread our sins underfoot and throw them into the depths of the sea, from where they cannot return to haunt us or accuse us. Perhaps we find it hard to forgive and forget, but God can—and does—for Jesus' sake!

Thank You, Lord God, for forgiving and forgetting my sin because of what Jesus has done for me; in His name I pray. Amen.

Carlos H. Puig

Luke 10:25–37

Caring

Go and do likewise. *Luke 10:37*

The story from which our text is taken, the parable of the Good Samaritan, tells us a lot about caring.

It is sometimes true that those who need our care are themselves to blame for their need. Perhaps it's hard for us to generate much care for people who have made a mess of their life.

Some of us act like the priest in Luke 10, who demonstrates that not everyone who worships God hears His call to help others. Then there is the Levite, so focused on taking his turn in leading the service in the temple that he was not motivated to take his turn in service to the man in need at the side of the road.

Enter the Samaritan. We note two things about this man, himself the victim of the prejudices of his day. First, he was ready and willing to help. Second, his credit was good. The innkeeper trusted him to pay the victim's bill.

The lesson is clear. Everyone who is in need is our neighbor. Feeling sorry for people less fortunate than we are is not enough. People bringing trouble on themselves is no reason for us to hold back our care and our assistance. God has heard our cry for mercy, though our need for it is our own doing and failure. And we are to hear and heed the cry for mercy of everyone in need.

Dearest Jesus, I want Your "go and do likewise" to guide my actions daily. Amen.

Leland Stevens

Numbers 12:1–8

Sketch of Similarities

With him [Moses] I speak face to face, clearly and not in riddles. *Numbers 12:8*

God chose Moses long before this leader was conscious of God's plan for him. God promised to be with him, and He doubled that promise by fitting him for his every task.

Moses was privileged to spend much time in God's presence. He ascended the Mount of God and walked right into His presence. He listened while God spoke to him "face to face, clearly," and in turn Moses pleaded the cause and needs of his people through fervent prayer, again in God's presence.

And so it is with us. God chose us to be His very own: "I have called you by name, you are Mine" (Isaiah 43:1 RSV). We too have spent many days and nights talking with God in prayer. It has not been a one-way conversation because God also spoke to us in His Word, the Bible, both at church and in the privacy of our home.

We think of Moses' position of leadership as unique, but really it wasn't much different from ours. We are called to lead our family circle or circle of friends and neighbors through the wilderness of daily challenges and momentary setbacks to the promised land of heaven's mansions. God is with us and does fit us for our task!

Lord God, we thank You for having spoken clearly to us in Your Word and for leading us through the daily challenges to the promised land; through Jesus Christ, our Lord. Amen.

Bernard H. Arkebauer

Luke 11:1–13

Read My Mind

We do not know what we ought to pray for, but the Spirit Himself intercedes for us with groans that words cannot express. *Romans 8:26*

"She can read my mind," the husband says of his wife as she provides for a need before he asks. Two people have become so understanding and intimate that they know each other's needs and wishes without naming them.

This describes our relationship to God by the power and presence of the Holy Spirit. The Spirit works on our behalf a relationship of total intimacy with the Father so our unspoken prayers are before the Father's throne even before we speak them, or even before we are aware of our needs. In ways that cannot be known, "with groans that words cannot express," the Spirit brings before the throne of a gracious and merciful God all our cares and concerns.

The prayers we offer, imperfect and jumbled, are presented before God in perfect order and making perfect sense. Our shortsightedness is eliminated; our self-centeredness is erased; our faith is presented full and clear. We can pray with confidence, knowing the Holy Spirit will present our prayers before God with the clarity and the respect we desire to show Him.

O Spirit, present before God our earnest prayers and praise; through our Lord Jesus Christ. Amen.

Paul J. Albers

Philippians 3:7–11

Examples to Follow

Follow my example, as I follow the example of Christ.
1 *Corinthians 11:1*

When a coach sets out to teach his team how to master a certain sport, he will usually demonstrate the different actions and plays to the players. He may point out some stars of the game and encourage the players to study their form and way of playing and try to pattern themselves after them. Often the coach will have a more experienced player show how it is done. Then, after the best possible instruction has been given, each player must get in the game and work at it. It takes example, instruction, practice, and more practice to learn the game.

In a deeper sense the Holy Spirit seeks through God's Word to coach us in the contest of life. Every believer in Christ will want to master the task of being a child of God and will welcome the aid and instruction of the Holy Spirit. Here too our "Coach" encourages us to study the greatest example of all, the life of our Lord.

Also He urges us to look closely at the lives of outstanding followers of Christ, the great men and women of faith, that we might learn from them. Finally He invites us into the fellowship of the church, where He provides examples of experienced Christians who can help us by advice and example better to play the game of life according to the rules of God.

O God, help us to become better followers of Christ through the example of others. Strengthen us in our efforts; for Jesus' sake. Amen.

T. A. Weinhold

1 Kings 21:1–16

Envy

Let us not become conceited, provoking and envying each other. *Galatians 5:26*

The apostle Paul in his great hymn of love (1 Corinthians 13) reminds us that Christian love does not envy. Such love does not become discontented at another's good fortune.

God has blessed each of us with material blessings. He has also blessed our neighbor. We can obtain our neighbor's possessions through purchase, barter, inheritance, or other ways that are pleasing to God. If we cannot obtain them "fair and square," we should not try to get them "by hook and by crook." God wants us to be content with the things He gives us and to be happy about our neighbor's good fortune.

We need to fight against envy. There is no reason for any of us to become envious. God has been good to us without any merit or worthiness of our own. With Jacob we must confess: "I am unworthy of all the kindness and faithfulness You have shown Your servant" (Genesis 32:10).

Only by God's grace are we the beneficiaries of His love in Christ. He has given us the gift of salvation for time and eternity. Far from envying anyone, we thank God for His undeserved blessings on us and those we love.

Thank You, Lord Jesus, for all Your gifts of love to me and my neighbor. Amen.

Andrew Simcak Jr.

Philippians 1:7–8

'Failure' Is Not Always Failure

What has happened to me has really served to advance the gospel. *Philippians 1:12*

Sir Winston Churchill failed twice to achieve an elected office during the early 1920s and had little political influence through the 1930s. But he continued to develop his talents, and in 1940 he became prime minister of England. Today he is regarded as a hero.

The apostle Paul had planned to go to Rome to preach the Gospel, but he was taken there as a prisoner instead. It looked as if he had failed. But in his cell he penned some of his outstanding epistles. He made many contacts. That is why he could write to the Philippians that everything had turned out for the advancement of the Gospel.

When our carefully laid plans fizzle, let's not give up. If we discover that we have blundered, we can correct our mistakes. If we have failed because of circumstances beyond our control, let's ask God to teach us what He wants us to learn, and let's trust more fully in His grace in Christ, who has accomplished our salvation and who would use us to pass on that good news to others.

"Success is failure turned inside out, The silver tint of clouds of doubt, So stick to the fight when hardest hit: It's when things seem worst that you must not quit" (Anonymous).

Lord Jesus, keep us faithful at all times. Amen.

Dennis A. Kastens

Proverbs 5:1–23

Sex—God's Gift

It is God's will that you should be sanctified: that you should avoid sexual immorality. *1 Thessalonians 4:3*

Thessalonica sounds a lot like our modern world. Apparently one of the greatest games to play was sex—just enjoy it anyway you can! Today's sexual attitudes befuddle us.

Do we forget that God created sex as a special gift for Adam and Eve? that the Bible actually celebrates human sexuality? Read the Song of Songs again. God intends for us to enjoy our sexuality. He uses marriage as a way to describe the deep forgiving love He has for us in Christ (Ephesians 5). Because He created sex, He knows best how it should be used so it will bless our lives. He sets the rules for us to follow, and those rules say clearly that sex is no game for us to play. It is a rich gift to be enjoyed between a man and a woman in their life of wedded love—to sustain them through years of marriage, enabling them to grow in love and understanding one for the other and to build a healthy family life on which society can become strong and secure.

That's not the popular view of sex in our world, but it's God's view, and He expects it to be the view of all who claim to follow Him.

Lord, thank You for Your gift of sexuality. Enable us to use it to bless our marriages and families according to Your will; for Jesus' sake. Amen.

Unknown

James 1:22–27

Busy Hands

Lazy hands make a man poor, but diligent hands bring wealth. *Proverbs 10:4*

God gave us hands to work for Him. Our verse today says it well, "Lazy hands make a man poor, but diligent hands bring wealth." Not hands for selfish gain like the man who built bigger barns, but hands for faithful stewardship of God's resources.

How easy for us to sit back and watch television, extend coffee breaks, and work halfheartedly. How prone we are to fill pews but never to do anything as a result. James questions such inactivity: "Do not merely listen to the word, and so deceive yourselves. Do what it says" (James 1:22). Busy hands are needed to work and to help those in need.

Because Jesus Christ's hands were pierced for us and our hands were made clean by His shed blood, we offer Him our hands for His tasks. With praying hands we seek His will and His strength. From His open hands we receive both the opportunities and the ability to be busy. At home with dishes and laundry; at work with wrench, computer, and assembly line; in our community with food basket, paintbrush, and snow shovel, we lend our busy hands to the ongoing opportunities for service.

Lord, forgive us for idleness. By Your death on the cross, empower us with busy hands in Your service. Amen.

Stephen J. Carter

Romans 10:14–17

Ears for Hearing

Blessed are your eyes because they see, and your ears because they hear. *Matthew 13:16*

After the apostles died, how did Christianity spread? Domestic servants spoke the Good News in homes where they worked. Shopkeepers shared it with their customers. Housewives spoke it to others across rooftops in the cool of the evening. Children did the same as they played together. That's how Christianity conquered the Roman Empire.

With our eyes we look for opportunities to present Jesus Christ. Our mouths are for confessing the Christian faith. Our ears are for hearing the Gospel and listening sympathetically to others. When we confess what we believe about Jesus Christ, someone else's ears are open to hearing the message—the Good News of Jesus Christ.

We may make excuses. When told to speak to Pharaoh, Moses complained that he had a speech impediment. Jeremiah excused himself by saying he was too young to be a prophet. Isaiah said, "Woe to me! I am ruined! For I am a man of unclean lips" (Isaiah 6:5). Jonah took a boat to go the opposite direction from Nineveh.

Yet touched by the Spirit of God, these men spoke the Word of God. We too can proclaim the Good News to waiting ears. The Gospel is for hearing.

Lord God, here am I. Send me to speak of Jesus; in His name. Amen.

Charles R. Birner

Philippians 2:1–11

All Arrows on Target

Your attitude should be the same as that of Christ Jesus.
Philippians 2:5

All who belong to Christ belong to each other. We have "one Lord, one faith, one baptism; one God and Father of all" (Ephesians 4:5–6).

God has not given each of us our own island to run. He has placed us into community. "You stand firm in one spirit, with one mind striving side by side for the faith of the gospel" (Philippians 1:27 RSV). One helps another in life's struggles.

This is the way we express our oneness of mind and purpose: (1) We walk together under God's Word. We strive to advance Christ's church in knowledge, in love of the truth, in purity of life. (2) We watch over one another. We cultivate love in the body of Christ, Christian sympathy, and courtesy. We are slow to take offense, always ready for reconciliation. (3) We contribute cheerfully to maintain the ministries of the church—the spreading of the Gospel through all the world, the relief of the poor and needy. (4) We maintain private and family worship, and we seek the salvation of our kindred and acquaintances. (5) We are just in our dealings with others, watchful in our manner of life. We refrain from everything that may bring reproach on Christ, who gave His life for the salvation of us all.

Lord Jesus, I want my example to spread the light, never casting shadows. May my words and deeds reflect my life in You. Amen.

Carl W. Berner

Psalm 100

Doubting God's Existence

The fool says in his heart, "There is no God." *Psalm 14:1*

"How can I know there is a God?" This question is often spoken in derision by atheists, rightly called fools by God. But this can also be the anguished query of a Christian attacked by doubt. This doubt is repugnant to our whole spiritual being, and we fear to dwell on it. Yet few are the Christians who have not been besieged by this doubt at some time in their lives. This doubt must be faced and can be conquered through the power of the Holy Spirit.

How shall we combat a doubt so devastating as this, a doubt that seeks to undermine the whole structure of our faith? Reason and logic, science and philosophy, our senses and our instinct can all be useful, but none of these can resolve the issue for us.

We can repulse these doubts only by going to God's Word, the Sacred Scripture, where the Holy Spirit speaks to us. He will never turn away from a single soul who seeks God in Christ Jesus. God fully reveals Himself through Christ. This Jesus entered human history at Bethlehem, born of the Virgin Mary, and became a tangible part of our history. In His life, His teachings, His miracles, above all, through His suffering and death on the cross and rising again as conqueror of our sins and death, He has revealed to us God as true God and Father.

Dear God, through the power of the Spirit we know You as our heavenly Father. Help us to live confidently in You; trusting You for Jesus' sake. Amen.

Arnim H. Polster

Genesis 8:15–22

Precise Creation

Who marked off [the earth's] dimensions? Surely you know! Who stretched a measuring line across it? Job 38:5

If the globe on which we live were just a few miles smaller in diameter, the density of its atmospheric blanket would be greatly reduced. The air would be so thin that when there was no direct sunshine, the earth would not retain enough heat to sustain animal or human life. On the other hand, if the diameter of the earth were a bit larger, the air would become correspondingly more dense, resulting in too much heat for living forms to survive. But God, who is infinitely wise, carefully measured the earth for optimum size and weight.

Our heavenly Father, who carefully maintains the physical universe, is also concerned about us as individuals. He not only cares for our earthly existence but also provides for our eternal destiny. Through His Son, our Lord Jesus Christ, He provides ransom from sin, rescue from ruin, pardon for all transgressions, and the promise of a resplendent eternity when this earthly life is past. He gives us a comfortable dwelling place here on earth, and He assures us a perfect home in heaven as we put our trust in Him. In creation we see His hand; in redemption we see His heart.

Thank You, gracious Father, for Your provision both for this life and for the next; in Jesus' name. Amen.

Dennis A. Kastens

2 Timothy 3:10–17

A Vital Question for Today

What does the Scripture say? *Romans 4:3*

Decisions, decisions, decisions! We are called on to make them every day. We make them in our business, in our free time, in our family life, and in church. Many times those decisions come back to haunt us. It is then we realize that perhaps we did not put all the data into our mind's computer, or perhaps we did not take time to make a rational decision. There ought to be some way that we could make our task much easier and far more effective.

There is! When our Lord was confronted with questions by either His friends or His enemies, when He was asked to make a decision, there was one source on which He never failed to draw: the Holy Scriptures.

It has often been said that the Bible has more psychology within its covers than any other book. Furthermore, when we are confronted by a perplexing situation and confused as to what path to walk, there is a question each of us can ask: What does the Scripture say? Above all, the Bible teaches us the way of salvation through faith in Christ Jesus, our Savior.

Holy Spirit, our Comforter and Counselor, guide us by Your Word when we must make decisions in life. Give us the wisdom we need in all situations. We ask this in Jesus' name. Amen.

Howard G. Allwardt

2 Peter 1:3–11

Kindness Is next to Godliness

When the kindness and love of God our Savior appeared, He saved us, not because of righteous things we had done, but because of His mercy. *Titus 3:4–5*

"Cleanliness is next to godliness" goes an old saying. It may be true, but St. Peter states that the Christian life is filled with many different characteristics. In that list, kindness is next to godliness. Where is kindness in our lives?

We often find it easy to be kind to those who are kind to us. Waiting for others to act first with generosity and friendliness makes it easy for us to respond in kind. We need take no risks that way. Such action, lacking in initiative, is actually motivated by selfishness.

The Christian lives by a different motive. By God's grace given to us through His Word and Baptism, we receive a new heart. We live by a different set of values. We have different goals. Faith in Jesus, our Savior, works by love and many other virtues: goodness, knowledge, self-control, perseverance, godliness, kindness, and love. These qualities are gifts from God, but St. Peter says that we must make every effort to add them to our lives. Lack of them makes us nearsighted, blind, ineffective, unproductive, and forgetful. Having them allows us to participate in Christ's mission.

Thank You, dear Father, for giving us everything we need for life and godliness. We trust Your promises to us; for Jesus' sake. Amen.

Norris G. Patschke

Faith for Works

Without faith it is impossible to please God. *Hebrews 11:6*

Which came first—the chicken or the egg? For ages this question has been asked, both seriously and in fun. The biblical answer is that the chicken, created by God, came first, then laid the egg.

People concerned with spiritual matters ask another question: Which comes first—faith or works? The biblical answer is that God first plants Christian faith in our hearts. Then in that Spirit-created faith we desire to do good works in Christ's service.

It's part of our fallen nature to think that you don't get something for nothing, that everything has a price, that there's no such thing as a free lunch. Such faulty logic concludes that God's forgiveness through faith in Christ cannot be free.

Other people don't worry about forgiveness at all. "Good food, good friends, and good wine make the good life," goes the saying. So why bother about either faith or works? God makes it quite clear that life without faith in Christ is at best an empty shell.

For Christians, life without faith in Jesus, our Savior, is unthinkable. For those who think heaven is earned, Jesus takes second place behind their works. Yet the Bible is quite clear: "By grace you have been saved, through faith … it is the gift of God—not by works" (Ephesians 2:8–9). Our works say "Thank You" to God, but they come after faith, not before.

Dear Lord, increase our faith in Your salvation, and multiply our works to Your glory; through Jesus Christ, our Lord. Amen.

J. Barclay Brown

2 Kings 2:19–25

The Days of Youth

Don't let anyone look down on you because you are young, but set an example for the believers in speech, in life, in love, in faith and in purity. 1 Timothy 4:12

The days of youth are a great time to be alive. They are a time for growing, for developing, for learning, for planning, and for action. The vigor and enthusiasm of youth, if harnessed for a worthy cause, lend themselves to accomplishing much.

St. Paul wrote two letters to young Pastor Timothy that contained wise words of guidance and instruction for his ministry. Paul said in effect, "Timothy, remember that the grace of God has made you who you are today—a redeemed child of God in Jesus Christ. God has given you gifts of wisdom and leadership, and He expects you to exercise those gifts. You are trained and called to be in God's service. So Timothy, if someone belittles you because you are young, put them to shame by your mature words of faith and loving conduct in life."

Young Pastor Timothy was an inspiration for many others—young and old alike—as he read the Scriptures and proclaimed the Good News of forgiveness through faith in the life, death, and resurrection of Christ Jesus. What an encouragement for each of us!

Heavenly Father, remind each of us how important it is to set an example as we live to honor You; through Jesus, our Savior. Amen.

Ernest L. Gerike

1 Corinthians 8:1–13

Our Father in Christ

For us there is but one God, the Father, from whom all things came and for whom we live. *1 Corinthians 8:6*

Perhaps the greatest but least appreciated privilege given to Christians is the opportunity to address God as "Father." Jesus Himself taught His disciples to address God with an intimacy and familiarity that was startling to the people of that day.

In one sense, God is our Father simply because He created us. But the basis for calling God "our Father" is that we are His children by faith in Christ.

We were prodigal sons and daughters who had squandered our inheritance, yet God called us back to Himself. He gave His Son, Jesus Christ, as ransom to buy us back from our slavery to sin. He has restored us to His family in Holy Baptism, and He clothes us with the perfect righteousness of Jesus Himself. He continues to shower us with His gifts, and He promises that for Jesus' sake we will inherit everlasting life in the Father's heavenly mansions.

In the context of our redemption and of our adoption by Him, we call on our Father with confidence and boldness, sure in our relationship and certain of His blessings.

Heavenly Father, we give thanks that through Your Son we can call you "Father." Continue to show us Your favor and mercy. Amen.

Irma S. Pinkerton

Micah 6:6–8

Keeping It Simple

What does the Lord require of you? To act justly and to love mercy and to walk humbly with your God. *Micah 6:8*

Albert Einstein once said, "You have never mastered something until you can say it simply." Whether you are talking about physics, sports, or the Christian faith, there is a lot of truth in his statement.

So try it out! Say simply, in 20 words or fewer, what it means to you to live a Christian life. It's difficult, isn't it? We describe it with so many things—praying, reading devotions, witnessing, worshiping, serving others, and the like. Things get complicated when we add society- or church-made rules calling for fasting, doing penances, or observing Sunday "blue laws."

But God did not intend for Christian living to become confusing or unduly burdensome. The words of Micah 6:8 are refreshingly simple—do what is just or fair, love mercy, and walk humbly with God.

If you are not sure where to begin, start at the cross. There is no better setting for seeing these words in action than in Christ's suffering and death for our salvation. In Jesus' life and teaching one sees justice, mercy, and humility in glorious simplicity. Faith in His work of reconciliation enables us to follow in His footsteps.

Lord Jesus, help me to simplify my walk with You in a way that brings joy to my heart and glory to Your name. Amen.

Barry J. Keurulainen

Matthew 6:19–24

Look Up

Set your minds on things above, not on earthly things.
Colossians 3:2

Think of the many different things on which we set our hearts. In childhood it may have been a certain kind of candy or a toy we saw in a store window. We wanted it more than anything else.

That desire for something special goes with us through life, though the object of our desire may change to clothes or houses or cars.

That's the trouble. The things we long for keep changing in importance as we move through life. What seemed important in our youth has little or no value when we grow up. What we wanted most when we were in our teens becomes irrelevant when we move into adulthood. And in the light of eternity, they all become trivial.

That's why Jesus told us to lay up treasures in heaven—not on earth, where rust and decay make them useless. And that's why the apostle Paul tells us to set our minds on things above and not on earthly things.

Jesus has a place for us in heaven. Through His death and physical resurrection He has freed us from the consequences of our sins. One day He will free us from all sorrow and disappointment, even from death. He wants us to be with Him forever. There's nothing more wonderful. Take time each day to treasure heaven.

Help us, Lord Jesus, to lift our eyes and think of heaven, where one day we will live with You forever. Amen.

Edgar Walz

Philippians 3:12–16

Courage for the Race

Let us throw off everything that hinders … and let us run with perseverance the race marked out for us. *Hebrews 12:1*

An athletic trainer tells us that there are many differences between winners and losers. Physical condition, hard training, mental attitudes—all of these are important factors. But more important than all of these is the will to win. Without that there is not much hope of developing a winner.

The apostle Paul seems to have followed the games of his day very carefully. He knew the language of the sports world, and he probably noticed that where the competitors were fairly evenly matched, the prize went to the one who really wanted to win, whose heart was set on victory.

This is what we are to do in the race of life. We are to persevere. We are not to let any side issues take our minds off what we are to become as Christians, as followers of Christ. All kinds of tempting offers come to us, and we are inclined to take a short run down the alley where riches are the prize or up the canyon where fame is offered. All of this throws us off our stride. We have only one prize and goal, to live in the Word of God and the sacraments we become more and more like Christ and finally win the victory, eternal life.

Dear Jesus, as we run the race before us, give us Your strength and desire to reach the heavenly goal. Amen.

Martin L. Kretzmann

Matthew 22:34–46

A Love-Hate Relationship

Dear friends, let us love one another, for love comes from God. Everyone who loves has been born of God and knows God. *1 John 4:7*

We cannot love God and hate a person at the same time. These two opposites cannot dwell in a human heart. The spirit God has given to His believing children through faith in Christ is a spirit of love, but a hater is a murderer because he kills someone with a slow death.

God wants us to love everyone just as He has. This doesn't mean God requires us to have a feeling of affection for everyone. Often we are not even fond of ourselves. Loving our enemy doesn't mean that we must think of her as an agreeable person. This should be a great relief to us all.

Even as we look at some things in ourselves with horror and shame, so we hate a person's actions, but not the person. As we hate our own cowardice, selfishness, conceit, greed, lust, and pride and still go on loving ourselves, so we should do the same for others. We are to feel sorrow for their evil and pray for their repentance. We are to love everyone, even though there is nothing lovable about them. When we find that difficult, let us remember that is what Christ has done for us. Some may not seem deserving of our love, but neither are we deserving of Christ's love. Let us love one another.

Heavenly Father, thank You for the love You showed us and help us reflect that same forgiving love to others; for Jesus' sake. Amen.

Carl W. Berner

Daniel 6:16–24

A Companion to the Angels

Praise the Lord, you His angels, you mighty ones who do His bidding, who obey His word. *Psalm 103:20*

A Christian is a companion to the holy angels. Angels do many things in service to God. The psalmist, in this great psalm that calls on God's people to praise Him, tells us that angels do the work of the Lord and listen to and obey His Word. Daniel experiences this when the Lord sent angels to do His will and spare his life when King Darius had ordered him thrown into the den of lions.

As Christians, redeemed by the shed blood of Jesus Christ and given new life in Him, we join the invisible angel messengers of the Lord in serving the Lord and praising His name. Empowered by the Holy Spirit and the good news of the Gospel, we are called into our Lord's ministry to do His work and obey His Word. The angels are models for us, showing how we should continually listen to God's Word and do His will.

What an awesome responsibility, but also what a glorious privilege—to do the work of the Lord! He who spared not His only-begotten Son will give us all things needed to carry out our Christian tasks in thought, word, and deed. Companions to the angels. It sounds nice. It is! It's a great life being a Christian.

Lord Jesus, at the cross and empty tomb You made me Yours. Assist me in gladly doing Your work. Amen.

David W. Hoover

Matthew 5:13–16

Salt Talk

You are the salt of the earth. *Matthew 5:13*

What should be the distinctive role of Christians in a country that is free? As grateful children of our heavenly Father we want to thank Him for the countless blessings He has showered on us and the freedom we have to worship our Lord Jesus Christ.

Our Lord, who gave His life for us, told us that we are to be "the salt of the earth." That applies not only to our private lives as individual Christians but also to our civic lives as Christian citizens. As salt, we help preserve the health of our nation, preventing corruption and moral decay and promoting integrity and justice.

How desperately our nation needs the salt of Christian witness! Dishonesty, greed, profanity, and sexual immorality are all around us. In concert with other God-fearing citizens we are to do all within our power to stop the corruption that threatens our land. Salt that is not applied is worthless. We are to pray, to speak, to give, to work diligently for our Lord, that many more may know His salvation.

God bless our native land!
Firm may she ever stand. Amen.

Herman W. Gockel

1 Corinthians 12:12–26

Finishing the Picture

The body is a unit, though it is made up of many parts … they form one body. So it is with Christ. For we were all baptized by one Spirit into one body. *1 Corinthians 12:12–13*

Workers were putting the finishing touches on the new church when a visitor walked in. The high wall behind the altar caught his attention. There an artist was working on a mural of Christ. Only His head and shoulders were visible.

"Will you finish in time?" asked the visitor.

"Oh, I'm finished," replied the artist. "The rest of Christ's body won't be on the wall. His members—His arms, hands, legs, and feet—will be in the pews."

Paul would surely agree with that artist. The illustration of the human body was a favorite of his when speaking of the church and its people with varied gifts and abilities—each one important, and all of them functioning together, with Christ, the Redeemer, as their head. Paul also mourned when individual members did not function as Christ intended or when there was strife between them.

Baptized into Christ's body, we each have been given the Holy Spirit, who endows us with gifts to be used for the good of the whole church. How important it is that we complete the picture of Christ as we take our place in the pew!

O Christ, help us as baptized members of Your body to work together for the good of Your whole church! Amen.

Raymond L. Hartwig

Ephesians 5:1–14

Guided by Love

Live a life of love, just as Christ loved us and gave Himself up for us. *Ephesians 5:2*

All of us want to control things in our lives. Parents control children. Teachers control students. Businesspeople control profits and losses. Farmers control weeds and insects. Children control toys. Drivers control cars.

As Christians, we want God's love to govern and direct our lives. Between God and His people there is a bond of love. So great is God's love for us that Jesus gave up His life for us on the cross. That love connection by faith brings response and change. Those who have been touched by God's love in Christ are so moved that they no longer live for themselves, but for Him.

Sacrificial love characterizes the Christian life. We are now controlled by Christ's love. Christ's love is God's power at work in our lives. Christ's love is God's way of governing His church to keep it radiant and vibrant.

The life of love has no hint of immorality, indecency, greed, or foul language. Rather it is a life openly lived to enable all to see the goodness, righteousness, and truth produced in it by the power of the Spirit.

"Love makes the world go round" is a song lyric. Christ's love also *brings* the world around. The power to love and to be controlled by love comes from God. We love because He first loved us.

God of love, connect Your loving Word to us so we may be guided by Your love; for Jesus' sake. Amen.

Carlton L. Riemer

2 Chronicles 1:1–13

Being Realistic

What do you have that you did not receive? And if you did receive it, why do you boast as though you did not? 1 Corinthians 4:7

This is a humbling question that greets us at every point as we take inventory of our assets. Our body, mind, and soul are gifts of God. Our faith is nourished by the Bible, given by inspiration of God, and by Holy Communion, the very body and blood of our Lord.

We live in cities and on farms that were made possible by the hardships of rugged pioneers. In our education we had access to the treasures of the ages, gathered by an untold number of scholars. Our personality reflects the influences that have come to us from parents, teachers, friends, and associates. In making our living we are dependent on a political and economic order that calls for the cooperation of many. Behind all these human activities is God, who rules and overrules for our welfare. Yes, what do we have that we did not receive?

This question also deepens in us the sense of responsibility. There is no such thing as absolute ownership. Therefore nobody can say: "This is mine to be used as I please." We are divinely appointed stewards. As such we are to invest ourselves, our talents, and our possessions to the glory of God, for the temporal and eternal welfare of others.

Heavenly Father, You are the giver of every gift. With humble and grateful hearts we thank You and ask that we might use Your gifts to be a blessing; in Jesus' name. Amen.

Charles A. Behnke

Matthew 7:7–12

....

Confident in Prayer

In the day of my trouble I will call to You, for You will answer me. *Psalm 86:7*

"God will answer me." Can we really be so confident? Yes—God assures us that He will answer our prayers. "Ask and it will be given to you," said Jesus (Matthew 7:7). He even promised us the ability to move mountains by prayer if this should be necessary. All that is required is faith in Him.

Yes, faith! How often do we pray halfheartedly, doubting that God will hear? How often Jesus had to rebuke His disciples for their weak faith! And how often, in connection with His miracles, did He commend people for their faith! Effective prayer and faith go together.

In praying for spiritual blessings—faith, salvation, the Holy Spirit—we pray without qualification, for we know that it is God's will to give these blessings. In praying for earthly blessings, we are not always certain what God's will is. So we commit the matter to Him, knowing that He will do what is best for us and our loved ones. He has proven His love by giving His only Son into death to redeem us.

Adding the petition "Lord, strengthen my faith" to a prayer will work wonders. "If you believe, you will receive whatever you ask for in prayer" (Matthew 21:22).

Lord Jesus, we trust in You to take care of all our spiritual and physical needs. Above all, strengthen our faith. Amen.

William A. Kramer

1 Corinthians 13:1–13

Stepping Aside for Others

Love does not insist on its own way. *1 Corinthians 13:5 RSV*

Sometimes mountain trails have stretches so narrow that two hikers can barely pass each other. Only as one stands still at the side can the other go by safely. If both insist on their own way, danger could turn into disaster.

Often on life's trail our desires conflict with those of someone else. Too often neither gives in willingly—with disastrous results for the relationship.

Jesus guides us in handling such situations. He inquired in Gethsemane whether a way other than Calvary might be possible. But He did not insist on His way. In keeping with His Father's will, He chose the way of the cross, suffering for us sinners.

Now, forgiven through faith in Him, we are able to forgive. Loved by Him, we also can love—not only God, but others as well. Part of this love is not to insist on our own way.

Of course, we must insist on God's way. When His Word clearly speaks, we must follow, no matter how much conflict results. But when it is merely a matter of my way instead of another, because of Jesus I can willingly yield for the other to pass.

Help us, heavenly Father, to yield to others when love requires it. We ask this for Jesus' sake, who gave His life so we might pass from death to life. Amen.

Theo E. Allwardt Sr.

Ephesians 4:22–32

Honesty in Business

The merchant uses dishonest scales; he loves to defraud. *Hosea 12:7*

We hear and read much about corruption and questionable tactics in the business world. The abuses are symptoms of humankind's greed, found in societies the world over.

Hosea describes this greed in the words of our text. He shows that the desire for gain, acquired by deception and at the expense of the buyer, occurs frequently.

The merchant who resorts to deceit, the storekeeper who gives customers short weight, the dealer who mislabels the goods, the salesperson who hides the defects of a product—all of these may deceive the buyer, but their craftiness does not escape divine scorn. The commandment "Thou shalt not steal" applies to the dubious deals that are passed off as "good business."

It is, of course, possible to be a Christian businessperson and to adhere to the principles of fairness and honesty. This is the only policy that wins divine approval.

Keep us always, O Lord, in the way of honesty and truth; through Jesus Christ, who came to be the way, the truth, and the life. Amen.

Thomas Coates

Romans 5:12–17

You Can Make a Difference

If, by the trespass of the one man, death reigned ... how much more will those who receive God's abundant provision of grace ... reign in life through the one man, Jesus Christ. *Romans 5:17*

What power one individual has for good or evil! Adam disobeyed God, and humanity was cursed. The human race was preserved through righteous Noah. Moses prayed, and God spared the entire nation. David killed Goliath, and the army of Israel won the battle.

The prime example of the influence of one is the Lord Jesus. As Adam brought sin and death into the world, Jesus brought forgiveness and life. If we trust in Jesus alone, God accepts us and assures us of eternal life.

We don't rank with Jesus, Noah, Moses, or David. We are inclined to ask, "What difference can *I* make?" A good answer is given by the person who wrote, "I am only one, but I am one. I can't do everything, but I can do something. And what I can do, by the grace of God I will do."

None of us is indispensable. Yet each is important. Some acts of kindness will never be done if not by us. Some lonely people will never be reminded of God's love, and certain people without Jesus may never come to believe in Him unless we invite them. May we uplift the spirit of those around us and encourage them to do better, to have hope, and to be of good cheer!

Lord Jesus, You have overcome sin and death for me. Make me an influence for good today. Amen.

Herbert and Alma Kern

1 Peter 2:4–10

Adopted Children

[God] predestined us to be adopted as His sons through Jesus Christ, in accordance with His pleasure and will. *Ephesians 1:5*

Thousands of children are adopted each year. Without the experience we cannot fully understand the joy and happiness that come to those who adopt a child.

All Christians are adopted. When we became Christians, God adopted us into His family through this means of grace— Word and Baptism. He made us members of the holy Christian church.

Only by God's undeserved love are we the children of God. None of us deserved to be in His family. By nature we were spiritual outcasts. Nothing in us made us worthy of His love. The sins charged against us made it impossible for us to be received as God's children if it depended on us. There was no earthly reason why God should adopt us.

But there was a heavenly reason—His love! Through the death and resurrection of His Son, Jesus Christ, our Father made it possible for us to have our sins forgiven, to become the blood-bought sons and daughters of God. We remain God's children by clinging in childlike faith to Jesus as our only Savior.

What a privilege to be adopted as God's children! May we, by the power of the Holy Spirit, live a life of thanks and praise in His family.

Father, let me ever be Your faithful child; through Jesus Christ. Amen.

Andrew Simcak Jr.

Revelation 1:4–8

Jesus—Timely and Timeless

Jesus Christ is the same yesterday and today and forever.
Hebrews 13:8

Jesus is unchangeable. He lives and reigns today without any change in personality since the days when He personally reached out in compassion to the weak and sinful and offered new life to the crushed and defeated. He remains the saving God. Glory be to His name!

But a distorted application can be made of His unchangeable nature. Some may picture Jesus in long robes and beard and cannot imagine the changeless Christ understanding computers or modern society and so dismiss Him from modern life. Or an inactive church member, knowing that Jesus never changes, believes that his childhood introduction to God was complete and considers any further religion repetitious or unnecessary.

It is a sad mistake to believe that Jesus is timeless but to forget that He is also timely. The words of Christ gave startling light to the world in which He lived, and they hold penetrating truth also today. The life and cross of Jesus, which offered amazing pardon to the first Christians, do the same today. Christ is not behind us but always before us. The closer we follow the more will we marvel at His infinite truth and grace, which apply to any world in any generation. Christ never changes. He is always timely and timeless.

O Thou who changest not, abide with me. Amen.

Victor L. Brandt

Matthew 25:14–30

Good Stewardship

The man who had received the one talent went off, dug a hole in the ground and hid his master's money. *Matthew 25:18*

In His parable of the talents Christ shows not only what faithful stewardship is but also what it is not. Three stewards received from their master different amounts of money in trust. Two stewards used the money wisely and won the acclaim of the master: "Well done, good and faithful servant." They were good stewards. The third steward was condemned by the master, not because he had lost or stolen the money, but because he had simply hoarded it. He had done nothing with his talent. He was discharged as a steward unworthy of the trust.

Luigi Tarisio had a possessive and obsessive love of exquisite violins. When he died, he left practically nothing but an attic crammed with 246 excellent violins. How sad! He deprived the world of the beautiful music they could have made.

God, who owns everything, has given us all we are and have: material blessings, skills, opportunities, and best of all, the gift of the Savior. We are not reservoirs in which God wants to store all this. We are channels through which these gifts are to flow to His glory and for the benefit of others.

May our gratitude for the many gifts You have given us, O Lord, prompt us to use them wisely and effectively; through Jesus Christ. Amen.

Armin C. Oldsen

Esther 4:4–17

For Such a Time

Who knows but that you have come to royal position for such a time as this? *Esther 4:14*

Have you ever thought of an age in which you might like to have lived? Was it the "good old days"—a time when the world seemed more peaceful, when the pace of life was slower? Whether there ever was such a time is hardly debatable, for sin was always present.

Esther lived in a troubled age. Although she was a Jewess, she had become queen of the Medes and Persians. Wicked Haman hated her people and plotted their annihilation. Esther had a choice. She could cling to her crown, or she could try to help her people at great risk to herself. God had placed her into the kingdom for such a time as this and expected her to do His will.

It won't help to dream of a better age when there was less violence, more respect for God and His Word, no television, fewer leisure options, and less money to corrupt people. God wants us to live in the world as it is. There is no other one. He knows these times and He knows us better than we do. He put us here and made us what we are because He knows what is good for us and what good He can do through us in His kingdom.

God, help me to live this day as Your child, mindful of the opportunities to do Your will; through Jesus Christ. Amen.

Louis W. Grother

Ephesians 6:1–13

A Privileged Role

Train a child in the way he should go. *Proverbs 22:6*

Babies do not come equipped with knowledge about what is right and wrong. They aren't born knowing who God is and what He is like. Infants do not automatically know Jesus as the one who came to save them from their sins. Babies start with a memory bank that is empty. For them to know, understand, and remember, they must be taught. Teaching, therefore, is essential to the development of a child. And if the right things are to be learned, then the right things must be taught.

Solomon, the wise author of the book of Proverbs, understood this. He knew that if children were to go in a certain way, it was necessary to train them.

We are sometimes led to believe that it is bad to train children biblically. What a lot of nonsense! The fact is that it is impossible not to. If parents don't influence their children, someone else will. The list of other teachers is endless: friends, TV, movie stars, and sports personalities. Someone will teach the growing child. Why not parents?

We have such wonderful things to teach our children: God's love, forgiveness, the Christian life. What a privilege this is!

Heavenly Father, we thank You for the children You have created. Help us to be faithful Christian teachers; for Jesus' sake. Amen.

W. Th. Janzow

Luke 10:25–37

Who Is My Neighbor?

Love your neighbor as yourself. *Luke 10:27*

Who is my neighbor? That is a good question. It can also be a most embarrassing one. Most people don't know the names of all who live in their immediate neighborhood. Some don't even care to know.

According to Christ's story of the Good Samaritan, all those are our neighbors who are in need of our help. We are to love them even as we love ourselves. This goes pretty deep.

The needs of our neighbors may be similar to the needs supplied to the man who was beaten on the Jericho road. Our neighbors have many needs. Some people are lonely. Others hunger for a word of warm encouragement. Death may have taken a loved one. Someone has lost a job. Another's son or daughter is in serious trouble. Gossip may be undercutting a neighbor's reputation. Others are living in unbelief and rejection of the Gospel message.

Helping others may mean going out of our way, causing us inconvenience and changing our immediate plans. It may even present some real problems. When God's love dwells in our hearts, it overcomes all barriers. Do you see a neighbor in need?

Heavenly Father, help us respond in love to those around us and in our actions to reflect Your love; for Jesus' sake. Amen.

John E. Hermmann

Deuteronomy 6:1–9

Future Saints

Go and make disciples of all nations. *Matthew 28:19*

God wants to make Himself known through His saints, those who already believe in Him, so other people can come to know Him and thus become saints in their turn.

It is a continuous process. The story of Jesus and the Good News of salvation must be told over and over so new generations of saints can join the body of Christ.

It is a worldwide process. There are always parts of the world that either have not heard or have forgotten what they once knew about Jesus. The Gospel must be proclaimed in every corner of the earth age after age.

It is a renewing process for the hearers and brings new life to them. Eternal death is what those without the Gospel know of life. To unlock the doors of eternal death with the Gospel is to enlarge, enrich, and expand life for all who believe it.

It is a renewing process also for the bearer of the Gospel. People who try to keep the Gospel for themselves will soon not appreciate it. Their faith will become lukewarm and perhaps fade entirely away. Speaking the Gospel renews faith in the speaker as well. Jesus made it clear that saints are to make new saints in every generation.

Holy Spirit, use my mouth and my life to honor my Savior's name and to bring others closer to Him; through Jesus Christ. Amen.

Hubert F. Beck

Luke 15:1–10

Dangerous Distractions

Martha was distracted by all the preparations that had to be made. *Luke 10:40*

It is easy to become distracted while driving. We get involved in a conversation; something beside the road catches our eye; the car phone rings. Distraction can lead to serious accidents.

On the journey of life there is much to distract us from focusing on our Lord and His Word. In our text Martha was distracted, showing hospitality toward Jesus instead of listening to His message. Distractions can stand in the way of a close relationship with Jesus. The devil entices us to place a higher priority on business or social activities than on spiritual health.

Few Christians wake up one morning and decide to abandon their faith. Falling away from God more often is a gradual process. Each time we skip a worship service or neglect our daily devotions or prayer life makes it easier to miss them again and again until God ceases to be meaningful at all.

Although we too easily become distracted from God on our journey, God always rejoices when we repent. He is ready and eager to welcome us back. He sent His Son to suffer and die for us to bring us back to Him. Keep focused on Jesus, and He in turn will rivet your focus on the God who loves us and helps us to fight off all that would distract us from Him.

Lord Jesus, help me keep my focus on You and Your Word. Amen.

Henry E. Fuelberg

Deuteronomy 6:4–7

My God Is

Acknowledge and take to heart this day that the Lord is God in heaven above and on the earth below. There is no other. *Deuteronomy 4:39*

I believe in God and I believe that I live in a moral universe that came from the mind and hand of a Creator who is still in charge, in whose keeping still lie all the issues of life and death. I am not a creature of chance, fate, Kismet, or Lady Luck. I am a child of God. I believe that God has made me and all creatures and still preserves us.

I believe that I am responsible to this God for my actions, that He has laid down certain unchanging laws in the Bible that are to guide my life. This God is personally concerned about everything that happens to me. He cares whether I laugh or cry, eat or starve, live or die. He is moved by love for me.

So when I cry out in prayer, I know that there is someone who hears and answers me. I know because He once visited this small planet in the person of Jesus Christ, who said, "Anyone who has seen Me has seen the Father" (John 14:9). This one Lord, He is God. And His love sent His Son to the cross that I might live with Him in glory.

Glory be to God the Father,
Glory be to God the Son,
Glory be to God the Spirit;
Great Jehovah, Three in One!
Glory, glory while eternal ages run! Amen.

Walter E. Kraemer

1 Timothy 6:1–10

Possessions

The love of money is a root of all kinds of evil. *1 Timothy 6:10*

According to an old fable, a fly discovered a tantalizing strip of flypaper. It looked so appetizing that he decided to claim it for himself. So, after chasing away all the other insects that threatened to share his find, he landed on its very edge and happily announced: "My flypaper!" Then he proceeded to partake of the tasty feast. However, in his desire to satisfy his appetite, he tried to walk around to get all he could. Soon his feet became firmly attached to the sticky surface. Realizing he couldn't move his legs, he began flapping his wings, but they too became mired. Finally, completely exhausted, he gave up. It was then that the flypaper proudly exclaimed, "My fly!"

This fable portrays what happens to those who get caught in the trap of materialism. At first they say, "My possessions!" But after catering to the trinkets and pleasures of this world, they themselves are the ones who have been taken captive. They are being possessed.

Though there is nothing wrong with material possessions in themselves, it's what priority we give them that makes the difference. Only when Christ and His salvation are first in our lives are we freed from bondage to what is perishable.

Lord Jesus, preserve us from enslavement to earthly things so our hope might rest in You alone. Amen.

Dennis A. Kastens

Acts 26:9–19

Let Your Conscience Be Your Guide

I too was convinced that I ought to do all that was possible to oppose the name of Jesus of Nazareth. *Acts 26:9*

Let your conscience be your guide. Who of us has not used that expression? Someone comes to us for advice. We make certain suggestions, and then, as if to summarize all we have said, we add: "Just let your conscience be your guide!"

Conscience is that small voice within that calls us to task, that challenges us to think, that takes issue with our judgment. It is the red light flashing its warnings at the crossroads of life. It is that irritating little summons that refuses to allow sin to become a pleasure. At times we wish we couldn't hear it.

But conscience has its flaws. God created Adam and Eve perfect. They knew God's will without it being put down on paper. But sin changed that, and conscience was dulled—not silenced, but twisted and bent to some degree. Where once it was a sure, reliable guide, it became unreliable.

So Paul confesses that even when he persecuted the followers of Jesus, he felt he was doing the right thing. His conscience led him to believe that he was championing the right. Only when he came face-to-face with the holy and blessed Christ did he realize that his conscience had misled him.

Conscience needs to be tuned to God's Word, the Bible, so it sends out correct signals and keeps one walking in the footsteps of the Lord. Yes! Let your conscience be your guide, but let it be an enlightened, Christian one!

O Lord God, attune my conscience to Your holy commandments; for Jesus' sake. Amen.

H. M. Schwehn

John 17:20–26

Alone, but Together in Him

Holy Father, protect them by the power of Your name—the name You gave Me—so that they may be one as We are one. *John 17:11*

We human beings are individuals. That is, we are each trapped within our inner self. We have forms of communication by which we reach out to others, but at best they allow us only a glimpse of others. We live with people in our own families for years, but we can never get to know what is really going on inside them. What is your mother's favorite color, her greatest fear? Even if she told you yesterday, is it still the same today? And would you even remember?

The problem is that we are each, by nature, the center of our own universe. We are more concerned that others should know us—our ideas, our feelings—than that we should know them. We are better talkers than listeners.

We are each born trapped within our own soul, but not for eternity. Jesus' death and resurrection are God's way of freeing us from that trap of self-centeredness. His love reaches out so we might be in Him and He in us. As He draws us closer to Himself through His Word and sacraments, His love reaches out through us to others and draws us together as the members of His body. In eternity we will form a perfect unity of individuals—one, as God is one.

Lord Jesus, our loving Savior, make us one through faith in You, even as You, the Father, and the Holy Spirit are one. Amen.

John M. Moe

1 John 3:11–18

Love's Labor Never Lost

Serve wholeheartedly, as if you were serving the Lord, not men. *Ephesians 6:7*

We have heard about the shoemaker who said, "My business is saving souls, but I mend shoes to pay expenses." While his zeal is praiseworthy, as a faithful Christian he also would have to make sure that he did the best possible job with the soles of his neighbors' shoes. Both through soul-winning and sole-repairing the cobbler shows love to his neighbor and helps God to provide His creatures with "clothing and shoes."

We are called to love and serve our neighbor for Jesus' sake. In our complicated society our neighbor's needs are complex. We all need food and clothes, homes, places of business, cars and roads, mail service and telephones, cotton and wool, aspirin and antibiotics. Nearly every occupation contributes to human welfare. By our jobs we are helping the neighbor whom God created and redeemed. It makes all the difference in the world when we view others as neighbors, as sisters and brothers in need. We love because Christ first loved us and gave His life to bring us back to God. One way to show this love is by our daily work, which helps meet our neighbor's need. This labor of love is never lost.

O Jesus, You understood the value of work. Bless our work. May it be done in love for You and our neighbor. Amen.

Robert K. Menzel

Acts 12:12–17

God Hears Prayer

[Peter] described how the Lord had brought him out of prison. *Acts 12:17*

God does the most surprising things. Look at Peter. Peter had not known that his fellow Christians had stayed up this night to ask the Lord to deliver him. It was the only thing they could do. They were absolutely helpless, and therefore they were all the more willing to let the Lord handle the matter. The result was that the Lord surprised them. They had not expected that their prayer should be answered. They had miscalculated; they had made God too small.

All of us need to learn this fact about our prayer. We are praying to the true God who loves us dearly. We are asking things of Him who can do all things. We usually feel that we should bring to the Lord only such things as are possible in our thinking. After all, God already has given us the strength, the talents, and the ability to do the possible. We need to have the courage to step to the throne of grace and ask God for the impossible. That is when our faith really begins to shine. Then we have acknowledged God to be the great God that He really is. Nothing pleases the Lord more than this.

We need to think about this especially in our church work, in the great mission work in which we are engaged. Let us pray God to do what we think is impossible, then we shall better understand that with God all things are possible.

Almighty God, forgive us for thinking You are too small to accomplish great things. Help us by Your Spirit boldly and confidently to call on You; in Jesus' name. Amen.

Martin J. Zschoche

John 1:1–14

The Word of God

In the beginning was the Word, and the Word was with God, and the Word was God. *John 1:1*

Dialog with God? We engage in it through prayer. And God speaks to us in His Word. How does the Word of God come to us? It is more than words, more than parts of speech. In one sense, God's Son is the Word. This Word is with God and is God. This Word created all things and became incarnate in Jesus Christ. God's will is done when He strengthens our faith and keeps us firm in His Word as long as we live.

We are also given God's Word, the Bible, which testifies of Jesus. By studying the Scriptures, by turning to them in all of life's circumstances, we find guidance and comfort.

The Word awaits us in the order of worship, especially in the Word that is joined with water in Baptism and with bread and wine in Holy Communion. God speaks to us also in Word-related sacred music, poetry, and art and in the beauty of His creation.

We hear the Word from our pastors, church workers, and fellow Christians. And because the Word is not just words but power, we see it at work in acts of love and forgiveness, patience and sacrifice. In all these ways we are kept firm in God's Word, and our faith is strengthened.

Jesus Christ, true Word of the Father, keep me firm in Your Word, that I may both hear and believe it. Amen.

Lillian B. Wehmeyer

Psalm 119:57–64

What Makes a Best Friend?

You are My friends if you do what I command. *John 15:14*

Which is more amazing—that Jesus desires to be our friend or that He wants us to be His? Jesus makes the best friend we could ever have.

What makes a best friend? Consider Jonathan and David (1 Samuel 18–23). The world celebrates theirs as the ultimate true friendship. They show that a friend is committed in words and actions (1 Samuel 18:4). A best friend is loyal, putting everything on the line to speak on the friend's behalf (1 Samuel 19:1–5). Jonathan was a faithful friend (1 Samuel 23:17), and he loved David as himself (1 Samuel 18:3).

Committed, loyal, faithful, loving—the marks of a best friend. This is the kind of friend Jesus desires and deserves. He wants friends who are committed in more than words. He delights in friends who are loyal to Him and speak up for Him. He wants friends who are faithful and true. He wants friends who love Him even as they love themselves.

What kind of friend are you to Jesus? Not nearly the best friend He is to you. Even when we fail as His friends, He forgives us and remains committed and loyal to us. He is faithful, loving us even to the point of dying for us so we may live forever. "What a friend we have in Jesus."

Jesus, You are my best friend. Help me live as Yours. Amen.

Barry J. Keurulainen

Romans 8:28–39

Human Life: A Burning Issue

[God said,] "Take off your sandals, for the place where you are standing is holy ground." *Exodus 3:5*

As Moses approached the burning bush in Midian's wilderness, he was stopped in his tracks by God's words in our text. The presence of God caused the ground on which he stood to be holy ground.

The presence of God will do that every time. Today we approach not a burning bush, but a burning issue: the sanctity of human life, ground that belongs to God as the Lord of both life and death. To snuff out young lives by abortion, or prematurely to terminate life by euthanasia, is to trespass on holy ground. The command of God to Moses applies to us as well: Off with those sandals!

How we personally approach this burning issue of our day is an important matter. It is helpful to remember again the value placed on every human life by God, the price established by the Creator Himself when He did not spare His own Son, Jesus Christ, but delivered Him up for us all. God values human life so highly that He gave His beloved Son to redeem every single person. That is the reason for us not only to take our sandals off, but to take a firm stand as we face this burning issue.

Grateful for our lives, O Lord, may we respect the lives of all other human beings; in the name of Jesus, whose shed blood purchased salvation for every person. Amen.

Raymond L. Hartwig

Psalm 20

Teach Us to Pray

One of His disciples said to Him, "Lord, teach us to pray."
Luke 11:1

What is prayer? What is its purpose? The purpose of prayer is to communicate with God. But a full and effective prayer life consists of more than a shopping list, a catalog of things you need or want. While God invites—yes, even encourages—us to bring all our requests to Him, He desires that we accept His will according to His Word as we pray. When our wills come into line with His, as they do when we pray, "Not my will, but Yours be done" (Luke 22:42), our lives are altered in a fundamental way.

The process of prayer is the heartbeat of our faith in our Lord. Are your will and desires in line with God's Word for your life? Make it a major part of your prayer life to submit your will, and then your actions, to His Word.

Oh yes, prayer makes a difference. God answers prayer according to His Word and will. He responds to our pleading and removes the obstacles that block our Christian way. God promises to hear and answer our prayers. But above all, when we pray He brings our wills into line with His through the Word and sacraments. God's will becoming your desire—glorious thought! Pray, indeed, that the Holy Spirit cause your will to come into line with God's as you pray, "Your will, dear Lord, not mine be done."

Heavenly Father, hear my prayers and by them bring my life into line with Your will; in Jesus' name. Amen.

Barry J. Keurulainen

Matthew 12:46–50

We Are Responsible

Do not follow the crowd in doing wrong. *Exodus 23:2*

This text teaches us that we are morally responsible human beings. As human beings we do not live in a vacuum. You and I, as social creatures, belong to certain groups: the family, the church, the community, the nation, the human family. This explains why we are so prone to "follow the crowd."

God does not say that it is always sinful to follow the crowd. But He does say it is sinful to follow the crowd "in doing wrong." Unfortunately this is the direction the crowd is likely to take.

When we follow the crowd to do evil, we somehow seem to feel that we are not as guilty as if we did wrong by ourselves. We seem to think the fact that many others do the same thing somehow makes wrong right, or if not right, at least okay.

God doesn't think so, and for this we have reason to thank Him. Because we are individually responsible, He sent Jesus for each of us. That is why in His Word, in Holy Baptism, and in Holy Communion, He gives to each of us the assurance of personal salvation and forgiveness. That is also why He offers each person the gift of a saving, personal faith in Christ.

We are individually responsible.

God, help us to face life's responsibilities and to confess, "I believe that Jesus is my Lord"; in His name. Amen.

Otto A. Geiseman

Matthew 20:17–28

Success Story

He humbled Himself and became obedient to death—even death on a cross! *Philippians 2:8*

From rags to riches, from office boy to president of the firm, from log cabin to White House—these are the great American success stories. Sometimes when I think of this, I say to myself, "When will you make your mark? Will you ever be a success?"

Then I think of my Lord's success story: from heaven to earth; from the right hand of God the Father Almighty to a peasant mother and a manger in Bethlehem; from popularity to indifference to hatred to crucifixion to death! And through it all I see my Lord Jesus busy serving everyone around Him. Guests at a wedding drank the wine He prepared for them; more than five thousand sat down on the grass and ate the bread and fish He served; scores of the sick received His healing; 12 chosen men sat around a table arguing about success while their master and Lord quietly washed their feet! Then came the highest service of all: ignorant soldiers jeered at Him, spiteful priests quoted the Bible at Him, cowardly disciples fled from Him as He hung by nails to a cross, bearing the sins of all, even of His enemies!

This was our Savior's success story. True, He also rose from the dead and returned to His throne in heaven. But the success of His redemptive mission was assured when from the cross He cried out, "It is finished" (John 19:30).

Lord Jesus, through the power of the Holy Spirit let the story of Your success move me to saving faith and humble service. Amen.

David A. Preisinger

1 Peter 2:4–12

Chosen to Be His Witnesses

You will be My witnesses in Jerusalem, and in all Judea and Samaria, and to the ends of the earth. *Acts 1:8*

The courtroom grows silent at the sound of the gavel. "Call the first witness," commands the judge. You hear your name and are asked to take the witness stand.

We have each been chosen—chosen by God to be a witness for Jesus. What do we know about Him? What exactly is our relationship to Him? How long have we known Him? When was the last time we were seen walking with Him? What have we witnessed Him doing in the time we have been with Him? Just what is the character of this Jesus?

Jesus sacrificed Himself to make us God's people so we "may declare the wonderful deeds of Him who called you out of darkness into His marvelous light" (1 Peter 2:9 RSV). Spectators surround us every day, listening and watching as we attest to Jesus in word and action. What are we declaring? Others grill us for details. Are we prepared to answer?

We sometimes fail as witnesses for the Gospel of Jesus, "no-showing" sometimes or saying the wrong thing. God assures us that "if anybody does sin, we have one who speaks to the Father in our defense—Jesus Christ, the Righteous One" (1 John 2:1).

O Great Defender, help us to be Your witnesses. Amen.

Gloria K. Lessmann

1 John 1:1–10

No Other Solution

I acknowledged my sin to You and did not cover up my iniquity. I said, "I will confess my transgressions to the Lord"—and You forgave the guilt of my sin. *Psalm 32:5*

In Psalm 32 David tells how he had been wrestling with enemy number 1—his guilt—and was taking a beating. He had tried the hiding game, but it just didn't work. He might be able to hide his sins from others, but how could he possibly hide them from God? There was only one way out: "I will confess my transgressions to the Lord," David says. Then God forgave the guilt of his sin.

This is the only solution to our own guilt problem. Instinctively we try to hide guilt, to bury it or wish it away, dance it away, drink it away, drug it away. Nothing works; the guilt still preys on the heart and brings regrets, worries, and fears.

David's solution is still the only one: honest, flat-out confession. No hiding, covering up, or shifting the blame but simply: "I will confess my transgressions to the Lord." That is step 1. Even more important is step 2: to believe with David, "You forgave the guilt of my sin." We must know God not only as a God of stern justice but also as a God of love—a forgiving God who welcomes us with the Good News of His grace in Christ, our sin-bearer. Trusting that Christ has made amends for us, we can rest assured that our guilt is really gone.

In the joy of Your salvation, Lord, let my soul find peace; for Jesus' sake. Amen.

Albert W. Galen

Hebrews 4:9–16

Morning

Sow your seed in the morning, and at evening let not your hands be idle. *Ecclesiastes 11:6*

Every morning begins a new day for us. The beginning of another day provides opportunity for new challenges. It is God's way of opening a door for us to get a fresh start, to make a new beginning, to have another chance.

In that sense each new morning symbolizes the Christian faith. Christianity could well be called "the religion of another chance." That's what it really is. No matter what we think or feel, no matter what we have done or not done, no matter what we have been or not been, always—without exception—God offers us His forgiveness. He wipes the slate clean so we can begin anew. There is no limit to that forgiveness, no end to those further chances. Always God is ready to say, "Try again. My grace in Christ surrounds you. I love you not because you do not fail; I love you despite your failures."

It is certainly true, as we all know, that "to err is human." We will never be perfect. It is equally true that "to forgive is divine." Because He is divine, God will never fall short in that. We live our lives, even through our mistakes, always with "another chance."

Thank You, Lord, for giving me another chance in Christ. Amen.

Wilbert J. Fields

1 Corinthians 12:1–11

The Spirit with Us in Our Gifts

There are different kinds of gifts, but the same Spirit.
1 Corinthians 12:4

The German theologian and pastor Helmut Thielecke once observed that when he told young people how gifted they were, they invariably acted as if he were complimenting *them.* But, he asked, had he not said that they were *gifted?* Does not that in turn remind us that a gift comes from someone else and that the giver of every gift is God? There is never any room for pride in our accomplishments.

God always comes as one who gives. When the Holy Spirit comes through God's Word and the sacraments of Baptism and the Holy Supper, He gives us faith. Then He gives us special abilities through which He will reveal His presence. The requirement made of us is that we remember that our spiritual gifts are always gifts. We either use them to the credit of the giver, or we throw them away in proud and selfish living.

Since it is God who does the giving, none of us should demand that He give the same gifts to everyone. If we are wise, we do not expect that each member in the family will have the same gifts. When people forget that the same variety of gifts exists in the church, then divisions and criticism arise. When they remember that there is but one Spirit who gives to all as He wills, then the church remains one. Above all, we must never forget that God gave the greatest gift in Jesus, our Savior.

Holy Spirit, help me to see and use the gifts You have given to me and to rejoice in what You have given to others. Let us all use our gifts in service to our God; through Christ, our Lord. Amen.

Vernon R. Schreiber

John 14:1–7

To Whom Shall We Go?

Simon Peter answered Him, "Lord, to whom shall we go? You have the words of eternal life." *John 6:68*

Millions of people are asking the same question—"To whom shall we go?" What a shame that so many do not know the answer! They are searching, investigating, hoping against hope that something, somebody, anybody will give them the true meaning and purpose of life. By nature we all want to know the answers to the three basic questions of life: Who am I? Why am I here? Where am I going?

Many flock to the New Age movement, to a guru, to astrologers. We are told that Americans spend large sums of money trying to find out the purpose and direction of their lives from fortune-tellers. Many people observe the positions of the stars and planets to help them make decisions.

Peter answered his own question with a beautiful confession of faith: "You have the words of eternal life." Jesus is our life. He who surrendered His life for us gives us new life, a life of forgiveness and eternal life with Him. We need to go to Jesus and His Word alone. He is the only way, the only truth, the only life.

Lord Jesus, keep my faith focused on You always, in times of perplexity and of peace. Amen.

Andrew Simcak Jr.

Ephesians 5:22–33

Husband and Wife

Enjoy life with your wife, whom you love. *Ecclesiastes 9:9*

A Christian marriage is not held together by laws and social customs that say, "You must remain married," but by strong ties of mutual love and respect that say, "We want to remain married."

Students of family life who do not fully understand Christianity sometimes are puzzled that a Christian husband and wife should be happily married despite great handicaps and misfortunes. How can a Christian husband and wife be so understanding, so forgiving, so helpful? How can they live in joy and peace when everything seems to be against them?

The love between a Christian husband and wife is patterned after the love of Christ for all believers. Paul wrote: "Husbands, love your wives, just as Christ loved the church and gave Himself up for her" (Ephesians 5:25). The love between a Christian husband and wife is not selfish. Rather it is sacrificial; that is, it seeks happiness not for self but for the other. A Christian husband wants to make his wife happy; a Christian wife wants to make her husband happy. That is why they strive to be understanding, patient, and forgiving.

O God, let our marriage always be one in which we, as husband and wife, dearly love one another as You love us; in Your Son's name. Amen.

Armin C. Oldsen

John 18:36–38

Learning the Truth

When He, the Spirit of truth, comes, He will guide you into all truth. *John 16:13*

How often we are tempted to excuse ourselves from Christian service by saying, "I'm too old" or "I don't know enough" or "I'm already doing my share." We can think of others who can do the job more easily or who are not as busy as we are. If we wait until Christian service is easy or the opportunity is perfect, we will never do all we can or should. Far better to realize that we live in an imperfect world and to trust the Lord to see us through.

We can trust the Lord to help. Has He not already done that which is greatest in sending Christ to atone for our sins and to assure us of forgiveness? Does He not promise the Holy Spirit's aid in our Christian life?

If we wait until we understand everything before we trust God or join the church or serve Him in the congregation, we will never do so. We trust Christ's promise that the Holy Spirit will guide us into all truth. Assurance comes to us from the Word of God by the power of the Holy Spirit as we strive to obey what we do understand.

Trust God's Holy Spirit to deal with you through God's Word, the Bible, and to guide you into all the truth you need.

Holy Spirit, be my guide, my strength, and my teacher; through Jesus Christ. Amen.

Omar Stuenkel

1 Corinthians 12:12–27

Side by Side

Stand firm in one spirit, with one mind striving side by side for the faith of the gospel. *Philippians 1:27 RSV*

"Where two or three come together in My name, there am I with them" (Matthew 18:20). This is the precious promise the Lord of the church gives to congregations of Christians. Through the centuries Christians have united in congregations, and congregations have united in church bodies, synods, and the like. In the days of St. Paul's ministry the churches were united in faith and doctrine. When the need arose to help the drought- and famine-afflicted people of the Jerusalem church, Paul encouraged the congregation to help the needy.

The assignment our Lord gives to His followers is a large one—the evangelizing of the world. No individual Christian alone can do this work. No congregation alone can do this. But let Christians and Christian congregations unite in their efforts and they will be able to do great things for Christ, their Lord.

Blessed is that congregation and church body where Christians, united in faith and doctrinal practice, stand side by side in working for Christ and sing, "We are not divided; All one body we, One in hope and doctrine, One in charity." That church will march like a mighty army, conquering the world for Christ. United in faith in Christ Jesus we stand side by side with our fellow believers, striving to bring the pure Gospel to all that they with us may have everlasting life.

Strengthen our church, dear Lord, that united, we may strive to do Your will; through Jesus Christ, our Lord. Amen.

Amos A. Schmidt

Matthew 15:21–28

The Gift of Faith

By grace you have been saved through faith—and this not from yourselves, it is the gift of God. *Ephesians 2:8*

Faith in Christ is no doubt the most important subject in the Bible. The Scriptures are brimming with references to it. One chapter, Hebrews 11, is devoted entirely to faith. There faith is defined as "being sure of what we hope for and certain of what we do not see" (11:1).

More simply, faith may be said to be the "receiving hand" that reaches out by the Holy Spirit's power to grasp God's gift of forgiveness and eternal life in Christ Jesus.

Faith is also the "gripping hand" that holds fast to God's promises no matter how deterring the obstacles or how desperate the situation. It is thrilling to read in the Bible about all that faith can do, as told in the inspiring record of the heroic action of people empowered by faith. In His ministry Jesus also cited examples of heroic faith, notably a woman of Canaan and a Roman centurion, both unnamed and both from outside the nation of Israel. Throughout the church's history, and still today, God has raised up countless other people of great faith.

Saving faith in Jesus is a gift so vital and so priceless, yet through God's Word and the sacraments of Baptism and Communion it comes to us absolutely free by the Spirit's power.

O most merciful God, replenish and renew in us the gift of faith in our Savior, Jesus Christ; in His name. Amen.

Albert W. Galen

Genesis 2:4–7

The Glory of Creation

By Him all things were created. *Colossians 1:16*

In the great laboratories of our age, scientists explore the secrets of nature. Now and then, more frequently today than ever before, there is a breakthrough, and humankind is given another open door to new resources for life on earth. It is a privilege to live in this age, to witness the amazing accomplishments of the mind, and to enjoy the benefits of new discoveries.

Now into all this pride of achievement comes the humbling thought that what the brilliant scientist is discovering is nothing more than what was already there. Long ago the wisdom and power of our Lord designed and created all things by the power of His Word. God made this world and filled it with all its riches. God created us to live in this world and to discover and use its resources. His is the greater glory and the greater wisdom.

Most of all, God made us for Himself. We are the objects of His deepest concern and of His greatest love, a love that finds its most convincing evidence in the gift of His own Son. To behold this glory, to be reminded of our origin and our destiny, to see ourselves in our relation to God as our maker and, most of all, as our Father in Jesus Christ—this we need to know through the Gospel and to remember in faith.

O Lord, how manifold are Your works! In wisdom You have made them all. The earth is full of Your glory; in Jesus' name. Amen.

Daniel E. Poellot

1 John 4:7–21

The Dynamics of Christian Stewardship

We love because He first loved us. *1 John 4:19*

Many different reasons prompt people to share their blessings with others: a lifeless habit; a means to impress others; a way to save on income tax; or even an effort to earn heaven. While we may at times be prompted, at least in part, to respond to such motives, they are not pleasing or acceptable to God. They are all devices of selfishness.

When God created everything, He used His unlimited power and boundless wisdom, but He was moved by His infinite love. That's where everything worthwhile begins: the love of God.

This great love of God must not flow into us as into a dead-end street. By the Spirit's power it flows through us and is reflected in our lives. Our love for God and for others, strengthened by gratitude for all God has done for us, especially for His gift of forgiveness and eternal salvation in Christ, is the dynamics, the driving power, behind the stewardship of our life.

We cannot possibly earn anything from God, nor can we pay Him for anything He has given us. All we want is an opportunity to show our love for Him and our gratitude. Stewardship is a wonderful way to do just that.

May our stewardship, O God, be a "thank You," spoken in a loud and clear way; in Jesus' name. Amen.

Armin C. Oldsen

Ephesians 4:17–32

Commandments in Stone

[Moses said:] "These are the commandments the Lord proclaimed. … He wrote them on two stone tablets and gave them to me." *Deuteronomy 5:22*

Between many of our nation's expressways there are concrete dividers. These are not meant to create hazards for motorists, but they are there for their safety. Yet as we drive along we see where cars have crashed into them, leaving black tire marks and evidence of metal scraping on concrete.

It is similar with the Ten Commandments, written by God on stone. Many people chafe under God's Law and, as it were, crash against it. Profanity, violence, and immorality are examples of such an attitude. The results are similar to crashing into an expressway divider. The offenders cause great damage to themselves and others. The commandments of God still stand as a curb, keeping His people safe.

God made His commandments clear and firm because He loves us. His love is made even plainer in the gift of His Son, who came to reclaim and renew the wrecks we make of our lives through sin. St. Paul writes, "God made Him who had no sin to be sin for us, so that in Him we might become the righteousness of God" (2 Corinthians 5:21). All who believe in Christ as their Savior are righteous in God's sight.

Lord God, out of love You have given us Your commandments. Help us to keep them because we love You; for Jesus' sake. Amen.

Walter F. Fisher

Ephesians 6:1–4

Family Ties

Do not exasperate your children; instead, bring them up in the training and instruction of the Lord. *Ephesians 6:4*

"God sets the solitary in families" (Psalm 68:6 NKJV). Just now the family, with its values and purposes, is under grave threat. The notion of a mother-father-child relationship seems arbitrary and random to many, and they are not beyond testing different forms of relationships.

But there is nothing arbitrary about the Lord's determination to make the family the basic unit to protect, educate, and fulfill the solitary souls of this world. Others may abandon the family unit in favor of some broader social organization or even the concept of total independence of individual, but God knew and knows what He is doing. And when He determined to establish the family as the structure for the nurture and growth and fulfillment of souls, He created a workable and functional pattern to assist and encourage the welfare of His world.

Christians must invest effort and time in the strengthening of the family. We are in the world but not of it. Family is assailed in our modern culture, and preserving its significance and worth becomes more and more difficult. Christians need purposely to employ every means to keep the family strong and to use it to bring up children and preserve one another in the faith.

Lord, help us to build our families on the foundation of Your will and Word, with Christ as the cornerstone; in His name. Amen.

Bonnie Schneider

Matthew 16:24–27

Are You Bored?

I have come that they may have life, and have it to the full.
John 10:10

Are you bored? Usually at one time or another we get into a rut and life becomes dull and uninteresting.

Why? Is it the sameness of each day that gets us? We sleep, we eat, we work. That is today. Tomorrow will be the same thing over again, back to the same old grind. Some people dislike their work and can't wait for payday.

Perhaps that is the problem. Perhaps we ought to take another look, not at our job but at ourselves. Perhaps we have forgotten that God wants us where we are because He has a special job for us to do. He has a life that we can touch when perhaps others could not.

Are you bored? Forget self. Turn to Christ, who says: "I have come that you may have life, and have it to the full." Turn to the cross because there the full life was made possible. The cross is the answer to life's boredom. Its vertical bar points us to God, and its horizontal bar points us to others.

Lord Jesus, take me away from myself. Draw me to You by the power of the cross. Amen.

Albert L. Neibacher

Psalm 78:1–7

Sharing the Gospel

Let this be written for a future generation, that a people not yet created may praise the Lord. *Psalm 102:18*

Lutheran Hour Ministries, a national organization dedicated to bringing the Gospel message to the world, has as its theme "Go ... tell a NEW generation." We have the responsibility and privilege to share the Gospel message with those who are new to the good news of salvation in Christ.

Begin at home. Share a prayer with a child. Help your children learn by your example that we can take everything to the Lord in prayer. Give your children Bibles of their own and help them read and understand the message of God's love in Jesus Christ. Our children represent the most accessible new generation.

You don't have to leave your own neighborhood. Your next-door neighbors may very well qualify as a new generation. Invite them to a special worship service, or invite a neighbor's children to vacation Bible school. Move out a little further to a co-worker, a client, or a clerk at the store where you shop.

Christianity will live in future generations. Its existence is in the hands of a new generation. There is no other way for the church yesterday to become the church tomorrow but through us who are the church today. May the Holy Spirit use us to "tell a new generation."

Dear Lord, help me eagerly to "tell a new generation" of Your love; through Jesus Christ. Amen.

Irma S. Pinkerton

Psalm 24:7–10

The King of Glory

Lift up your heads, O you gates; … that the King of glory may come in. *Psalm 24:9*

God's people sang this song long ago. How happy they were as they marched up to the temple-church on Mount Zion! They welcomed Jehovah, their hero. How often He had used His shining presence to rescue them!

Today joy also wells up in us because this God of glory sent His glorious Son, Jesus, as our deliverer. Jesus stepped through the broad portals of heaven and quietly slipped down to our earthly life. Stable doors creaked as they opened for the Lord of glory in His virgin mother's arms!

Years later the old gates of Jerusalem swung open for Him. A beast of burden carried Him through. People glorified His name. But that same week the city gates opened for Him the last time. People watched as He allowed Himself to become a beast of burden and carry a cross. But they did not see another heavier weight on His innocent shoulders—the burden of the guilt and evil of all people of all ages. Outside the city, this Lord did battle with our sins as He died on the cross at Golgotha.

We Christians go joyfully through church doors today. There the Lord lets us hear His glorious Gospel. His Spirit uses this Word to open any doors of our heart that our inner self wants closed to Him. Through the power of the Spirit, He comes into more and more areas of our thinking, feeling, and will. His presence today gives us a foretaste of our eternal glory.

Redeemer, come! By God's grace, I open wide my heart to You. Amen.

Arthur M. Vincent

Revelation 5:11–14

Campaign of Whispers

Blessed is he whose transgressions are forgiven, whose sins are covered. *Psalm 32:1*

A commentator on national radio stated that if he were the prince of darkness, he would take over the country with a campaign of whispers. To the youth he would whisper that the Bible is a myth, that what is bad is good, and what is good is outdated. He'd educate authors on how to make lurid literature exciting so anything else would appear boring. He would encourage the entertainment industry to produce more sexually explicit movies and television programs. With flattery and promises of power, he would get the courts to vote against God and in favor of pornography. "If I were Satan," he said, "I'd just keep on doing what he's doing, and the entire world would go to hell."

Into this world Christ came to release us from the influence of Satan. He is the Lamb who was slain to overcome the demon who wielded the power of death. On the cross of Calvary Christ gained our forgiveness. Is it any wonder that the psalmist speaks about the blessed happiness of the person who knows God's forgiveness?

To counteract the whisper campaign of Satan, we need what St. Paul calls "the full armor of God," including "the shield of faith, with which you can extinguish all the flaming arrows of the evil one" (Ephesians 6:13, 16).

Lord, by the power of Your Word help us overcome and resist Satan; through Christ Jesus, our Savior. Amen.

Rudolph A. Ritz

Luke 17:11–19

Giving Thanks

Give thanks in all circumstances, for this is God's will for you in Christ Jesus. *1 Thessalonians 5:18*

To say "thank you" is not very difficult. These probably were some of the first words your parents taught you to say. But often, a sincere expression of gratitude involves action. It calls for doing something besides mere talk.

A friend says "thank you" with a handshake or a hug. A baby says it with a gurgle and a coo. The boss says it with a raise. A child says it with a squeal and a shout. A flower says it with beauty.

But how do you say "thank You" to the Lord who made you, redeemed you, and gives you abundant blessings now, followed by eternal life? We give thanks regularly, and we mean it. We appreciate all of God's bountiful blessings.

Ultimately, our thanksgiving shows itself in the way we live. We give thanks with our gifts of love to the Lord and to others. We bring to God our hearts and demonstrate our love as we faithfully worship Him, follow Him and His leading in His Word, and care for others in true compassion, even as God in Christ cared for us.

Don't let your "thank You" just be words! Let it be from your heart as you give God the credit for all you are and have.

O Lord, let my heartfelt "thank You" show forth in manifold ways as I live for You; through Jesus Christ. Amen.

Luther C. Brunette

John 15:1–17

The Right Reason

If anyone loves Me, he will obey My teaching. My Father will love him, and We will come to him and make Our home with him. *John 14:23*

It is simple to do the right thing for the wrong reason. Our motives are not always pleasing to the Lord. They may be polluted with selfishness. "What's in it for me?" "Maybe she will help me later." "I will make a big impression."

Why do we try to do God's will? What motivates us to love God with all our heart, all our soul, all our mind? What is our motivation for loving our neighbor?

We love God because He first loved us. It was not possible for us to love Him, for we were dead in trespasses and sins. "But God demonstrates His own love for us in this: While we were still sinners, Christ died for us" (Romans 5:8).

We respond to God's love by keeping His commandments, by doing His will. His death and resurrection motivate us to present ourselves to Him in a life of service. We live a Christ-pleasing life because we love the Lord Jesus, who first loved us.

May His love motivate us in all that we do, think, and say!

Jesus, help me to live for You out of love to You, for You first loved me and gave Yourself for me. Amen.

Andrew Simcak Jr.

Romans 8:12–17

Sons and Daughters of the King

Now if we are children, then we are heirs—heirs of God and co-heirs with Christ. *Romans 8:17*

There is a legend about a king who was trying to solve the problems of a grubby and unhappy village. The village people were always bickering and quarreling with each other. The king came up with a plan. He issued this proclamation. "Somehow, at birth, there was a switch in babies, and my son or daughter is living in this village. I will be back to claim the child."

Life began to change. Each family wondered whether among its children might be a prince or princess. Parents became more patient and understanding. Children were treated with love and care. The dreary, unhappy village began to flourish, and it became a pleasant place to live.

We are all sons and daughters of the King. Remembering that *everyone* is the creation of God and that He has sent His Son so all may be saved, might we not treat each other differently? Living is not always an easy task. There are schedules to meet, chores to complete, and daily consideration of the needs of others above our own to regard. To maintain mutually fulfilling relationships takes effort and patience. Remember, the King is returning to claim His children—each of us.

Dear Lord, help me by the power of the Spirit to treat all people as precious in Your sight and in need of Your grace and love; in Jesus' name. Amen.

Irma S. Pinkerton

Isaiah 55:1–13

Christian Concern

I will bless you ... and you will be a blessing. *Genesis 12:2*

All of us heed the flashing lights and siren of a speeding ambulance. We pray that the patient receives prompt medical help and recovers quickly. Our Christian faith teaches us to have sympathy for the sick and injured. Jesus Himself taught concern and compassion for the needy.

Heathen religions demonstrate little regard for the afflicted. The ancient Greeks murdered deformed babies; other cultures eliminated their sick and aged. But because of the influence of a Christian woman named Fabiola, who lived in Rome in A.D. 390, the first public hospitals were established. Since then, Christians, recognizing their great responsibilities toward the suffering, have united their efforts to provide health care.

Most church bodies today support agencies of mercy and offer assistance to the physically and mentally disabled, the sick and dying, aged, homeless, needy, and abused. Jesus, the Savior of sinners, is primarily revealed as the true healer for life's desperate afflictions. Only He can cure our souls and make us right before God. Christians are to be generous in their support of healing ministries—out of concern for the spiritual and human needs of the helpless.

Lord Jesus, enable me to help lighten the pain of others. Amen.

Herbert G. Walther

2 Corinthians 4:5–11

Clay Pots

We have this treasure in jars of clay to show that this all-surpassing power is from God and not from us. *2 Corinthians 4:7*

Paul had just told the Corinthian Christians that God, who had made the light to shine out of darkness, had now shined into their hearts with the glorious Gospel of His Son. This, he said, was their greatest treasure. Then he is quick to add: "But we have this treasure in jars of clay"—the ordinary, unadorned crockery that was very much in evidence in every ancient home. The jars were useful but were seldom an item of art or beauty.

Why this language? To remind them (and us) that the power of the Gospel lies in the God-given *treasure* (His life-giving Word) and not in its frail and fragile containers—not in you and me who are merely the conveyors of the good news of His saving love. We are merely vessels. Pots! But we are pots that carry treasure of inestimable worth.

Not our eloquence, not our personality, not our winsomeness! But, as Paul says elsewhere, it is the Gospel of Christ, and nothing else, that is "the power of God for the salvation of everyone who believes" (Romans 1:16). May we both hold and share that precious treasure!

Lord, You have entrusted us with the treasure of Your Gospel offered in Your Word and sacraments. May we always prove faithful to that trust; for Jesus' sake. Amen.

Herman W. Gockel

Revelation 15:1–4

The Broken Watch

Could you not keep watch for one hour? *Mark 14:37*

Last year, a church in California hit on an idea to increase church attendance. It advertised that one of the services each Sunday would last fewer than 30 minutes. They were right. Attendance did increase.

Nothing in Scripture suggests the proper length of a worship service, but most today are in the one-hour range. Just because you occupy a church pew for an hour on Sunday mornings doesn't mean that you have kept watch with Jesus. What might distract you? Planning next week's menu? Letting your mind wander during the sermon? Anticipating the excitement of the afternoon's football game on TV? Reflecting on last week's business deals? Preparing a mental outline for the research paper due next week?

Jesus' question, "Could you not keep watch for one hour?" is just as appropriate for us as it was for the disciples in the Garden of Gethsemane before His arrest and crucifixion. If our answer is an embarrassing no, we pray for forgiveness and also ask for alertness and concentration in the future. No matter how long your worship service is, use the time to hear God's Word, pray, and sing praises.

Lord of the Sabbath, help me watch with You one hour; in Jesus' name. Amen.

Dave and Carol Ebeling

1 Peter 1:13–21

The Priceless Christ

You were bought at a price. *1 Corinthians 6:20*

Have you ever considered the value of a human life? Have you ever thought about *your* true value? People are likely to forget this in our age of violence and killing. To some governments the lives of people are cheap and used or abused at will by those who are in power. In our country too many people forget the real value of life. And all of us at times fail to recognize our own true worth.

The Lord Jesus Christ—and thank God for that—understood the value of a soul. So clearly was this impressed on Him that He was willing to sacrifice Himself that our life, not just our body, but our whole being, might be redeemed by God. We were bought not with gold or silver, but with the holy, precious blood shed by God's innocent Son. Our God and Creator, who is beyond and above all values, gave Himself that we might have everlasting life.

Priceless indeed is our Lord Jesus Christ! And we are priceless too. All the wealth of the world is valueless when compared with a single soul. What dignity the priceless Christ bestows on the sons and daughters of clay! No human being, certainly no Christian, should ever again despise life, either one's own or that of any other. We should consider how expensive we are, how much was paid for us. And when we realize that, a most wonderful confidence and self-respect comes to us. We will regard every other human being with the same respect, knowing that all are bought with the price of the priceless Christ.

Heavenly Father, thank You for making us valuable in Your sight, through the precious blood of Your Son; in Him we pray. Amen.

Edwin P. Nerger

Matthew 6:25–34

Some Rush and Some See

Look at the birds of the air. … See how the lilies of the field grow. *Matthew 6:26, 28*

Once on a trail we met some hikers whose main purpose seemed to be how quickly they could walk those miles. We wondered how much they actually saw as they rushed along. Oh, no one could miss the big views. But what about the little beauties God created—the wildflowers, the birds, the varieties of mushrooms?

Some people seem to be that way on the trail of life. They rush from one experience to another, demanding that everything be exciting.

But what about the little things of life? And what about the fact that life is not always exciting? What about those times in life when we agonize with pain or heartache?

That's when we need to appreciate the little beauties God gives us—the smile of a stranger, the listening ear of a friend, quiet conversation with a loved one, a delicate flower, a gentle rain, a glorious sunset.

Exciting experiences can also be gifts from God, but those are usually few and far between. But the little things are always here to encourage us if we only take time to see them. Most of all, Jesus is with us always, forgiving, comforting, guiding as our beautiful Savior.

Thank You, Lord, for the little beauties You have placed along my trail of life. Amen.

Theodore E. Allwardt Sr.

John 14:1–7

Going Ahead

The Lord Himself goes before you and will be with you; He will never leave you nor forsake you. Do not be afraid; do not be discouraged. *Deuteronomy 31:8*

"There's a long detour on Highway 18. Why don't you take 35 over to 90 instead? You'll probably make better time."

Someone has been there ahead of us and tells us of the detours. So too the Lord goes before us and knows what lies ahead. Whether it is surgery, a job change, or continuing an education, the Lord goes ahead of us. He is already there, preparing the doctors, filling the new office with His presence, softening the hearts of the teachers.

When we are there, He will see us through the hard times, directing us around or through the detours. He will bring us to our goal.

We trust in Jesus' ability to do this because He has already gone before us to the cross. He has taken the punishment that should have rightly been ours for the sins we commit. He has endured more pain and sorrow than we will ever face. He can tell us about the detours and distresses of life from His own experience, then add His love and direction to it.

Without Christ's strength and guidance offered through His Word and sacrament, how could we ever endure the changes and challenges of life? With it, we can do all things.

Lord Jesus, help me to trust that You have been before me in anything I will face today. Prepare me and direct me. Amen.

Gary and Christine Dehnke

1 Corinthians 7:32–35

A Word to the Single

To the unmarried and the widows I say: It is good for them to stay unmarried, as I am. *1 Corinthians 7:8*

Marriage is not for everyone. Not everyone desires to be married. Not everyone who wants to get married has the opportunity to do so. Some people, because of their chosen vocation in life or because of circumstances that would make married life difficult for them, voluntarily decide to forego marriage. God gives them this right.

It may come as a surprise to some to learn that Paul himself was single. One of the few things about his personal life that he shares with us is the fact that he did not have a wife. What is more, he can even write to those in his congregation in Corinth who were not married that it would be "good for them to stay unmarried."

Those of us who are married should be sensitive to the situation and needs of those among us who remain single. All of us who have been baptized, single and married alike, belong to Christ's body. We are therefore all members of His household and of His family. In a spirit of mutual encouragement that comes from Christ, let each of us help and support one another in our pilgrimage through life. We do it for the sake of Christ, who in love died for us.

Lord Jesus, help us at all times to be sensitive to the needs of others; for Your sake. Amen.

Samuel H. Nafzger

Luke 3:7–20

Coward or Hero?

For John had been saying to Herod, "It is not lawful for you to have your brother's wife." *Mark 6:18*

The world of John the Baptist was anything but rosy. The spiritual leaders were corrupt; the occupation troops were oppressive; and King Herod was living in flagrant adultery.

If immorality cannot be tolerated in low places, then certainly it cannot be condoned in high places. With privilege comes responsibility.

The will and the Word of God had touched the heart and soul of John. He could not remain silent. He spoke out against the evils of his day, though it meant imprisonment and death in a foul Roman dungeon. Thomas Carlyle said that everyone must answer the question: "Wilt thou be a hero or a coward?" Perhaps we all have a bit of both in us.

We live in a day when circumstances are not always conducive to decency and truth. Do we remain strangely silent in the face of the tremendous racial, social, moral, and spiritual problems of our day? As those who have been cleansed by the blood of Jesus and enlightened by the Holy Spirit, do we have a testimony to share? Do we have the courage to stand for the truth regardless of the consequences?

Dear God, help me to face reality and the problems of this day in the spirit of Jesus, my Lord; in Him I pray. Amen.

Stratford Eynon

1 Peter 2:9–12

Living Letters

You show that you are a letter from Christ. *2 Corinthians 3:3*

Our function as Christ's followers in the world is to serve as His witnesses. While it is true that the Gospel is the only means the Holy Spirit uses to convert sinners, it is also true that people are attracted to Christ as they see Him at work in His followers. Christ speaks of us as being the light of the world, and He encourages us to let the light of our Christian faith shine before all people.

Scripture also reminds us that as Christians we are living letters that others read. Our speech and conduct, the principles for which we stand, the ethics we follow, the hopes and ideals we express, and whatever else constitutes our life expresses whether Christ lives in us and whether we live in Him. People study our lives as they read a book. And what they see and hear attracts them to Christ or repels them from Christ.

Being disciples of Christ goes far beyond attending worship services and contributing from our material wealth for the work of the church. By God's grace it involves giving ourselves to Christ, dedicating our lives to Him, and glorifying Him in all we think and say and do.

Lord Jesus, make us legible and living letters of Your mercy, love, and grace. Amen.

Remus C. Rein

Romans 7:13–25

Strength for the Soul

What a wretched man I am! Who will rescue me from this body of death? *Romans 7:24*

Have you ever felt like that? Do you ever share this dark and dismal feeling of the apostle Paul? Do you ever feel that life is a fizzle, a failure, a fraud? Does your conscience nag and gnaw at you or beat you down with a long list of failures, sins, and short-comings?

Like Paul, we struggle with sin. We struggle with our "old Adam," as Martin Luther describes it. We review and reflect on this past week—the encouraging word we didn't speak, the ugly gossip or profanity that came from our mouth, the unkind thoughts and words and deeds. "What I do is not the good I want to do; no, the evil I do not want to do—this I keep on doing" (Romans 7:19).

There is help and healing. There is the gift of forgiveness. There is strength for the soul. It is the good news of God's glorious Gospel. Let's go to church and bask in the blessings of this Gospel! The cross of Christ will be preached and proclaimed. Jesus died there for you and for me. That message will lift us up and give strength to our souls.

Dear Lord Jesus, we thank You for the gift of free and full forgiveness through Your merit. Strengthen our souls as we gather for worship in God's house. Amen.

Victor F. Halboth Jr.

John 6:16–24

Act of God

We rejoice in the hope of the glory of God. *Romans 5:2*

Many people believed in Jesus when He gave sight to the blind and when He fed a huge crowd with a handful of food. These and other signs signaled God's presence in the world in the person of Jesus Christ.

Today God still signals His presence. Paul writes, "And now these three remain: faith, hope and love" (1 Corinthians 13:13). What miraculous signs these are! What is more extraordinary than the consecrated lives of ordinary Christians? What is more remarkable than the day-to-day dedicated work of God's people? What is more significant than our continued confidence in Jesus and His promise of salvation?

"But the greatest of these is love," declares Paul. The Holy Spirit produces the miracle of patience, kindness, and humility in us in the middle of a society that glorifies quick results, personal power, and self-promotion. We testify by our lives to trust and perseverance, contrary to trendy beliefs and changeable values. It is a miracle that the truth is still taught, preached, and believed in its purity, despite the proclamations of those who would rewrite the Word of God.

Miracles, signs, and wonders? The greatest miracle is that miracle of love that God forgives us for Jesus' sake. By the power of the Holy Spirit, we see them! We live them!

Jesus, work in us the miracle of Your Spirit. Amen.

Pat Mitchell

Isaiah 44:24–28

A Wonder of the World

I praise You because I am fearfully and wonderfully made; Your works are wonderful. *Psalm 139:14*

A Christian is a wonder of the world. Compare yourself to the rest of God's creation. It's amazing! What a wonder our bodies are! There is no doubt about it. They are carefully crafted by the all-knowing mind and powerful hand of God. In 24 hours your heart beats 103,689 times and your blood travels 168 million miles. In addition to that, you breathe 23,040 times, inhale 438 cubic feet of air, move 750 muscles, and exercise 7 million brain cells. The body's entire structure is a miracle of precision engineering and production. "Your works are wonderful," Lord! It is surely evidenced in my body.

But far greater than all that is the fact that God not only created me as a wonder of the world but also redeemed me, a lost and condemned creature. While I was yet a sinner, Jesus Christ died for me. Through the gift of saving faith in Christ I have forgiveness, salvation, and new life. That too makes me a wonder of the world—and a wonder of the world to come, where I will live with Him forever in heaven. We speak of the seven wonders of the world. Let's add an eighth wonder—the Christian, created and redeemed by the Lord.

Thank You, Lord, for creating and redeeming me. Help me to honor my body as the temple of the Holy Spirit; in Jesus' name. Amen.

David W. Hoover

John 15:1–12

We Live by Faith

For to me, to live is Christ. *Philippians 1:21*

There is a real danger that life can quickly pass us by. It depends on how we live our lives. We can so easily make the highlights of our lives temporary, passing pleasures of this world—a party, a concert, a trip, a football game. We can set our sights higher and concentrate on making money, gaining social prestige, advancing in position or profession. For many people, life is lived one day simply to live another day "tomorrow," until the tomorrows are no more. But is any of this real living?

By God's grace, it is possible to live our lives in such a way that every day is vital and meaningful, rich in purpose. If we can say with St. Paul every day of our lives that living itself is Christ, then each of those days takes on tremendous significance. Then our day is tied in with the meaning of eternity, and the power of God fills our lives.

A life in which Christ has been the motivating power cannot be insignificant, even if it should go completely unnoticed by the world. The most humble duties take on some of the glory of heaven when performed for the glory of God. Our lives can be filled with the glory of God when by faith we live in Christ and He in us.

Lord Jesus, dwell within our hearts and fill us with Your love, Your glory, Your purpose. Amen.

Arnim H. Polster

Proverbs 22:2–11

A Christian Home

Train a child in the way he should go, and when he is old he will not turn from it. *Proverbs 22:6*

It's a great advantage to live in a Christian home and take part in Christian home life. We are concerned about maintaining a Christian atmosphere in our homes. What are some of the ingredients of the Christian home life?

1. The love Christ has for us and we for Him shows in the respect members of a Christian household have for each other.

2. Forgiveness, like the forgiveness we experience through Christ's suffering and death on Calvary, is practiced and expressed.

3. Prayers, Bible readings, and Christian music are part of daily living.

4. Moral values based on biblical truths are taught and practiced.

5. There is a sense of fellowship, belonging, and security.

6. There is trust, love, and affection.

No home is without conflict. The difference in a Christian home is how we deal with it. Christian family members deal with each other in a manner that reflects the love of Christ. Indeed, the love of Christ, His for us and ours for Him, is at the very heart and center of a Christian home.

Dear Lord, endow our families with Your love. Amen.

Irma S. Pinkerton

Rest Awhile

Come with Me by yourselves to a quiet place and get some rest. *Mark 6:31*

For many people the sense of work is overwhelming. The term "workaholic" identifies them as victims of the earnest desire to work constantly. For some it is an intense drive to get ahead, to climb the ladder to success. Occasionally some use work to keep from facing other concerns in life such as family responsibilities or spiritual obligations. Others are seemingly driven by a sense of duty towards work that makes them feel guilty when they take time off.

It is not a sin to take a vacation or to relax. The heavenly Father designated a time for quitting our labor. Christ called His disciples to rest and thereby be "re-created."

Sometimes in the home the work that never ends takes its toll. Mothers who have a deep sense of dedication to their calling can be trapped in the constant pressure of caring for families. They are fatigued and yet also have guilt feelings, because many also have jobs outside the home. A wise and considerate family needs to take frequent stock of its goals, its division of duties, its periods of recreation. To rest and to worship are God's design for our well-being.

Restore me, Lord, through rest and prayer; for Jesus' sake. Amen.

Victor L. Brandt

John 17:20–26

Called

Open your eyes and look at the fields! They are ripe for harvest. *John 4:35*

He lived in Capernaum and worked for the Romans. It was taken for granted that he would steal from the locals by overcharging them on their taxes. Not exactly the kind one would expect Jesus to recruit for work in His harvest field.

Matthew sat at his tax collector's booth when Jesus walked by. "Follow Me," Jesus commanded, right out of the blue. And Matthew got up and followed (Matthew 9:9). The call of Jesus changed Matthew. He never returned to his booth or profession. Starting right then and there, he followed Christ and spent his whole life spreading the Gospel of God's love.

God has called us through His Word and Baptism. He has heard us pray for workers to be sent into His harvest field. He answers our prayers with a simple "Go." Our Lord is acutely conscious of souls who wait to hear the Gospel from us. Surely if He can use Matthew, He can use you. He changes the hearts of the corrupt, strengthens those who are fearful, and speaks through the mouths of the shy. He has chosen you. He will radiate His glory through what you do and lead you to those who are ready to be "harvested" for His Kingdom.

Father, lead me to be an eager witness and to go joyfully into Your harvest field; through Jesus Christ, our Lord. Amen.

Bonnie Schneider

Matthew 6:5–15

The Royal Castle

The Lord's Prayer is like a magnificent royal castle. With the words "Our Father in heaven" we knock at the great door. Through faith in our Lord Jesus Christ it is opened to us at once.

As we enter, the angels stand singing: "Holy, holy, holy," and we too honor Him. "Hallowed be Your name."

We step into the great hall of His throne, where all the saints who have gone before us bow in adoration, and we pray, "Your kingdom come." We ask Him to keep us in the faith and lead many others into His kingdom.

We now enter His private cabinet, where He issues His commands and where His messengers go out to do His will. Humbly we pray, "Your will be done on earth as it is in heaven."

We proceed to the royal storehouse where the sun receives heat and the soil strength, and we pray, "Give us today our daily bread." We know it is His hand that feeds and sustains us.

Moving on to His treasury, where the bills are presented and paid, we plead: "Forgive us our sins." Though undeserving, our debt of wrongs are paid in full and we pledge to forgive others who have wronged us.

With our plea, "Lead us not into temptation," He opens His armory where we are equipped to find the right path and escape hidden snares of the enemy.

We humbly ask, "Deliver us from evil," and He brings us into His royal garden to view the crystal fountain.

"The kingdom, the power, and the glory are Yours now and forever. Amen."

C. W. Berner

2 Timothy 1:3–14

Energizer for Living

I can do everything through Him who gives me strength.
Philippians 4:13

The poster read, "Energy is nothing more than a love of life." This is especially true for us whose hope is in Jesus, the resurrection and the life. Energetic living hinges on drawing our strength and love from Him. Jesus offers the vitality and stamina to live in God's service. Through His means of grace—Word and sacraments—He supplies each Christian with a readily available source of energy: His Spirit. When we live for Him who has redeemed us, we experience exhilaration and rejuvenation because the Spirit is lifting us above the way of the world with the divine breath of life.

An energy crisis results from working at tasks that He would not have us perform. Or relying on our own power when the job requires His. Either way blocks out the Holy Spirit, causing Him to ebb instead of flow in us. Both are red flags that warn us to return to His Word and an active prayer life.

The study of God's Word, the remembrance of our Baptism, and frequent attendance at the Lord's Supper—all accompanied by a fervent prayer life—keep life flowing in our spiritual veins and equip us for living with joy and enthusiasm. We too can do everything through Him who gives us strength.

O God, our Strength, provide energy equal to the tasks You have given us as we seek to do Your will; for Jesus' sake. Amen.

Norman W. Stoppenhagen

1 Corinthians 15:3–11

I Am What I Am

By the grace of God I am what I am, and His grace to me was not without effect. *1 Corinthians 15:10*

Most of us have days that leave us with the frustrated feeling that we would have been better off staying in bed. The whole day seemed to be a waste.

Too often on such days we may look at God and ask, "Why have You made me like this?" We wish God had made us as wise as others we know—and as strong, as talented, as ambitious.

We find ourselves disgruntled by the limited abilities we think we have and the poor opportunities offered us to make use of them. The best cure for this attitude is gratitude.

Each of us should say, "I did not choose the circumstances of my birth, my parents, my intelligence, my body characteristics. All these vital components were chosen by God for me." Each of us can say, "I am a beloved child of God. All that I am and have is a gift from Him."

People should not take credit for what they look like, the things they have acquired, their abilities or the chance to use them. These are undeserved gifts of God. This keeps us humble. But to be humble does not mean to feel inferior, to downgrade ourselves. We are worth much, and to say this is to honor God.

We thank You, heavenly Father, for the gift of life. Help us to use the gift wisely; for Jesus' sake. Amen.

Alma Kern

Psalm 98

Asking for Heaven!

When you pray, say … "Your will be done on earth as it is in heaven." *Luke 11:2 NKJV*

Paradise was lost when man first said, "My will be done." The clashing of the wills of humankind perpetuates and compounds the turmoil and the trouble, the darkness and disorder of this world.

Someone has said, "The world resembles an orchestra gone berserk, each musician playing his own favorite tune." Anyone who has listened to an orchestra tuning up before a concert knows the result. There is noise instead of music, discord in the place of harmony. If there is to be music, the musicians must submit to the will and direction of the conductor.

When Jesus asks us to pray, "Thy will be done," He is not asking us to give in and give up all that is precious and good in life. On the contrary, He tells us how we can make our corner of the earth a bit more like heaven.

To pray "Thy will be done" is to ask for heaven. It is asking God to change our discord into concord and the nerve-jangling noise of earth into a harmonious symphony of sound. "Thy will be done on earth as it is in heaven." Heaven is a place of joy because in Paradise the ordered will of God is always done. There God conducts, and the whole company of heaven plays the tune He calls.

Our Father, make us unafraid to ask for heaven; for Jesus' sake. Amen.

Jack H. Ruff

Genesis 39:1–23

Faith Overcomes Temptation

How then could I do such a wicked thing and sin against God? *Genesis 39:9*

Genesis 39 reads like a well-developed soap opera. The characters represent Egypt's high society: Potiphar, the wealthy official in Pharaoh's court; his flirtatious wife; and Joseph, the handsome, industrious Israelite slave. This biblical account would have become even more sordid had not the Lord given Joseph a keen sense of what is morally right.

Joseph could have given in to his master's wife and remained secure in his position. But he knew that to sin against God was to risk losing the Lord who was with him. By God's grace, he chose to do what was right, even though he was falsely accused and imprisoned. He preferred to be in prison with the Lord, rather than in power without the Lord. But his gracious Lord eventually exalted him to an even higher position.

Jesus was faithful to the Father who had sent Him, never succumbing to temptation. He too was falsely accused and punished. But Jesus' suffering earned pardon for all who give in to temptation. Christ then was exalted to the right hand of the Father, where He ever pleads for us. May we all strive to be faithful to our Lord, who is with us in Christ, our Savior.

O God, enlighten us so we may see the clear path of Your will and not stray from it; through Jesus Christ, our Lord. Amen.

Gordon A. Beck

John 6:1–14

The Power of One

Here is a boy with five small barley loaves and two small fish, but how far will they go among so many? *John 6:9*

One young boy did not seem very significant that day in a crowd of five thousand people. His supply of bread and fish would not have gone very far even if he had been willing to share or sell them. But the boy became a good example for us because he made his bread and fish available to Jesus. Jesus' power then multiplied them so they were able to feed the vast throng.

Most of us may not feel significant. The abilities we have and the things we possess may not seem very important in relieving the misery of the world. Yet today, as in the past, God can do much with our little, if we let Him.

One act of kindness can brighten the whole day for several other people. Those who were helped come into contact with others and can multiply the effect of that one kind deed. One work of forgiveness or encouragement sometimes sets the direction of an entire life.

Let us remember the power of one person—the influence for good that each of us has if we are willing to be available when God wants to use us. Through one person God can bless a whole family, change a community for the better, and inspire an entire congregation.

Lord Jesus, help us to seize every opportunity You give us today to love You through loving others. Amen.

Alma Kern

Romans 10:5–13

What Shall I Do?

What shall I do, then, with the one you call the king of the Jews? *Mark 15:12*

The moral law confronts us with our sin. That can make people very uncomfortable. We do not like to be confronted with our sin. After all, most people in this world aren't even sure how to define "sin." In a world where the watchwords are "do your own thing" and "if it feels right, it is right," the followers of Jesus do not always know what to do. We echo the words first spoken by Pilate when he was confronted by Jesus, "What shall I do, then, with the one you call the king of the Jews?"

What shall I do, then, with the one who calls me the salt of the earth? What shall I do, then, with the one who tells me to go make disciples of all nations? What shall I do, then, with the one who assures me that even though I die, I will live? What shall I do, then, with the one who would have all people to be saved and to come to the knowledge of the truth?

What we shall do is accept from our heavenly Father the gift of forgiveness through the suffering, death, and physical resurrection of Jesus. What we shall do is respond to God's love by telling others about the Savior. What we shall do is thank and praise, serve and obey our Lord. What we shall do, by God's grace, is spend eternity with Him in heaven.

My precious Jesus, build in me the faith and confidence to proclaim Your love to those who are closest to me. Amen.

Dave and Carol Ebeling

Ephesians 5:15–20

Sing!

Speak to one another with psalms, hymns and spiritual songs. Sing and make music in your heart to the Lord, always giving thanks to God the Father for everything. *Ephesians 5:19–20*

Singing is an act of worship by which we praise and glorify God for His mercy and goodness. We are encouraged to speak to one another with psalms and hymns and spiritual songs. We edify one another in this way. Christian hymns touch some of our deepest personal needs.

We may not remember much of the sermon we heard, but a line from a well-known hymn will lodge in our mind and comfort and strengthen us. We may come to church in a pessimistic mood, but the music dispels our negative thoughts and directs our attention to God. Often we catch ourselves humming a familiar tune or mentally reciting a favorite stanza.

The Holy Spirit also uses hymns to open hearts to the Gospel message of salvation through faith in Jesus Christ. God's people have so many wonderful blessings to sing about. Even the smallest child can sing and understand "Jesus loves me, this I know, for the Bible tells me so." That's the greatest theme we can ever sing about.

Enable us, dear Lord, to use music and hymns to glorify You and to benefit ourselves and others; in Jesus' name. Amen.

Oscar J. Klinkermann

Ephesians 6:10–20

The Average Dare

[Caleb said,] "We should go up and take possession of the land, for we can certainly do it." *Numbers 13:30*

Not a moment's hesitation for Caleb! The land of Canaan lay ahead, and no gloomy scouting reports would hold him back! The children of Israel were afraid. Only Caleb and Joshua had sufficient daring to want to go ahead and occupy the land.

I am strangely attracted by the quality of daring. Yet my life seems too ordinary and commonplace to provide opportunities like Caleb's. Heroism seems out of place in a placid daily routine.

Are there no things for me to dare? No ventures lying ahead this week? No land of Canaan to conquer? Perhaps I overlook the fields I need to occupy, the challenges of the average life.

There is the venture of prayer, which calls for boldness in coming to the throne of grace. I dare to confess my sins to You today and expect them to be conquered by Your forgiveness in Christ! Will I dare to use Your Spirit to crush the faults that plague me? Will I be bold today to be Your person in all I do and say? Will I offer myself in love to those in need, stand up for the oppressed, resist the pressures of gossip and "group thinking"? Will I dare to accept the challenge of witness, the adventure of work in my church?

It is the average dares I need to recognize, and I seek the everyday boldness to meet them.

O Lord, clothe me with Your armor, and pour out Your Spirit on me to make my life a bold venture in Christ; in Him I pray. Amen.

Nicholas B. May

Ephesians 5:1–20

Redeeming the Time

Redeeming the time, because the days are evil. *Ephesians 5:16 KJV*

We are a time-minded people. Time is a tyrant in football games, in travel schedules, in work output. By watches chained to their wrists, people shackle themselves to time. Clock hands point not so much to minutes and hours as to people and say, "You concede to us!" All the while, time was made for us, not the other way around.

Time that is past and time yet to come cannot be bought. Yet Paul tells us to redeem the time. To redeem means to buy back. When we put a new value on time and on the things we do in time, we are in effect buying it back. When we "understand what the will of the Lord is," we are redeeming time. When we love God and serve our neighbor, we are giving a new value to our time and are thus buying it back. The same is true when we visit the sick, befriend the lonely, help the oppressed, and do good to our enemies. What better way is there to redeem the time than to pray daily and study God's Word?

Time needs this reevaluation "because the days are evil." Jesus foretold that between His ascent into heaven and His return there would be evil days. But He assured us also: "I have overcome the world" (John 16:33). Thanks to His victory, we can redeem the time and turn evil days into good days.

Lord, You have given us the gift of time. Help us to use it wisely in service to You and others; for Christ's sake. Amen.

George W. Bornemann

Exodus 2:1–10

Moses' Pro-life Parents

By faith Moses' parents hid him for three months after he was born. *Hebrews 11:23*

It is refreshing to read of committed parents such as Amram and Jochebed (Exodus 6:20). They recognized that children are gifts of God whose lives are precious. Moses, their baby son, would grow up to become the one through whom God would deliver His people. The attitude of these parents contrasts sharply with that of many today who resort to the evil of abortion to terminate unwanted pregnancies. Is not such a spirit in our day similar to that of the Egyptian Pharaoh, who ordered that the newborn males be cast into the Nile River? Abortion kills infants before they see the light of their first day.

How different is the view of Jesus! He asks that little ones be brought to Him so He can bless them. In Holy Baptism, they are born anew as His children. He came to seek and save everyone from sin, including infants, who also need His forgiveness. Jesus gave His own life as the ransom for all. Does it not take a special measure of faith for a woman with an unintended pregnancy to bring that new life into the world, then nurture and bring her child to Christ, the Savior? May God give all women the strength of faith for reaching God-pleasing decisions. May all of us give them our love and support.

Lord, may we ever treasure and care for the precious lives You commit to our keeping; in the name of Jesus. Amen.

M. D. Hilgendorf

John 15:18–24

Pupil, See Your Teacher

A student is not above his teacher, but everyone who is fully trained will be like his teacher. *Luke 6:40*

When it comes to spiritual matters, who are our teachers? They are our parents, our pastors, our grandparents, our Sunday school and religion instructors, our church leaders, and every Christian who leads a godly life according to God's Word.

The thought that we should be fully like them may cause us some misgivings. Think of Peter's denial and the disciples' fear. We should be like *them?* It does not take much scrutiny to discover that our parents and teachers commit many sins against God and others. We hear them regularly acknowledge their sins and ask for forgiveness in their prayers and confessions.

To see our Christian teachers only as weak and sinful is not to be fully taught. For faithful teachers do not presume or claim to be perfect. Their endeavor is to point us to the great master and teacher, Jesus Christ. Their desire is to show that He has forgiven them by His saving cross and that He has this forgiveness for us. They want us to know this teacher, Jesus Christ, that we may learn of Him and follow in His steps as dedicated Christians.

Lord Christ, make us faithful disciples who seek to bring others to You that You might be their teacher and Savior too. Amen.

Karl E. Lutze

Luke 14:12–14

Why Do It?

Whatever you do, work at it with all your heart, as working for the Lord, not for men. *Colossians 3:23*

There is a reason behind every action one does. We cannot always tell what it may be, just as we cannot always know what prompts some of our own actions. What looks like a kind act may have an unkind motive behind it. In Jesus' short sermon to the Pharisee who had invited Him to dinner, the Lord warns against doing good things to get some reward.

What the Lord cautioned against does not sound strange to us. We find ourselves tied up in that kind of thing. We often do things because we think we can get something out of it for ourselves. In a little while we find ourselves going around in circles, measuring out very carefully what we will do for someone and what the chances are for getting an equal return. The sad thing is that the circles get smaller and smaller until we find ourselves serving ourselves. And that is not a pretty sight.

Why do Christians work at the daily job? Why do they show love for others? Why do they do this willingly and enthusiastically? For only one reason. Christians know they are serving the Lord Jesus. They don't expect a reward. Reward does not matter. What matters is the confidence that they are doing this for Christ. All of life is laid at the feet of the Lord.

Dear Lord, teach us to live heartily to You and serve You alone; for Jesus' sake. Amen.

Martin L. Kretzmann

Mark 2:1–13

In a Crowd

Since they could not get him to Jesus because of the crowd, they made an opening in the roof. *Mark 2:4*

It isn't always easy to get through a crowd. If you have ever tried to elbow your way to a sale table or leave a sporting event with the throng, you know how rude and pushy a crowd can be. The crowd in the account as related by Mark was in the way, making it impossible for the paralytic's friends to get him in front of Jesus or even into the same room with Him. It took ingenuity and a lot of determination to climb to the roof, remove some of its tiles, and lower their friend in front of the master.

What stands in your way and keeps you from bringing your friends to Jesus? Is it the crowds of those who surround us, who do not know Jesus and who make sharing Jesus with friends uncomfortable? Is it the temptation to put off sharing Jesus and His love to a better time or more suitable place?

This man's friends were persistent. Sharing Jesus with others calls for persistence. May the Spirit help us clear the way for things that would keep our friends from coming to Jesus. May the Spirit help us be ready to speak to them the words that share the message of forgiveness, life, and salvation. May the Spirit help us determine that nothing will stop us from bringing our friends to Jesus and Jesus to our friends.

Jesus, make me a determined and persistent witness so I might bring my friends to You. Amen.

Charles A. and Jeanette Groth

Ephesians 1:3–10

Our Greatest Problem Solved

In [Christ] we have … the forgiveness of sins. *Ephesians 1:7*

Sin is our worst problem. For that reason the Bible addresses itself so fully to it. It tells us that the believer's sins are

1. *confessed*—"If we confess our sins, He is faithful and just and will forgive us our sins" (1 John 1:9);

2. *forgiven*—"Your sins have been forgiven on account of His name" (1 John 2:12);

3. *cleansed*—"Though your sins are like scarlet, they shall be as white as snow" (Isaiah 1:18);

4. *behind God's back*—"You have put all my sins behind Your back" (Isaiah 38:17);

5. *removed*—"As far as the east is from the west, so far has He removed our transgressions from us" (Psalm 103:12);

6. *cast into the sea*—"You will … hurl all our iniquities into the depths of the sea" (Micah 7:19);

7. *blotted out*—"I, even I, am He who blots out your transgressions, for My own sake, and remembers your sins no more" (Isaiah 43:25);

8. *forgotten*—"Their sins and lawless acts I will remember no more" (Hebrews 10:17).

What more do we need to love, serve, thank, and glorify our Lord?

Thousand, thousand thanks are due, dearest Jesus, unto You. Amen.

Carl W. Berner Sr.

2 Corinthians 6:1–10

A Perfect Day

This is the day the Lord has made. *Psalm 118:24*

The most difficult thing in life is to live in the present. Many of us diminish the joy of the present moment by regretting the mistakes of the past or by anticipating the troubles of the future. Hence the present moment, with its opportunities and responsibilities, escapes us.

In contrast to this, the word of the psalmist comes to us: "This is the day the Lord has made." This is the day in which we are living. All the past days are gone forever; those to come have not yet arrived. So we live for this one.

This day is weighty. This day you must face your problems squarely; this day you seek to be a faithful spouse, a concerned parent, a conscientious employee, a true disciple of Christ. This day is weighty because God made it; He is in control of it.

What has God done to enable us to live not only in the present but also in His presence? In eternity God planned our salvation, ordaining that His Son be born, suffer, die, and rise again on set days to save us. Because there were such days, we are at peace with God today. Each day now comes as a precious gift of God, and we can rejoice in it.

Lord, help us see that this is the day of salvation; through Jesus Christ, our Lord. Amen.

Henry C. Duwe

Exodus 3:9–14

You Don't Mean Me!

Who am I that I should go to Pharaoh and bring the Israelites out of Egypt? *Exodus 3:11*

God imposes many interesting challenges on us through the responsibilities of life. These come to us in business, in the church, in our personal lives. Unfortunately, many people try to excuse themselves from these challenges. By not using fully their abilities, many people deny themselves a rewarding experience.

Moses tried to do this very thing. God called him to lead the children of Israel out of Egypt. Moses said, "Who am I?" He told God that He must have gotten hold of the wrong man. Surely God could not mean him! Had God accepted his excuse, Moses would have been buried a forgotten shepherd.

How often we seek to run away from the challenges and opportunities that God in His wisdom gives us! The Lord dares us as Christians to live the life of heroic faith and service. He wants us to give of our gifts and ourselves to build the Kingdom. He promises blessings to us through the obligations we meet. How often do we excuse ourselves and say, "Surely, Lord, You do not mean me!" Let us learn to accept God's challenge.

By God's grace, we shall rise to the full stature of our being as Christians, redeemed for a life of service by our precious Savior, who came to Bethlehem, humble and poor, to enrich our lives now and in eternity.

Gracious heavenly Father, through Christ Jesus You have redeemed us and shown us how to accept every challenge that You place before us. For His sake grant us the grace to do Your work. Amen.

Edwin E. Nerger

Proverbs 16:1–9

Perfect Planning

"For I know the plans I have for you," declares the Lord, "plans to prosper you and not to harm you, plans to give you hope and a future." *Jeremiah 29:11*

Prior planning prevents poor performance. Anyone who has planned a successful event will vouch for that. And those who have resorted to last-minute preparation with no prior planning can relate stories of disastrous results.

Prior planning is simple for the Christian: begin with God. He is the great planner. "In the beginning," God planned and effected all creation. Through His Son, God devised and implemented a plan of salvation for the whole world. God announced His plans to send the Holy Spirit for all believers prior to Jesus' return to heaven. What a perfect planner!

But God is also a personal planner for every one of us. Before we were formed in the womb, God chose a plan and purpose for each of us (Jeremiah 1:5). It makes perfect sense to consult God in prayer to discover His plans before we initiate ours. Too often we make our own plans, then ask God to fit Himself into them. That's not a good idea. "Many are the plans in a man's heart, but it is the Lord's purpose that prevails" (Proverbs 19:21). God works out His will despite our selfish plans, but prayerful planning with God spells purposeful performance.

We commit our work and ways to You, O Lord. Establish our plans according to Your holy will; through Jesus Christ, our Lord. Amen.

Gloria K. Lessmann

Philippians 1:3–11

Enjoying People

I thank my God every time I remember you. Philippians 1:3

Do you enjoy the people God has placed into your life? Do you enjoy the person to whom you are married? Do you like to be around your co-workers? Peter Drucker, often called "the father of American management," says the number 1 characteristic of leaders is that they enjoy other people.

The apostle Paul enjoyed people. When he thought of others, he remembered the positive blessings God had given to them. While he had many problems in Philippi (he was arrested illegally, beaten, humiliated, and run out of town), Paul remembered the good things about his Christian friends there. Having been forgiven by God through Christ, he was able to forgive others. In other words, by God's grace he was enabled to "remember the best and forget the rest." God empowered Paul to bring those people before God's throne of grace in thanksgiving.

Life is too short not to enjoy the people God has placed in our lives. May we take Paul's lead in thanking God for the blessings of the people around us. The love of Christ will overflow in us, causing us to find joy in caring for others.

Dear God, thank You for the people You have placed in my life. Help me remember the good things You have done through them; through Your Son I pray. Amen.

Luther C. Brunette

Luke 17:7–10

Valuable Service

Serve one another in love. *Galatians 5:13*

We are saved to serve. We do not only take and receive; we also give and share.

Servants give themselves. It is more blessed to serve—to give oneself—than to give things. Foreign missionaries give their lives. They uproot themselves from family and friends, from their culture and security. They go to strange lands with different cultures and languages. It is simple for most of us to give money for their support. That is a blessed service, of course, but it is a different level from the service of self.

God accepts our service of things. He talks about feeding the hungry and giving a drink to the thirsty. He accepts these actions and things, done in love and faith, as good works. Most of that comes easily, but He also talks about housing the stranger, assisting the sick, and visiting the prisoner. Volunteers serve by cleaning the church. Others give a donation. A member visits the jail and ministers to its inmates. Others finance a chaplain, and that also is good. But it is the giving of ourselves in service that is most costly and difficult.

Every service given, whether of ourselves or of our possessions, is motivated by our love for Christ. He enables us to serve. As He empowers us through His Word and sacraments, our service becomes a privilege and a joy.

Lord Jesus, increase our love for You so we may serve both You and one another. Amen.

Edgar J. H. Otto

Matthew 9:35–38

God's Fishermen

"Come, follow Me," Jesus said, "and I will make you fishers of men." *Matthew 4:19*

Have you ever wondered why some Christians wear a pin with a fish on it? The early Christians had an expression in Greek: "Jesus Christ, Son of God, Savior." In the days of persecution they abbreviated these words, using only the first letter of each word. These letters spell *ichthys*, a Greek word for "fish."

God has made us His fishermen, and "the kingdom of heaven is like a net that was let down into the lake and caught all kinds of fish" (Matthew 13:47). How privileged we are to be selected as His fishermen! We have a joyful task even greater than that of the angels as we witness for Christ among people here on earth.

Few of us consider fishing a tiresome chore. We eagerly await and enjoy every opportunity to use our rod and reel. As fishermen for Christ, we should seek out every opportunity to tell others that Jesus Christ is our only Savior from sin.

Let us react as the disciples did when Jesus told them He would make them fishers of men: "At once they left their nets and followed Him" (Matthew 4:20). We too follow Jesus when we share with others the message of God's love and forgiveness in Christ.

Lord Jesus, thank You for making me a fisher of men; in Your name I pray. Amen.

Andrew Simcak Jr.

Matthew 28:16–20

The Reason for Reasoning

"Come now, let us reason together," says the LORD. *Isaiah 1:18*

Politicians believe that effective government requires occasional compromise. Concessions to opposing viewpoints are necessary if our system is to function properly. Winston Churchill judged democracy, despite its flaws, to be the best form of government.

Many Protestant churches are democracies. At local or national levels policy is decided by majority vote. Often these decisions displease people, and "politics" enters the process. But God lets fallible humans do His kingdom work as best they can, despite a flawed system.

Policy votes determine the priorities of church programs. Mission outreach, educational facilities, staff salaries, and other topics are discussed in lengthy debate. But finally it is a democratic consensus that determines the wisest way to do specific projects.

The democratic process works well in deciding policy issues, but God's Word alone settles spiritual questions. God's great purpose for the world was revealed in Jesus Christ. "Reasoning" with God means admitting our sins and trusting Jesus as our personal Savior. No vote or church action dare ever infringe on this loving policy of our almighty God.

Dear Lord Jesus, use us to carry out the work programs of our local and international church; for Your sake. Amen.

Herbert G. Walther

Colossians 3:1–4

The Wellspring of Life

Guard your heart, for it is the wellspring of life. *Proverbs 4:23*

We are apt to regard our thoughts as fleeting and unimportant and, as a result, imagine that it matters very little what we think as long as we say and do what is right. Yet, in the last analysis, everything depends on our thoughts.

It is true that our thoughts are the products and proofs of our character. But they are infinitely more than that. They are the very materials out of which our character, lives, and destinies are built. Evil thoughts mar and destroy. Good thoughts build up, elevate, and refine. What we shall be in the future is based on what we think today, for what we think today provides the basis from which all our words and actions spring.

Above all, as Christ rules in our hearts His radiance beautifies our thoughts. He enables us to lift our thoughts above all that is sordid and sinful and to keep them steadily in the presence of God. Paul had this in mind when he said, "Whatever is true, whatever is noble, whatever is right, whatever is pure, whatever is lovely, whatever is admirable—if anything is excellent or praiseworthy—think about such things" (Philippians 4:8). This is the peace that Christ earned for us by His death on the cross and that enters our hearts by faith in Him.

"Create in me a pure heart, O God, and renew a steadfast spirit within me" (Psalm 51:10); for Jesus' sake. Amen.

Unknown

Romans 12:3–8

A Melting Pot of Cultures

In Christ we who are many form one body, and each member belongs to all the others. *Romans 12:5*

One fascinating aspect of life in New Mexico is how much it truly is a melting pot of cultures: Native American, Hispanic, and Anglo cultures contribute most, yet Asian and African add some spice to the mixture. There isn't perfect harmony, but because each has had to live with the others for so long, each has influenced the others to give the state a fairly harmonious blend.

In our individual congregations we may not see too many different colors or cultures. Because we each have different abilities and personalities, however, God intends each congregation to be a "melting pot," which combines each one's uniqueness with the others into a living tool for Christ, who is both true God and true man in one living person. The church is His body.

Our congregational "pot" is not an accident of geography or history. By the guidance of the Holy Spirit, we have been brought to the particular congregation of which we are members. And what is His purpose? That we, who are saved, might help each other be more faithful to Him as individuals and as a congregation that serves Him.

Help me, Lord, to appreciate the role You have given me and each one in my congregation; for Jesus' sake. Amen.

Theodore E. Allwardt Sr.

Joshua 24:1–15

Who Sets the Priorities?

Seek first His kingdom and His righteousness, and all these things will be given to you as well. *Matthew 6:33*

A Christian counselor often hears someone say: "I don't know what the Bible says, but I think ..." This may apply to domestic problems, to making moral decisions, yes, even to doctrinal matters. It seems that more and more people are making judgments and decisions based on their own reason, even their own feelings and desires.

This would be good, except that He who made the heaven and the earth and all that is in them, including human beings, has given us a set of guidelines. We are to follow them if we are to attain happiness and avoid much of the misery that we bring on ourselves.

Who sets the priorities? God does, in the Holy Scriptures. There we find guidance for life—for a happy marriage, for uprightness in business, and for right relationships in all our social dealings. Above all, in the Holy Scriptures we find Jesus Christ, who lived, died, and rose again to save us. That leaves us just one route to follow. Jesus said, "Search the Scriptures!" They are the unerring guide for all of life. They set this priority: Christ and His kingdom first!

Father in heaven, thank You for supplying us with all that we need to know to live to Your glory and to find happiness; in Jesus' name. Amen.

Howard G. Allwardt

1 Corinthians 13:1–13

Love, the Greatest Gift

These three remain: faith, hope and love. But the greatest of these is love. *1 Corinthians 13:13*

God is love. The supreme self-revelation of God is to be seen in the love of Christ. So it is not surprising that St. Paul declares love to be the greatest of all things. It is the one thing that abides forever. Necessary as faith is in this life, love is greater because faith will end in seeing. Precious as hope is, love is greater because hope will end in fulfillment. Love is greater than all other gifts and blessings. It is greater than eloquence, than prophecy, than all learning.

See how powerful love is and how wonderful are its effects! Love teaches us to be patient and kind and generous. It keeps us from being envious and arrogant and proud. It makes for courtesy and unselfishness. It puts the best construction on everything. It dwells on the good rather than on the evil.

Christian love is the greatest civilizing and refining agency. No matter how great one's knowledge or power or fame, unless love is the moving force, no life is really good or great. The abundant life of which Jesus speaks is a life that is "rooted and grounded in love" and that knows "the love of Christ which surpasses knowledge" (Ephesians 3:17, 19 RSV). Whoever lives in this love is a truly spiritual person.

Dear Father, grant us an ever larger appreciation of the wonders of Your love in Jesus Christ. Amen.

Walter E. Bauer

1 Peter 2:11 –17

The Real World

He has given us this command: Whoever loves God must also love his brother. *1 John 4:21*

A Christian may be a citizen of heaven, but he must first live on this earth. He dare not drown in a sea of mysticism; he must not lose contact with the realities of his present situation. In his union with God he should not drop out of the fellowship of humanity. He has duties and obligations toward other people in this world.

What it means to be a good Samaritan on a person-to-person basis is clear. But how are we to carry out the commandments of God in respect to social justice? Should love for fellow human beings prompt the Christian to participate in demonstrations on their behalf? Should the Christian be active politically in the same cause?

We know that in our dealings with other people the law of love is supreme. No legalism, no selfish considerations, no personal dislike of one's neighbor must stand in the way of our helping her in every way possible. That's what we're here for. Our assignment is to serve people, as the Son of Man came to serve. He died on the cross for all, but only those who believe in Him shall see life eternal. We who believe must do all we can to get this Gospel to everybody.

Open our eyes, O God, to the needs of our brothers and sisters, and by the example of Your Son, Jesus, teach us to minister to them. Amen.

Herbert F. Lindemann

Matthew 28:18–20

Make Use of Today

There is a time for everything, and a season for every activity under heaven: a time to be born and a time to die, a time to plant and a time to uproot. *Ecclesiastes 3:1–2*

A motivational plaque declares, "Yesterday is but a dream; tomorrow is a vision of hope; look to this day for it is life." This saying can be used to express the urgency of our lives as Christians. If yesterday were Christmas, today Easter, and tomorrow was Christ's second coming and the end of time as we know it, would we be living differently?

In C. S. Lewis' *The Screwtape Letters*, the devil meets with his under-devils to plan how best to combat Christianity. Each under-devil is assigned the challenge to come up with a catchy slogan. One suggests, "There is no God." The devil feels this would be hard to promote. Another suggests, "There is no devil." Again the idea is rejected as not possible. The last little devil comes up with the slogan, "There is no hurry." The perfect slogan to defeat Christianity!

We always feel that there will be time. We do not feel the urgency to share the Gospel today. Would it make a difference if we knew that Christ was coming tomorrow? Whom do you know who needs to hear of Christ's birth, death, resurrection, and second coming? There is a valid warning in that slogan from *The Screwtape Letters*. Christianity is impacted in a most negative way by Christians who feel there is no hurry.

Dear Lord, help us live today as if it were our last day on earth and the end of time to share our faith; for Jesus' sake. Amen.

Irma S. Pinkerton

1 Corinthians 15:1–11

An Eyewitness Report

We were eyewitnesses of His majesty. *2 Peter 1:16*

Detractors of the Christian faith often dismiss it as merely pious myths, having nothing to do with reality. They forget that the very first propagators of the faith were eyewitnesses of the miraculous events that they proclaimed: the miracles of Christ, His transfiguration, His death, His post-resurrection appearances to the Eleven, an appearance to more than 5,000 at one time, and finally His visible ascension into heaven. Not myths, but facts! Not dreams, but reality!

The writers of the New Testament letters stress this again and again. John, who was closest to the Savior, writes: "That which was from the beginning, which we have heard, which we have seen with our eyes, which we have looked at, and our hands have touched" (1 John 1:1)—that is what the apostles declared to us.

Our faith, then, is based on the very words and works of Christ, transmitted by reliable witnesses who both saw and heard the precious Gospel as it unfolded before their very eyes. It was to them that Christ said: "Go ... preach the gospel" (Mark 16:15 RSV). Thank God, we have received the Gospel from those whose eyes had seen the events they recorded!

Lord Jesus, we thank You for sharing the "good news" with us through witnesses whose eyes have seen. Amen.

Herman W. Gockel

Luke 11:1–13

God's R.S.V.P.

Before they call, I will answer. *Isaiah 65:24*

Sometimes we get an invitation that asks us to let the host know if we're coming. The card often has "R.S.V.P.," a French abbreviation for "please respond." God invites us to pray and promises to answer every one of our prayers. Isaiah tells us that sometimes God answers even before we ask! This may seem impossible, but remember that we pray to a God who is able to do all things.

Does the Savior know all our needs and wants? Surely He does, but He still invites us to pray about any and all of them. God is capable of granting us anything He wants to and fully answers all our petitions according to His good and gracious will.

Naturally God does not desire to grant His beloved children things that would harm us, so at times He is compelled to answer no. But He always answers, and always in our best interest, just as a loving father will answer his child—sometimes yes, sometimes no, and even sometimes wait—but always in love.

Notice how in the Lord's Prayer Jesus encourages us to call on our heavenly Father for all things, especially for our spiritual needs of forgiveness and deliverance from evil. God always replies, and it's always for our best!

Grant, dear Father in heaven, that when I pray I accept Your reply in faith and trust Your good will. Amen.

J. Barclay Brown

Genesis 12:1–3

Blessed to Bless

I will bless you; I will make your name great, and you will be a blessing. *Genesis 12:2*

What a wonderful promise the Lord gave to Abraham, the father of the Hebrew people and an ancestor of Jesus: "I will bless you, … and you will be a blessing." God blesses us too that we may bless others.

Can we hear? Let's listen to others with a sympathetic ear. Can we speak? May we use the gift of speech in a constructive way—to heal, enrich, and build up self-esteem. Has God blessed us in a material way? Let us share our possessions and be generous to the church. Do we have a skill in business, music, teaching, working with children and youth, or some other talent? May we use our God-given ability in the church and elsewhere to improve other lives. If we are healthy, we may assist the weak. If we are frail and sickly, we can benefit others by praying for them.

Have we in time of trouble and sorrow experienced the help of God and the love of people? Let us share the strength and support we have received, showing understanding to people who are troubled. Let us tell how God has sustained us in time of difficulty. Do we know Jesus as personal Savior and friend? Let's pass on the good news. All of us have been blessed in some way. May we in turn be a blessing.

Father, You have been good to us for Jesus' sake. Empower us through Your Word and sacraments to touch other lives with Your goodness. Amen.

Herbert and Alma Kern

James 4:13–17

God's Will

You ought to say, "If it is the Lord's will, we will live and do this or that." *James 4:15*

Does the old phrase "the good Lord willing" still play a part in our planning? Most of us have heard stirring graduation speeches or motivational seminars where we are told, "You can be whatever you want to be." The intention is to inspire higher goals and greater ambition. While we appreciate encouragement, as Christians we are wary of any promise that leaves God out of the picture.

James noted that even we Christians are tempted to make plans without considering the will of God. He reminds us that we who live under a loving God depend on His good pleasure. When we plan for the future, we must seek guidance and direction from Him. When we add "If the Lord wills," we are doing much more than tacking on a pious phrase. Those words express our willingness to change or abandon our plans in favor of God's design.

Life brings disappointments and questions: What was wrong with my plan? What is God's will for my job, education, or marriage? Because we know the master planner, we can accept His ways for us. To all our dreams and wishes and prayers we can add, "If the Lord wills." The God who sacrificed His own Son to redeem us will not let us down!

Teach us, Lord, to trust Your good and gracious will for us; in Jesus' name we pray. Amen.

Norbert V. Becker

1 Samuel 20:12–17

Reliable

Show me unfailing kindness like that of the LORD as long as I live. *1 Samuel 20:14*

We would want it said of us that we are reliable. We want friends and family to be able to depend on us to react predictably when some specific situation arises or when "the pressure's on." People want to be able to count on us. They want to know that we will be as good as our word and unchanging in our support and friendship.

To be reliable is a basic ingredient of any friendship. C. S. Lewis observed that few of us have many friends. We have acquaintances. In a mobile and fast-paced society, building lasting friendships is difficult. Self-interest takes precedent over concern for others. We curve in on ourselves.

King David in Psalm 12 decries the lack of faithfulness among people and talks about deceit and deception. But David also knew the reliability of lasting friendship. He had found that in his relationship with Jonathan.

Jonathan, in turn, likened the love he wanted from David to the kind of reliable love he had experienced from the hands of God. That kind of reliable love and friendship is not only like the love of God but also stems from that love. God's love authors our kindness and love for others.

Lord Jesus, I can count on You, my best friend, for forgiveness and strength. Help me to be a friend others can count on as I count on You. Amen.

Leland Stevens

1 Samuel 17:32–37

Who Wants to Go?

Then I heard the voice of the Lord saying, Whom shall I send? And who will go for Us? *Isaiah 6:8*

There is no silence so deep, none so embarrassing, none so penetrating as the silence that usually follows the question, "There is work to do! Any volunteers?" Those at the meeting sit very still in their chairs, eyes cast down, as the chairman searches the group for some sign of willingness to serve. The poor moderator, at that moment, has some inkling of the pained silence in heaven as God too seeks servers.

God does seek servers! Not because He needs our response. Not at all. Messengers by the millions, the angels, yearn to do His bidding. Yet for the love of humankind He gives us opportunities to share in His plan for the world. God permits us to give food to the hungry, wisdom to the ignorant, healing to the sick, forgiveness to the penitent, and hope to the confused. He wants to use us so we may have the joy of participating in service. It is regrettable that the most common response to His call is silence. Instead of an eager "I'll go!" the loyal sons and daughters of the loving Father too often sit mute.

Who wants to go and serve God by telling sinful humankind that God gave His only Son on Calvary's cross to set us free? By God's grace, let each one of us say with Isaiah: "Here am I! Send me!"

O Lord, call us to mighty service and by Your Holy Spirit strengthen us to respond willingly; for Jesus' sake. Amen.

Charles S. Mueller

John 17:20–26

Prayer Plus Response

I have prayed for you, Simon, that your faith may not fail. *Luke 22:32*

A son hearing his father pray that the wants of the poor might be supplied said, "Dad, I wish I had your grain." "Why, Son? What would you do with it?" asked the father, a farmer. The son replied, "I would answer your prayers."

Is it not true that answers to our prayers sometimes lie in us? We pray for the worldwide mission program. A proper response to this prayer would be to support missions with our personal witnessing and generous offerings. We pray for good government. Again, a proper response to such a prayer would be that we strive to be law-abiding citizens. As parents we pray that the faith of our children may not fail. A proper response to such a prayer would be that we teach them the Word of God with all diligence.

Jesus prayed and then acted. He prayed for the apostles and for all believers through the centuries. His prayer was followed by action, for He went to the cross, suffered, died, and rose again for the salvation of the whole human race. He prayed for His disciples that their faith would not fail and then lovingly encouraged them to faithfulness. If the answer to some of our prayers lies in us, may God lead us to action!

Lord, help us to respond properly when we have prayed; for Jesus' sake. Amen.

Leonard H. Aurich

Acts 2:37–42

The Power of the Pulpit

[Jesus] said, "Blessed … are those who hear the word of God and keep it." *Luke 11:28 RSV*

Preaching is the most powerful form of communication in all the world, not because of the preacher (sometimes even in spite of him) and not because of the sermon itself as a human effort; it is because the preaching of the Word is in a very special way the voice of the Spirit of God. Through preaching, people are won for Christ.

On Pentecost the Holy Spirit established the Christian pulpit and made the Gospel it proclaimed the power of God for salvation. That's why Jesus told His disciples to go into the whole world and preach the Gospel. To be sure, their mission would involve them in other things, but none was as important as the preaching of Christ, crucified and risen from the dead. This is also why Martin Luther explained the commandment to remember the Sabbath Day in these words: "We should fear and love God that we may not despise preaching and His Word, but hold it sacred and gladly hear and learn it."

Our Lord caps the matter for us by saying, "Blessed … are those who hear the word of God and keep it"—keep it in good and honest hearts.

Lord, may Your Word always be a lamp to our feet and a light to our path; for Jesus' sake. Amen.

Frederick C. Hinz

Romans 6:1–4

New And Improved

[You] have put on the new self, which is being renewed in knowledge in the image of its Creator. *Colossians 3:10*

You've seen the ads claiming that products are "new and improved." That also describes Christians.

St. Paul talks about some of the works of the old nature: sexual immorality, impurity, evil desire, anger, malice, and slander. These words characterize the sinful nature in all people. But later Paul lists some traits of the new nature: compassion, kindness, meekness, patience, love, and harmony. That's quite an improvement! Actually, it's more than an improvement; it's a radical change brought about by the Holy Spirit, who renews us so we become more and more like Christ, our Savior.

Periodically we should look at our lives and ask which nature is most evident: the old or the new. Are our lives characterized by anger, impatience, selfishness, jealousy, and envy? Or do words like gentle, kind, and loving describe who we are?

"All of you who were baptized into Christ have clothed yourselves with Christ" (Galatians 3:27). The Christian life is a constant struggle to put off the old nature, with which we were born, and to live according to the new nature, given us in Baptism. By the power of the Spirit dwelling in our hearts, God renews us, making us truly new and improved.

Lord Jesus, make us new in You and like You. Amen.

Bruce W. Biesenthal

1 Corinthians 6:9–20

Our Body Is God's Temple

Do you not know that your body is a temple of the Holy Spirit, who is in you, whom you have received from God? *1 Corinthians 6:19*

Alexander the Great was ruler of Macedonia at the age of 16, a victorious general at 18, and king at 20, but he died a drunkard before age 33. He could not conquer himself.

Excessive use of alcohol contributes to crime, divorce, family disintegration, accidents, and highway fatalities. Billions of dollars are lost by employers each year because of absenteeism, much of which is caused by workers who cannot control their alcohol intake.

Many hearts, homes, and lives are being destroyed because too much alcohol is being consumed. The toll continues to rise.

Our body is the dwellingplace of the Holy Spirit. God gave us our body. It belongs to Him by the right of creation. He redeemed our body through the death and resurrection of His Son, Jesus Christ. It belongs to Him by the right of redemption.

By creation and redemption God owns our body. It is not ours to do with as we please. It is a trust from Him. We must strive not to harm our blood-bought bodies in any way. They are special in God's eyes; they should be special to us.

Lord, whether I eat or drink, work or play, let me do it to Your glory and for my own good; in Jesus' name. Amen.

Andrew Simcak Jr.

Romans 8:18–39

All Things for Good

We know that in all things God works for the good of those who love Him. *Romans 8:28*

How many confirmands have had this text as their confirmation verse? And how many have had the opportunity to test the truth of this divine statement as they suffered disappointments, losses, illness, or death? One can hardly be blamed for asking: Does God really, in all things, work for our good?

What do we mean by "good"? "Good" does not mean the total achievement of all our desires but rather something that becomes a part of the tapestry God is weaving of our lives— something that builds character, leads us to recognize His mercy, exercises trust, teaches us patience, or thrusts us into opportunities for service. Then indeed all the experiences that befall us "who have been called according to His purpose" are truly good for us in some way that may not now be apparent.

Also this is told to us to assure us of God's goodness in dealing with us: "He who did not spare His own Son, but gave Him up for us all—how will He not also, along with Him, graciously give us all things?" (v. 32). Knowing that attitude of God toward us, someday we will say: "So that was how He meant it for my good!"

Teach me, O Lord, to trust You for my welfare in all things; for Jesus' sake. Amen.

Jaroslav J. Vajda

Mark 4:21–25

Listen!

Take note of this: Everyone should be quick to listen, slow to speak and slow to become angry. *James 1:19*

We are bombarded with noises and voices. Since much of what we hear is unpleasant or unimportant, we often don't listen carefully.

There are times when love demands that we listen. When someone is hurting, it may be even more important for us to lend an ear than a helping hand. That person may not want or need advice—just someone to listen with patience. A few well-chosen, encouraging words may be helpful.

When there has been a disagreement between people, there must be some honest speaking and loving listening if the relationship is to be healed. Often we are anxious to say some very honest things but are not willing to listen to one another.

Good listening does not mean just being silent while others speak. A good listener tries to see the problem the way the speaker sees it. He tries to feel for him, experience with him.

We tend to do all the talking also when we pray. It's hard for us to listen to God when He says "forgive"; "be angry but do not sin"; "speak the truth in love"; and "love others as yourself"! If we really listen to God as He speaks in His holy Word, we'll be better listeners to other people.

Lord Jesus, by Your suffering You reconciled us to Your Father.
Fill us with Your Spirit that we may listen with patience. Amen.

Alma Kern

Galatians 2:16–21

"Up to Speed"

If anyone loves Me, he will obey My teachings. My Father will love him, and We will come to him and make Our home with him. *John 14:23*

Individuals who know what is going on around them and are able to size up a situation and then can deal with it are sometimes referred to as "up to speed." Corporations are always looking for people who measure up. Universities search out students who, they feel, will be able to cope with college academics successfully. Sales managers are in constant search for talented people who can sell themselves as well as their products.

Our gracious God is always looking for those who in their lives reflect their love for Him. They do so by becoming involved in His Word and then applying it to their lives. They are the people of God who ask the question "What does my Lord want me to do?" not "What's in it for me?" They eagerly accept responsibilities in His church to show their appreciation for what He has done for them in Christ, the Savior from sin.

Christ makes this great promise: "My Father will love him, and We will come to him and make Our home with him." It is thrilling to have a national figure as an intimate friend but to share the intimacy of God is breathtaking.

Lord, help us to come up to Your expectation in our love for You and Your Word, for we want You to live in us; we ask this in Jesus' name and for His sake. Amen.

Howard G. Allwardt

Philippians 2:5–11

To the Ends of the Earth

You will receive power when the Holy Spirit comes on you; and you will be My witnesses in Jerusalem, and in all Judea and Samaria, and to the ends of the earth. Acts 1:8

Jesus commissioned us to be witnesses to Jerusalem, Judea, Samaria, our own cities and towns, and to the ends of the earth. On one hand we say the world is getting smaller with satellites circling the earth and jets crossing the oceans in a matter of hours. What happens in one part of the world is known instantaneously through a vast communication network.

But the world is also getting bigger. Fifty years ago there were just over two billion people in this world. Today there are more than five billion. And only one-fourth of them know, or profess to know, Jesus as their Savior. Christians must be ever more diligent and determined in proclaiming Jesus Christ and His cross. It is to be part of our very nature to herald Jesus and His word of reconciliation to those with whom we live and to those whom we don't know and have never and will never meet. Jesus said, "You will be My witnesses." He did not say "you ought to be" or "you should be," but "you will be." Each Christian, by the power of the Holy Spirit, is equipped and committed to share the love of Jesus with others, at home, in the neighborhood, and across the world.

Send me, O Lord, send me; for Jesus' sake. Amen.

Paul J. Albers

Galatians 6:7–10

You Can Do It!

Since we are surrounded by such a great cloud of witnesses … let us run with perseverance the race marked out for us. Let us fix our eyes on Jesus, the author and perfecter of our faith. *Hebrews 12:1–2*

After he had run all 26 miles of the New York City Marathon, one runner had this to say of the cheering crowds along the way: "My goal was to make the 16-mile mark, but the inspiration the people gave made me think twice about not finishing. The winner had passed by an hour before, but the crowd stayed on cheering us all. 'You can do it,' they yelled. How could I give up in front of this throng? I was beginning to feel sore in my thighs and hips. I had no energy left, but I plodded on to that faraway finish line."

All of us need encouragement in the daily race of our Christian life. That's why God puts us with other people. We can cheer one another on. Our congregations are meant to be support groups. In them we do bear one another's burdens.

Through God's Word and sacraments we can encourage those who tire of doing good, lift those who stumble and fall, and comfort those who ache and hurt from the blows of life. We tolerate stress and pressures better if at least one other person knows about it and cares.

Lord Jesus Christ, we thank You for taking the burden of our sin on Yourself and for letting us know You care also about our pains and problems of daily living. Give us strength and courage. Use us today to demonstrate Your love to members of our church family. Amen.

Alma Kern

Acts 1:6–14

The Best Is Yet to Come

When I go and prepare a place for you, I will come again and will take you to Myself. *John 14:3 RSV*

When a farmer sets out to plow the first row of an uncultivated field, he fixes his eyes on some landmark and heads for it without looking down at the ground beneath him.

By His glorious ascension to the right hand of the Father, our risen Savior has provided all of His followers with a landmark, a goal: our eternal home with Him. When Christians fix their eyes on that glory, their entire life will be uplifted and headed in the right direction. Materialists, on the other hand, have their eyes glued to the earth and end up going around in circles.

For those whose treasure is stored away in the heavens, life is an adventure, each day filled with opportunities to see the love and glory of God and occasions to witness that love and glory to others. Every act of service becomes an anonymous meeting with Christ. Try living your life with your hope on heaven, and it will become filled with memorable experiences of God's power and joy. Be conscious of the ascended Savior at your side, lean on Him in every need, and be in constant communication with Him. Then your "walk is heavenward all the way."

Victorious and ruling Lord Jesus, whom we are privileged to know as Savior and brother, be praised forever. Amen.

Jaroslav J. Vajda

Luke 18:18–30

Before the Face of God

Whoever loves money never has money enough; whoever loves wealth is never satisfied with his income. This too is meaningless. *Ecclesiastes 5:10*

One of the wealthiest men in the world, when asked how much money he needed to live comfortably, answered, "I would starve on $2,000 a week." We never seem to have enough. We buy a house and promptly want to remodel. We get a raise and shortly find ourselves living to the limit of our higher income. We buy a new car and covet the newest models as soon as they hit the market. This is our fate as long as we chase after earthbound goals. Contentment is a handmaid to the attitude that sees wealth and possessions as gifts through which to give God glory. "If we have food and clothing, we will be content with that." (1 Timothy 6:8).

There is nothing wrong with a fine home, a reliable car, or a comfortable income. All these may be used to glorify God. The trouble comes when they begin to take a preferred place to God on our list of values. "The love of money is a root of all kinds of evil" (1 Timothy 6:10).

God has a special plan for our lives. He is the giver of all good things. He grants us places to live and clothes to wear. But He gives us the grace to love Him above all else. His Son has taught us to live before the face of God with humility and gratitude, contentment and gratification.

Dear God, give us such values that place Your Son first in our lives; in Jesus' name we ask this. Amen.

Bonnie Schneider

1 Peter 1:18–25

Right and Wrong

The grass withers and the flowers fall, but the word of the Lord stands forever. *1 Peter 1:24–25*

We are living in a world of unprecedented change. In one generation we have gone from horse travel to the space shuttle. Technology continues to accelerate, making possible more advanced computers, new medical procedures, and conveniences unthinkable years ago.

There is nothing wrong with progress. But we must take care amid the rapid changes occurring today that we do not drift from our Christian moorings. God and His Word, the Bible, never vary. They are our secure anchor during life's tempests.

Recently we heard a Christian defend unethical business practices: "That's what you have to do these days to get ahead." A church member who fell into sexual sin said apologetically, "I know the Bible says it's wrong, but it feels natural and right." Such statements are symptoms of an age that suffers from the disease of relativism. However, God tells us that what's wrong is wrong, and His Word is right. People and their ideas flower quickly and fade with time, but God's Word is permanent, enduring forever.

Thank God that in our changing world we have His changeless promise of forgiveness through our Lord and Savior Jesus Christ!

Lord, guide me by Your changeless Word. Help me shun evil and seek that which is good; for Jesus' sake. Amen.

Herman W. Gockel

Colossians 3:12–17

Harmony in the Home

How good and pleasant it is when brothers live together in unity. *Psalm 133:1*

The choir sang in beautiful four-part harmony. If just the sopranos or tenors had sung, they would have sounded good, but the four voices together enriched each other.

People in a home are like a choir. To live in harmony, they don't all have to be alike, look alike, or act alike. In fact, it is good when they are different and complete one another. Family members who live in harmony enjoy companionship. They share joys and sorrows.

A harmonious home life requires much effort. We must put up with others when they are irritable. God paid dearly to make our forgiveness possible. His perfect Son shed His blood for our faults. As He forgives us, we daily forgive one another.

It is wrong to dig up the past, to put other members of the family down, or especially to criticize them in public. We ought not make comparisons or take each other for granted. We are to thank and commend one another. Daily we need to turn to the Lord for strength to make harmony in the home a habit. Let us stick together and work together so that as a family we may walk in the way of the Lord.

God our Father, let our home be a place where we may retreat and daily refuel for life's journey; in Jesus' name. Amen.

Herbert M. Kern

Luke 16:19–31

When Did I See You?

They also will answer, "Lord, when did we see You hungry or thirsty or a stranger or needing clothes or sick or in prison?" *Matthew 25:44*

It isn't that they had not seen hungry, naked, thirsty, or distressed people. That isn't their point. They argued that they had not seen a hungry, naked, thirsty, distressed Jesus. Had they seen Him, they argue, their response would have been very different. But Jesus will have none of their reasoning. He answers: "If you fail to help those you see in need, you fail to help Me!" He identifies Himself with those in need of help.

For us the application is simple. In circumstances of need it's not who cries out but that the cry is uttered.

God has placed into this world enough of everything to satisfy the real needs of all people. Ours is now the joy of doling out the goodness of God in response to the needs of man. This requires that God's people become concerned with "social" questions. We take the word *social* seriously. It comes from a Latin word meaning "friend," "ally," or "associate." Social questions affect our friends, allies, and associates. We can abandon social questions only if we have first abandoned the ones whom these questions touch, and the one who comes to us wrapped in the dirt, thirst, nakedness, and need of man. To fail them is to fail Christ.

O Lord, open our eyes to see, and then open our hands to give as You, in love, gave Your very life for us; for Your sake, Jesus. Amen.

Charles S. Mueller

Acts 2:36–41

"This Corrupt Generation"

Save yourselves from this corrupt generation. *Acts 2:40*

Was the apostles' generation more corrupt than ours? It would serve no purpose to debate the degrees of corruption of various civilizations. TV shows and news reports certainly indicate that the term "corrupt generation" does indeed fit our times.

The need of our generation is the same as that of the Pentecost Day crowd to whom Peter spoke: to escape from the evil and Godlessness around us. But God does not call us to completely withdraw from the world or wall ourselves in. While we should avoid temptation and bad company as much as possible, our major strategy has to be a positive one: We are to be light and salt in the world, proclaiming the Gospel of Christ! We are to stand for His truth. We are to reflect Jesus' love in daily dealings with people.

Like a winning team in sports, we must have both a good defense and a good offense. Defensively, to escape being caught up in this corrupt generation, we need to be on guard against the evils around us. On the offense, we need to attack evil and champion the truth with the "sword of the Spirit, which is the word of God" (Ephesians 6:17). The Word's power comes from our loving God, who sent His Son to deliver us from all evil.

Save us, Lord, from the evil around us. In this dark world, enable us to be Your light; for Jesus' sake. Amen.

Norbert V. Becker

Acts 11:19–26

I Will Build My Church

I will build My church. *Matthew 16:18*

To 12 men with little know-how of building and possibly even less money, Jesus says, "I will build My church." He owned no home, not even a place to rest His head, yet He declares, "I will build My church." Anyone who has had a part in building a church realizes that much time, effort, planning, and financing are required to erect even a modest building. But our Lord is not speaking of a modest building.

He would build a church not made with hands or earthly materials but made of living stones: men, women, and children. He would erect a structure for eternity. He is speaking of His holy temple, the church of the living God.

The erection of this building will be costly. Before people can be a part of that temple, Christ must suffer and die for them. They must be purchased with His holy, precious blood and His innocent suffering and death. By the power of His Spirit they must be brought to faith. Through the long centuries Christ has been building His church through the Word and Baptism. When eternity dawns, the church made up of all believers of all times will stand complete and resplendent in His glory. The Lord calls and urges those who are His to lend a hand in building His church. Are we builders with Christ?

Gracious Savior, strengthen our hands and hearts that we may build Your church with You. Amen.

Amos A. Schmidt

1 Corinthians 2:9–16

The Use of Leisure

As a Christian I may do anything, but that does not mean that everything is good for me. *1 Corinthians 6:12 Phillips*

What the Christian does is not so important as why he does it. Almost anything is proper if it harms neither him nor his neighbor and glorifies God. But we must choose our pastimes thoughtfully.

What will give us a change of pace? What will refresh us in body and spirit? Martin Luther had all kinds of interests—hobbies, we might call them today. He loved to garden, especially with exotic plants from Morocco or Spain or England. Chess was a good sport, he thought, when the rain poured; and bowling on the green, when the sun shone. A dog was pleasant too if there was room and if the little critter did not chew up the books, as one of his did.

Singing was excellent, he thought, at home or on the road, alone or in a crowd. Music in any form was to be valued. He also liked paintings and statues and folk dancing on the village green.

A good conscience before God, a healthy change from routine life, a chance for useful exercise, a wise use of money and time—for us, as for Luther, these are all factors in considering how we spend the time God has given us.

All our time on earth, O Lord, is Yours. Teach us to use it wisely; for Jesus' sake. Amen.

Theodore J. Kleinhans

2 Corinthians 8:8–15

Sharing Generously

God is able to make all grace abound to you…. You will be made rich in every way so that you can be generous on every occasion, and … your generosity will result in thanksgiving to God. *2 Corinthians 9:8–11*

In each worship service we are again reminded of what God has done for us and of what we can do in serving God. We need that reminder.

Our heavenly Father does not supply our needs on a strict percentage basis. He does not distribute His gifts according to a carefully worked out budget. God gives royally, lavishly, despite our unworthiness, without asking how much we deserve.

But how much shall we give? Mindful of God's generosity, we are helped to a decision by two simple questions, sincerely and carefully answered: How great is the real need? How much do we have that we could give?

A few may be able to build a cathedral. Practically every one of us can give a piece of bread, the kind of gift Christ will commend on Judgment Day. Our gift will probably be between a cathedral and a piece of bread. God does not tell us precisely how much. We ourselves must decide. It is our New Testament freedom. One word ought to describe our contribution: generous—in the eyes of God, that is. He knows!

Keep reminding us of Your generosity, our Father, that we may be generous too; in Jesus' name. Amen.

Armin C. Oldsen

Romans 8:26–30

God Guides the Outcome of Life

Joseph said to his brothers, "I am about to die. But God will surely come to your aid and take you up out of this land to the land He promised on oath to Abraham, Isaac and Jacob." *Genesis 50:24*

Joseph's jealous brothers sold their young brother into slavery. Despite this evil deed Joseph was, in time, led by the Lord to become prime minister of mighty Egypt. When his brothers came to Egypt to buy food for their families, Joseph revealed his identity to them and forgave them. "You intended to harm me," he said to them, "but God intended it for good to accomplish what is now being done, the saving of many lives" (Genesis 50:20).

Our God has laid out His plans. He foresees the schemes of evil men and plans around them, turning evil into good. Peter proclaimed on Pentecost that Jesus, crucified and killed by the hands of lawless men, was delivered up according to the definite plan and foreknowledge of God. But God raised Him up, "freeing Him from the agony of death, because it was impossible for death to keep its hold on Him" (Acts 2:24).

Knowing this, we can be certain that our Lord is turning apparent evil into good also in our lives. We can fully trust that God is in control—of the world and of our lives.

Lord Jesus, You have a plan for our lives. Help us to trust You and follow Your guidance in the unfolding of this plan. Amen.

Alvin H. Franzmeier

Luke 15:28–32

Anger: Spiritual Disease or Not?

In your anger do not sin. Do not let the sun go down while you are still angry. *Ephesians 4:26*

Anger is so often followed by violence against ourselves or others that it is hard to believe that one can be angry and not sin. If anger grows out of selfishness, it will always lead to sin. But if it results from outrage over wrong, it has a better chance of being followed by mercy. Some people hide their anger and deny they have it, but it eventually leaks out in ways harmful to themselves and others. Christians sometimes don't want to admit to themselves the anger they feel because they think anger in itself is sinful. They do not recognize that feeling sorry for themselves or feeling "hurt" can be a veiled way of expressing anger.

The cure for sinful anger is honest confession, forgiveness, and love. These come from God, not from inside us. Jesus Christ is God's evidence of His forgiveness and love. On the cross God's anger is poured out in a healing way for us. God is no longer angry with us but loves us sinners, even while He hates our sin and waits for us to repent. We can learn to live with our anger by being honest with ourselves and by living under the relief of Christ's forgiveness toward us.

Lord, help us face our anger honestly and find the healing grace to forgive and love again; in Jesus' name. Amen.

Richard C. Eyer

1 Kings 3:5–15

More than We Ask

I will give you what you have not asked for—both riches and honor. *1 Kings 3:13*

In one way, praying is the easiest thing in the world. We know that we have a Father in heaven who is able and willing to give us everything we need. All we have to do is ask in faith and trust. In another way, prayer is the hardest thing to do, just because we often don't know what it is we really need.

King Solomon had a dream shortly after he succeeded to the throne of his father David. God appeared to him and said, "Ask what I shall give you." Solomon remembered all the goodness God had shown to David. Many things Solomon could have asked from God. But in his heart of hearts he knew that he needed one thing above everything else, and he asked for an understanding mind to govern God's people. It was then that he received the answer in our text, that God would also give him what he had not asked: riches and honor above all other kings.

We need to think about this when we pray. Do we ask for things for ourselves, or do we ask for things which will help us serve our fellowmen better and bring them the love of God? We can be sure that when we ask for those things which will help us bring God's love to others we will also receive many gifts from God we didn't ask for.

Lord, teach us to pray for the things that lead to the eternal welfare of our fellow human beings; for Jesus' sake. Amen.

Martin L. Kretzmann

Acts 5:25–42

Backbone

Peter and the other apostles replied: "We must obey God rather than men!" *Acts 5:29*

We lack backbone. We bend, compromise, sell out, and look the other way. Society preaches a new morality and lives permissively. Abortion on demand, pornography, corruption, and ruthless business practices abound. We lack the courage to stand up and be counted. Spineless wonders!

In the first days after Pentecost the disciples of Jesus faced stiff opposition from the religious establishment. Peter and John were arrested and told to keep quiet about their faith in Jesus Christ. They could have played it safe and gone underground. But by God's grace these apostles displayed backbone. Arrested again for preaching Christ crucified, they replied, "We must obey God rather than men!" They continued boldly proclaiming the good news of Jesus. No spineless wonders, the apostles!

We confess our lack of backbone because of our weak, sinful flesh. God points us to His Son, who endured the cross, despising the shame. With backbone He drove the money-changers out of the temple and exposed the sham of the Pharisees. Risen, He offers us forgiveness and strength in the Gospel to stand up for Him and obey God rather than men. Reinforced by Word and sacraments, we step forward with backbone to proclaim Jesus as Savior and Lord in today's society. No longer spineless wonders!

Lord, give us backbone for Jesus' sake. Amen.

Stephen J. Carter

Romans 10:14–17

Hearing God's Word

Faith comes from hearing the message, and the message is heard through the word of Christ. *Romans 10:17*

Sunday means a variety of things to different people. For Christians, Sunday is the main day of church worship because Jesus rose from the dead on that day. But some consider Sunday as a time for rest and recreation, for a picnic or golf game, or for enjoying nature. "Walking in the woods brings us closer to the Creator," they say.

It is true that nature does reveal some of God's majesty, but we need more than that. It is not enough to know God as our Creator; we also need to know Him as our Redeemer and Sanctifier. For that, we need the Word of Christ and the Holy Spirit, who works through that Word.

When our ears and hearts hear the Word of Christ, the Holy Spirit strengthens our faith. Christian faith is trust in the forgiveness of sins that was earned for us by Jesus Christ when He died on the cross. And that message was confirmed when our triumphant Lord burst forth from the tomb.

We must eat to strengthen the body. We must hear God's Word and receive His Holy Meal to strengthen the soul. It is only the Word of Christ that nourishes our faith and is the sustenance of life eternal.

Lord God, bless my hearing of Your Word so my faith in Jesus Christ, the only Savior, might be strengthened. Amen.

Roy C. Krause

Genesis 50:15–21

Rebuilding the Ruins

I will … restore its ruins, and build it as it used to be. *Amos 9:11*

Constantine's Arch is a tourist attraction in Rome. Unlike many such monuments, it was not built of new material. Constantine, the first Christian emperor, used the ruins of ancient Rome to build his triumphal arch. It stands as a symbol of a Christian empire rising from pagan rubble.

Joseph's life was in ruins. His own brothers had turned on him, and he faced a bleak future as a slave in Egypt. But when Joseph could no longer control his life, God stepped in. And Joseph became a great man who saved many people, including his own family.

God delights in taking the ruins of our lives and rebuilding them into His temple. It's when, by God's grace, we see our utter helplessness that we let Him take over. And as we give our lives to Him, He takes those broken stones and one by one, step by step, builds a beautiful cathedral, a life dedicated to His worship and praise.

Today I take the rubble of my life—the willfully destroyed relationship, the pride that won't let me admit I made a mistake, the jealousy that has replaced love with hate—and bring it to Christ for forgiveness and rebuilding. He delights in making a temple out of me!

Direct Your steps, O Lord, to the ruins I make of my life, and work Your salvation in the midst of them; in Jesus' name. Amen

Louise Mueller

Acts 17:22–31

The Earth Is the Lord's

God blessed them and said to them, "Be fruitful and increase in number; fill the earth and subdue it." *Genesis 1:28*

The wanton use of the natural resources of the earth is not a sacred "right" that we possess. When God said that man should subdue the earth, He was talking about responsible use, not irresponsible pillage.

As we walk on this earth, we tread on God's good earth. Every one of us has to remember that God has not sold us a free and clear title to this earth. He has not gone off to some other part of the universe, leaving us with our own private plaything. We have it from God—we have His Word for it—that everyone is responsible to God for the way he or she uses the resources of the earth. We shall either be good stewards, or we shall suffer the consequences. Divine judgment rests on every human irresponsibility, on every area of human life. It is true that we have responsibilities to ourselves, to our families, and to our neighbors. We have a responsibility also toward God for all He has given us to use.

In Christ there is forgiveness. And in Him there is power to live responsibly in the world. In Him there is life, a new kind of life with healthy attitudes toward the world that is now and with hope for what is yet to be.

Lord, help us to respect the world You have made; we pray in Jesus' name. Amen.

Oswald C. J. Hoffmann

Ephesians 4:16; 1 Timothy 1:8–14

Worthy of God's Calling

I urge you to live a life worthy of the calling you have received. *Ephesians 4:1*

"What's your calling?" an older lady asked a young man about to enter into the work force. "Oh, I'll make my money programming computers, Madam," he replied.

"I didn't ask you how you'd make a living; I asked what your calling is," insisted the lady.

There is a difference, you know. One's calling has a heightened, almost sacred ring to it. It signifies a purpose for existence, a mission.

You have a calling. It isn't identical to your job; it supersedes it. It encompasses work all right, but also life itself. It is expressed in living out a twofold relationship: The first is that you are united to God. Christ has paid for sin that would separate you from Him. Thus, you can live reflecting your union with Him. Second, you are united in Him with other believers. By the Holy Spirit's power your life can demonstrate a union with every believing Christian. This is your calling. God's grace makes your life sacred in Christ Jesus. No matter what you are going through, your calling is to reflect your union with God and your solidarity with His people. It is a sacred calling indeed. It prompts us to live in conformity with it.

Help me, Lord God, to live worthy of this noble calling; in Jesus' name. Amen.

Norbert C. Oesch

Ephesians 4:17–32

Swift—slow

Everyone should be quick to listen, slow to speak. James 1:19

If we ever fancied that we could get along without God's Spirit, even for a moment, we probably did not make this mistake in connection with the way we listen and talk. Who has not said on any number of occasions, "If I had only listened!" Or "Why can't I keep my big mouth shut?" If James had said, "Let everyone be quick to speak and slow to listen," we would have no problem at all.

Quick to listen. Listen to what? Events in the days of our loved ones, helpful counsel, the whole truth, both sides of a question, a plea for help, a request for forgiveness—all of these, of course. But as we listen carefully, we also hear utterances of disappointment, pleas for love, and sighs of sorrow that we alone can answer. These are special messages from our God, who cries in the pain of the world, "I am hungry … thirsty … in prison … sick."

Slow to speak. About what? A friend's shortcomings, office gossip, dissatisfaction with church, school, and community—all of these, of course. But here James is counseling us to "count to 10" before talking back in a budding argument. Our Savior had these words written of Him: "No deceit was found in His mouth. When they hurled their insults at Him, He did not retaliate; when He suffered, He made no threats" (1 Peter 2:22–23). His example and power are ours that we may follow in His steps, in the way of peace.

Lord Jesus Christ, let me listen and speak in love. Amen.

Edward C. May

Acts 8:25–40

Time

Be very careful, then, how you live—not as unwise but as wise, making the most of every opportunity, because the days are evil. *Ephesians 5:15–16*

Time is money. Many people bill us for their services according to the time spent. Parking and taxi meters, time clocks at work, lawyers, the telephone company, the auto mechanic—all meter the minutes and convert them to dollars.

While Christians recognize the value of each minute, they measure time not in terms of money, but as providing opportunities to serve God. A Christian businessman in Illinois had a reputation for getting things done. His secret? Before he wrote a letter, made a phone call, or interviewed a client, he focused intently on the job at hand. He prayed for God to help him be wise, fair, and honest. Then he made the most of his limited time.

The Ethiopian eunuch (Acts 8:26ff) used his travel time to read the Holy Scriptures, which make us wise to salvation through faith in Christ Jesus. Today we may play Scripture recordings or Christian music as we travel. Philip took advantage of the opportunity to speak to the Ethiopian about Jesus and baptized the eunuch into the Christian faith. Opportunities abound for us as well to share the message of Christ, if only we are wise and redeem the time.

Lord, teach us to spend our time wisely, redeeming the days for good, not evil. Our times are in Your hands; in Jesus' name. Amen.

William W. Griebel

Matthew 5:13–16

As Lights in the World

In a crooked and depraved generation … shine like stars in the universe as you hold out the word of life. *Philippians 2:15 RSV*

Christians fail more often than they succeed in being lights in this world because they are still sinful human beings. They often display a remarkable talent for wasting time, for squandering their talents, and for overlooking their opportunities. It must take a great deal of patience on God's part to use such weak and frail instruments. It seems to be such a contradiction that the perfect God should choose to use such imperfect people as His children, as His lights.

No matter how often we fail to shine or how frequently we displease our Lord with our words and deeds, the assignment itself does not change: Believers are lights in this world. It is always time to remember that God did not choose us because of our ability or strength but only out of love. He prefers to kindle the light in our hearts and lives.

God is fully aware of our weakness and frailty, our need for strength and encouragement. To that end He has provided the Word of life. Herein is the message of forgiveness when we fail, the dynamic inspiration to try again, and the standard by which to determine our conduct and direction. The times we do shine as lights will be achieved by His grace and will serve as an expression of thanks.

Let Your Word, O Lord, be a lamp to my feet and a light to my path; for Jesus' sake. Amen.

William H. Kohn

1 Corinthians 12:14–27

Built Up in the Body of Christ

Speaking the truth in love, we will in all things grow up into Him who is the Head, that is, Christ. *Ephesians 4:15*

Bodybuilding calls for intense discipline and consistency in exercise. Bodybuilders are dedicated to developing the most muscular, well-defined, and symmetrical physiques possible. To attain that goal, proper nutrition and frequent intense exercise are necessary.

Christians are part of the body of Christ, the church. We are to "grow up into Him [Christ]," that is, to know Christ better, serve Him more faithfully, and glorify Him always. This growth is accomplished through proper spiritual nutrition: regular worship in the communion of saints, where God's Word is preached and the Lord's Supper is served; daily study of the Scriptures and prayer; and frequent, intense exercise of our faith despite persecution, including bold witnessing to the Savior.

Jesus' life, death, and physical resurrection created the church and are her foundation. The continuing presence of our risen Lord empowers us, as members of His body, to keep growing. "From Him the whole body, joined and held together by every supporting ligament, grows and builds itself up in love, as each part does its work" (Ephesians 4:16).

Jesus, help me grow stronger in faith so I may contribute to the building up of Your body, the church. Amen.

Frederick G. Boden

Matthew 23:13–36

Happiness Is Being a Realist

Watch out for false prophets. They come to you in sheep's clothing, but inwardly they are ferocious wolves. *Matthew 7:15*

In the text Jesus warns against false prophets, against fakers, phonies, and plastic people. According to His Word, we are to be real, and that means that we emerge from behind our facades and fronts, our pretending and playacting, and speak and act with honesty. We are also to be realistic. That means we possess the ability to detect the spurious, the fake, and the dishonest. Realists do not look at life through rose-colored spectacles or through a glass darkly. They go by what is there, not by their own wishes, hopes, or fears.

Being real and realistic is a gift from God. The reason we can be real is because we have nothing to hide. Christ's death makes amends for our sins, and our Baptism gives us His righteousness. We can be realistic because we have learned to view life through the eyes of God. We don't blink at evil. How can we in the light of the cross? But we are not pessimists and gloom-spreaders. How can we be in the light of Easter? Yes, at times we are "sorrowful, yet always rejoicing" (2 Corinthians 6:10).

Gracious God, help us to be real and realistic; for Jesus' sake. Amen.

Herbert E. Hohenstein

1 John 3:11–18

Sharing with Others

If anyone … sees his brother in need, but has no pity on him, how can the love of God be in him? *1 John 3:17*

God is most generous in sharing with us the very best He has: His earth, His Son, and His heaven. He gives us life and what we need to sustain and enrich it; strength and skill to work and provide for our daily needs; special talents and aptitudes to better the quality of our lives; experience for living wisely; abundant resources we can manipulate for our comfort and pleasure; opportunity to grow in knowledge, both temporal and spiritual; hope, comfort, and courage to sustain us in life's dark hours; faith to live by and to die by. He does all this not only that we may live fully and well but that others also may benefit from His gifts to us.

God delights in giving each of us a special variety of gifts. In doing so, He always has the interests of a larger group in mind, not just the success of one individual. Even those whose gifts are limited, He gives opportunity for sharing.

A well-known scientist stated that man has now discovered that he is made for cooperation. It's about time! God has been saying that for ages: "Love one another and share with one another."

O God, we are often slow and stingy in sharing when we are able and there are so many needs. Give us a generous heart and a willingness to share what we have with others; for Jesus' sake. Amen.

Armin C. Oldsen

Jonah 1–2

Me, Lord?

Moses said to God, "Who am I, that I should go to Pharaoh and bring the Israelites out of Egypt?" *Exodus 3:11*

God must get awfully tired of human beings—and their excuses. Paging through the Bible we seem to find nothing but reluctant warriors for the Almighty. Instead of Isaiah's "Here am I. Send me!" the more common reply to God's call is "Me, Lord? Not me! Send him!"

Moses was like that. Confronted with God's call to service, he offered the human excuse. He pleaded inadequacy, unpreparedness, and indisposition. But God wanted Moses. Without his knowledge, God had prepared Moses for a task and mellowed him through the years. God was ready to act—through Moses. It was Moses who wanted to hold back.

God still equips those whom He would use. Through the Holy Spirit, operating in Word and sacraments, God supplies divine power. Using other men and women, God equips us through good example, adequate training, and steady encouragement. In this way He prepares fathers and mothers, citizens and workmen, pastors and teachers. All are to do His will, telling the story of Christ.

God urges us to let our light shine. When the divine order comes to blaze forth, we may be sure that He has already supplied the wick, the oil, and the match.

Call us to service, Lord, and by Your Spirit show us how we have been equipped by You; for Jesus' sake. Amen.

Charles S. Mueller

Hebrews 13:4

Let's Not Spend the Night Together

Marriage should be honored by all. *Hebrews 13:4*

Ask almost any pastor of a biblical, confessional church what one of the most difficult aspects of ministry is today, and he will answer, "Ministering to couples who are living together and come to me to be married." The situation is like a double-edged sword. Cutting one way, cohabitation outside of marriage is a sin that must be challenged and the couple led to repentance. Cutting the other, a pastor wants to encourage the couple to develop a healthy and legitimate relationship in marriage.

Thankfully, secular research has come to the support of Godly standards. A study headed up by Yale University professor Neil Bennett discovered several years ago that a connection between cohabitation outside of marriage and divorce after marriage can be made. "By no means are we saying that cohabitation causes higher divorce rates," said Bennett, "but the kind of people who are attracted to cohabitation are also more likely to divorce when a marriage goes sour. They have less of a commitment to traditional institutions such as formal marriage." Our God is displeased by conditional arrangements, temporary agreements, and shallow devotion. He is eager to bless, but He blesses within the boundaries of His will.

Lord, keep me from compromising Your standards; in Jesus' name. Amen.

Richard Lieske

James 2:14–17

Words Are Not Enough

What good is it, my brothers, if a man claims to have faith but has no deeds? Can such faith save him? *James 2:14*

Words are the lifeblood of our daily existence. Words express our emotions and desires. Without words there would be no civilization, no community, no business.

Words also make our religious life possible. God's Word tells us of salvation in Jesus Christ. We respond by confessing our faith in Him. But words are not enough. When we deal with others, God demands concrete actions, not just pious expressions from our mouths.

We cannot do anything directly for God. God has everything—all the riches of the universe. He has no need for anything we might offer to Him. We can, however, do something directly for others. In our relationships we must not only say that we love our neighbor but also do things that help him. Our good sentiments must be followed by real assistance.

Without good works flowing from faith, faith would be useless. Christians are concerned about feeding and clothing the poor, especially fellow Christians—because of their love for Christ, who died to make them His own that they might serve Him.

Lord, give me a faith that is always ready to help others, not in order to be saved, but because I am saved; in Jesus' name. Amen.

David P. Scaer

Colossians 1:24–29

Stewards of the Gospel

This is how one should regard us, as servants of Christ and stewards of the mysteries of God. *1 Corinthians 4:1 RSV*

When we think of stewardship, we usually don't think of stewardship of the Gospel. Usually we think of the "three t's": time, talent, and treasure. But what about the Gospel, the Good News of what God has done with our sin through Jesus Christ? Paul put it this way: "I consider everything a loss compared to the surpassing greatness of knowing Christ Jesus my Lord" (Philippians 3:8). The Gospel—the Good News of salvation, forgiveness, and eternal life through faith in Jesus Christ—cannot be surpassed by any earthly possession. Thank God for the Gospel!

But what are we doing with this gift from God? Paul tells us to be stewards of the mysteries of God, that is, of the means of grace (the Gospel and the sacraments) that bring Christ to us. You and I are called to take the Gospel mystery, revealed to us in the God-man Jesus Christ, and share it with others. It's what we call evangelism. As stewards of the mysteries of God we are entrusted with the Gospel so we might share with others what we have seen and heard concerning Jesus Christ. Where? At home, at work, at play. We look for opportunities to be good stewards of that priceless treasure. Him we proclaim. It's part of stewardship.

Lord Jesus, make me a good steward of the Gospel, making known to others what is revealed there of God's love. Amen.

David W. Hoover

Hebrews 10:19–25

Worship the Lord

Come, let us bow down in worship, let us kneel before the LORD our Maker. *Psalm 95:6*

In worship we express our love for God; we honor and adore Him "for He is our God and we are the people of His pasture, the flock under His care" (Psalm 95:7).

We can worship God in public and in private. In either case, faith and a feeling of gratitude to God for His blessings motivate our worship.

Worship involves thanksgiving and praise. "Enter His gates with thanksgiving and His courts with praise,"the psalmist invites (Psalm 100:4). Worship includes great joy and yearning for God. "How lovely is Your dwelling place, O LORD Almighty! My soul yearns, even faints, for the courts of the LORD; my heart and my flesh cry out for the living God" (Psalm 84:1–2).

Sometimes these feelings are not as strong as they should be. But the more we worship with our fellow Christians, the more the joy will come—through Scripture reading, the Lord's Supper, the pastor's message, prayer, hymns of praise, and the encouragement of fellow Christians.

We do not go to church because we have to. We go to thank and praise God and to receive new spiritual strength in Christ through Word and sacraments.

Dear Father in heaven, give us joy in worship. We know that You love us, and we love You for our Savior, Jesus Christ. Amen.

William A. Kramer

Hebrews 12:9–14

Strive for Holiness

Make every effort to live in peace with all men and to be holy; without holiness no one will see the Lord. *Hebrews 12:14*

Spiritual growth is exhilarating. How can we grow spiritually, become more holy and more dedicated to God's will? Only by the power of God's Spirit!

Jesus teaches us to pray for the Holy Spirit. "If you, then, though you are evil, know how to give good gifts to your children, how much more will your Father in heaven give good gifts to those who ask Him!" (Matthew 7:11). The Spirit works through His Word. Daily we need to mediate on that Word so God's thoughts and truths can control our thinking and govern our actions.

By God's grace, as we open our lives to the influence of the triune God, we grow spiritually. We pray more for others, forgive more easily, and have more peace within. We are less money-minded, less worrisome, and are more grateful. We are less jealous, less critical, and more understanding. We are less often depressed and more cheerful. We will never be all that we ought to be, but we can make progress. Each of us can say with conviction, "By the power of Christ's Spirit working through the Gospel, I can and will be better than I now am."

Spirit of the living God, thank You for giving us faith in our crucified, risen Savior. Help us to strive for holiness; in Jesus' name. Amen.

Herbert M. Kern

Matthew 13:24–35

The Beauty of the Sunset

He wraps Himself in light as with a garment. *Psalm 104:2*

On our evening drives in the country or to the lake we have opportunities to enjoy the beauty of the sunset. We feast our eyes on the gorgeous harmony of colors, see the mighty architecture of embattled clouds, and note the changing splendor of the western skies.

No two sunsets are alike; all are rapturously beautiful. Science has an explanation for this phenomenon of nature, but a Christian knows that behind the laws of nature is the omnipotent hand of God. His paintings at sunset are absolutely perfect.

Our Lord is a Lord of beauty, and He desires that we worship Him in the beauty of holiness. Our lives should reflect the glory of His kindness, love, wisdom, and strength. From day to day we are to be changed into the image of Him who created us. For this purpose He has given us His Good News of salvation.

The beauty of the sunset lasts but a short time. However, it is repeated every day. How abundant is the goodness of our Lord of creation! The enchanting hues of the sunset are given by God for our enjoyment, and He never tires of lavishing beauty before our eyes.

The beauty of the Lord is reflected in the skies. He asks that His light also be reflected in our lives. We are to shine daily before others in abundant deeds of love so that they, seeing our good works, will glorify our Father who is in heaven.

Heavenly Father, enable us by Your Spirit to shine for You; for Jesus' sake. Amen.

Walter E. Hohenstein

1 Corinthians 3:1–17

God's Plan for You

We are God's fellow workers …. Each one should be careful how he builds. *1 Corinthians 3:9–10*

Rosa J. Young, the first black Lutheran missionary in the Black Belt of the South, repeatedly told her students, "God has a plan for every one of you." It was her prayer and desire to encourage young men and women to follow God's calling and enter God-pleasing vocations.

We say to everyone who is choosing a vocation, "Look at that skyscraper towering high above the surrounding buildings. It didn't just happen that it is that kind of a serviceable structure. It had an architect who designed every part of it. Builders and skilled workmen followed the architect's drawing. The structure took shape. So it is in your life. God is the architect of your life."

We build on Christ, the sure foundation. We have been admonished to take heed how we build, whether with "gold, silver, costly stones, wood, hay, or straw." The apostle goes on, "His work will be shown for what it is …. the fire will test the quality of each man's work." God's beautiful and wonderful creation did not just happen. God planned and designed it; His signature is on every part of His creation. It is also on you, for He planned your life.

Lord God, heavenly Father, You are my maker. Teach me Your plan and purpose for me in Christ Jesus, my Savior. Amen.

Walter H. Ellwanger

Luke 1:5–13

Children—Gifts from God

Sons are a heritage from LORD, children a reward from Him.
Psalm 127:3

The Bible teaches that children are gifts from God and a sign of His favor. God blessed Adam and Eve and said, "Be fruitful and multiply" (Genesis 1:28 RSV). Throughout Scripture children are regarded as special blessings from God. The psalmist calls them a heritage and a reward. He refers to children as "arrows in the hands of a mighty warrior." He concludes: "Blessed is the man whose quiver is full of them" (Psalm 127:4–5).

Today children are regarded by many as liabilities instead of blessings. Just as we are learning so much more about the beautiful mystery of God's creating hand at work in the formation of a new human life, child abuse is on the rise. The sad plight of "unwanted children" is seriously held up as a justification for killing them before birth.

What has happened? Could it be that we have forgotten that children are a "heritage from the Lord"? Let us never forget not only that God is the giver of children but also that His own Son became a child in the womb of the Virgin Mary to become the Savior of all children—including us.

Lord Jesus, help each of us see in every child a gift from You. Amen.

Samuel H. Nafzger

Matthew 5:13–16

Lights in Dark Places

You are the light of the world. A city on a hill cannot be hidden. *Matthew 5:14*

How have we been discharging the duties of citizenship in our great and blessed land? Is our country, our city, our town, our neighborhood, our *street*, the better for our having lived here? Have we by our Christian witness and by our daily actions made a constructive contribution to the betterment of our community?

Or have we merely been the passive and ungrateful recipients of all the bounties, both spiritual and material, that God has showered on us through our land, its institutions, and its government?

In His Sermon on the Mount Jesus said that Christians are to be lights—not sponges! They are to give forth—not merely soak up. They are to show the way to others—not obscure it.

God puts His lights in dark places so they may spread their rays where they are needed. The world today—our nation, our community—needs nothing more than the light of the Gospel, which God has put into our hands. Wherever we are, God has placed us there "for such a time as this" (Esther 4:14).

May the light of the Gospel shine forth from our lives into the land we love the most.

Dear Lord, "Bless our native land;
Firm may it ever stand!" for Jesus' sake. Amen.

Herman W. Gockel

Philippians 1:12–18

Circumstances and Motives

What has happened to me has really served to advance the gospel. *Philippians 1:12*

"I just can't figure out what God is getting at!" wailed one friend to another. "Just what is He trying to accomplish?"

Perhaps we have uttered a similar cry when our carefully laid plans and objectives have had to be modified because of unexpected circumstances. Sometimes it seems to us that God is intervening in a way that is counterproductive to His own stated objectives.

St. Paul may have thought so when his work of proclaiming the Gospel was curtailed by his arrest and imprisonment. Yet he discovered that God's objective of advancing the Gospel message was being met in two ways: (1) the soldiers who guarded him came to know the Gospel through his witness; and (2) other Christians, encouraged by Paul's example, stepped forward to take a stand for Jesus also. Although their motives were mixed (some were self-serving), God's objective of advancing the Good News of salvation in Christ Jesus was still accomplished.

Today, perhaps one step at a time, one encounter at a time, one person at a time, let God have His way in advancing the sweet message of the Gospel—in any way He chooses.

Father, use me as part of Your plan to bring others to faith in Your Son, my Savior, Jesus. Amen.

Daniel and Donna Streufert

Colossians 3:12–25

We Are All Teachers

Teach and admonish one another. *Colossians 3:16*

Every follower of Jesus is to be not only a lifelong learner, but also a teacher of others. God told Israel's fathers and mothers to teach their children diligently everything He commanded. The great teaching commission in Matthew is not intended only for pastors and teachers. The letters to the Ephesians and Colossians teach that the whole membership of the church is a fellowship of teachers for mutual growth in spiritual things.

We teach each other in the congregational worship service, in the discussion at Bible class, in the meetings of boards and committees, in youth or adult groups, in the give and take of family living. We also teach by the way we meet success and failure, by the way we work, by the ideals we have, and by the interests we pursue. We are in fact always teaching someone.

What are you and I teaching the children who come in contact with us? What spiritual light and guidance are we giving to our youth? Are we strengthening or breaking down the faith of the adults with whom we have dealings?

Let us rely on the Holy Spirit, working through Word and Sacrament, to teach us (Luke 12:12) so we in turn can teach and mentor others. And when we fail to set the right example, to speak words that build up, to encourage, or to share God's love let us look to Jesus who is not only the greatest teacher of all but also the one who paid for all our failures on the cross. In Him we have forgiveness for our sin and new strength to start again.

Dearest Jesus, enable us to be good teachers of others. Help us to share Your love in word and deed; for Your sake. Amen.

Oscar Feucht

John 1:10–14

Children of the Most High

To all who received Him, to those who believed in His name, He gave the right to become children of God. John 1:12

An outstanding statement in the Bible promises that we can be and are children of God. When we consider the statement from our side, it is easy enough to comprehend. We have or have had parents. We understand that relationship, and we have had the opportunity to share ourselves and our experiences with these dear relatives. They have always been willing to listen, to give advice, and even at times, to chastise and correct us when that was for our good.

But we certainly need to hang on to our hats when we begin to think about a Father-and-son or a Father-and-daughter relationship with God. Isn't He the Creator of all things? Doesn't He sustain and maintain everything with His almighty power so the stars do not clash with one another and the earth produces its fruit in due season? I can understand being His creature, but His child? His son? His daughter? Unbelievable!

But is it? Jesus affirmed this relationship in Matthew 6:6–9, and He should know! He brought about the Father-child relationship when He reconciled us to God by taking all our sins on Himself as we were baptized into His name.

Thank You, Lord, for making me Your child and for the inheritance that relationship guarantees to me; for Jesus' sake. Amen.

Carlos H. Puig

Philippians 2:1–11

Maximizing Life's Value

I consider my life worth nothing to me, if only I may finish the race and complete the task the Lord Jesus has given me—the task of testifying to the gospel of God's grace. *Acts 20:24*

There is a growing trend in this day and age to regard life with little value. People thoughtlessly place themselves in harm's way by indulging in the perils of drug abuse. The proliferation of suicide indicates a groundswell of contempt for the value of life. There is little regard for the preciousness of other people's lives. Cruel, senseless murders are reported in every newscast. Minor irritations prompt ruthless homicide on our streets.

But life is a gift from the hand of God. Its worth is surpassed only by our new life in Christ and our everlasting life at God's side in heaven. Christians cherish life most highly and protect it vigorously. But Paul suggests that even so valuable a gift as life is nothing unless it is enriched by what we do with it. No end of possibilities exists. People who have no appreciation for the value of life are themselves a magnificent field for the investment of our lives. To confer new value on them by loving them, by sharing with them the discovery that they are "precious in God's sight," by taking them hand in hand to Calvary and showing them the love of God in Christ Jesus—all these things maximize their worth. Life assumes its greatest value if we complete the task that Christ Jesus gives us.

Dear Lord, help us complete the task You give us; in Jesus' name. Amen.

Irma S. Pinkerton

Matthew 7:21–29

Castles of Sand

The world and its desires pass away but the man who does the will of God lives forever. *1 John 2:17*

On the seashore or along the beach most of us have seen castles of sand carefully erected by youngsters, only later to be utterly demolished and destroyed. Beholding these disintegrated edifices reminds us of the "castles of sand" that men and women erect in real life. They spend not just a few hours but precious years, thinking they are really accomplishing something. But then comes the night, and the tides of time swirl in, and soon their cherished "castles" disappear.

There is only one way to build a life that counts and a "work" that endures. It is to found it on the rock, Christ Jesus, our Savior, and to do so with eternity's values in view. To rear and educate your children to succeed in this life is fine, but what are you doing to help them prepare for the life to come? To be successful in business and receive the praise of people may give temporary pleasure and satisfaction, but what are you doing for eternity? Are you building a castle of sand or a work that abides?

Whatever we build in faith on the Word and work of Jesus Christ will remain, for He is the same yesterday, today, and forever.

Holy Spirit, remind us that there is but one life that will soon be past; only what is done for Christ will last. Amen.

Dennis A. Kastens

Ephesians 5:21–33

A Model for Marriage

Be subject to one another out of reverence for Christ. Wives, be subject to your husbands, as to the Lord. … Husbands, love your wives, as Christ loved the church and gave Himself up for her. *Ephesians 5:21–22, 25*

The apostle Paul in his letter to the Ephesians presents a beautiful model for marriage. To the women in the congregation the apostle says, "Be subject to your husbands, as to the Lord." Note that he does not tell men to keep their wives in subjection. Rather, women should willingly recognize and accept the head-ship of their husbands, just as the church recognizes Christ as its head.

To the men Paul writes, "Love your wives, as Christ loved the church and gave Himself up for her." This is what it means to exercise headship—to have a love for the beloved that is willing to die for her.

Lest anyone misunderstand his instructions, the apostle expressly commands that all, men and women alike, are to "be subject to one another out of reverence for Christ." Where this model is implemented, a beautiful marriage, in which each partner becomes a blessing for the other, is assured. And together they become a blessing to their children.

Lord Jesus, You have provided us with a demonstration of the love we should manifest in our marriage relationship. Forgive us when we fail to follow Your example. Amen.

Samuel H. Nafzger

Luke 10:30–35

Proclaiming Good News

Suppose a brother or sister is without clothes and daily food. If one of you says to him, "Go, I wish you well; keep warm and well fed," but does nothing about his physical needs, what good is it? *James 2:15–16*

God has sent each one of us to proclaim good news in the mission field—a mission field that begins at the end of our nose. As Christians we know the best news is the Good News of the Gospel of Christ's cross. But many people do not know that. In the account of the Good Samaritan, the man who fell among robbers was not interested in hearing the Gospel right there on the road. He had needs that seemed more pressing. The Samaritan provided first aid, food, and shelter. Now that was good news for a half-dead man along the side of the road.

Take a look around. Perhaps a child needs the comfort of a hug or a fellow worker could use a pat on the back. A teenager wants time to talk; a lonely neighbor longs to share a meal; a friend needs a hand with a home-improvement project. A hug, a pat on the back, some time, a meal, and a helping hand are all good news to those in need.

By providing "good news" as others perceive it, we share God's love. In this way, God opens the door for proclaiming His Good News, the story of what His Son has done for the people who need Him as their Savior and Lord.

Lord, use us to proclaim good news and Good News in our personal mission fields; for Jesus' sake. Amen.

Gloria K. Lessmann

Daniel 3:1–18

Fear or Courage?

We must obey God rather than men! *Acts 5:29*

Biblical examples of human cowardice far outnumber the accounts of courageous behavior. The Israelites feared the Egyptian army at the Red Sea, even though a loving God had just rescued them from 400 years of slavery. Peter confessed undying loyalty to Jesus shortly before denying Him three times. Unwarranted fear has always been a major flaw in the lives of God's people.

We Christians are no different than the people mentioned above. When trapped in places where allegiance to Christ might bring us ridicule or harm, we find it safer to deny Him. A national magazine recently demonstrated that most people lie constantly to protect jobs, reputations, and themselves. Fear of opposition may weaken us spiritually and hinder our positive actions.

Jesus always told the truth, even though it gained Him enemies and cost Him His life. It took courage to chastise the religious leaders of the day and the Roman government itself. It took immense courage to face suffering for the world's sin and an agonizing death on the cross.

Christ's courage gained Him the victory of His resurrection on Easter, and we now share that prize. His example becomes our own as bold confession erases fears. With Christ beside us, we dare confidently boast that even the gates of hell cannot overcome us!

Lord, grant me courage to stand at Your side; in Your name, Jesus. Amen.

Herbert G. Walther

Psalm 46

A Great Document

If you hold to My teaching, you are really My disciples. Then you will know the truth, and the truth will set you free. *John 8:31–32*

The Declaration of Independence has changed the course of human history. Many books have been written that have altered society's way of thinking and living as well.

Towering over every document and book written, there is one book, which has done more than any other to change the world. That is the Bible, the Word of God spoken through God's chosen writers. Jesus, the Son of God, asks us to believe this Word.

We are asked to search God's Word for meaning in life. All of the great fundamental problems of humankind are answered in the Bible. Why are we here in the world? Where are we going? Is there a God? What kind of God do we believe in? What is sin? Does God care for us? Why do people have sorrow and heartache? What is true happiness? What happens after death?

When we read the Bible, we obtain answers to these and many more questions. We know God's truth through His Law and Gospel. We learn that because of Jesus' death and resurrection our sins are forgiven and we are free of guilt. As a result, we discover the happiness that comes from the promise of heaven.

Dear Lord, increase our desire to study Your Word through which we learn of Your will and especially of Your Son, Jesus, our Savior; for His sake. Amen.

Alfred P. Klausler

John 15:1–8

The Sustaining Christ

Apart from Me you can do nothing. *John 15:5*

Power plays an important role in our lives. Strength that sustains is the concern of everyone. People buy vitamins, herbs, health food, and all sorts of exercise equipment to keep them strong and well. Many emphasize exercise of every description to develop more physical strength. To live the full, abundant life, a person must have a full and confident faith. Many have discovered that while they were physically strong, they allowed themselves to become weak, frightened, and powerless because of their misdirected thinking.

When the will of man is misdirected and the mind of man is confused, confident power is missing. Faith in Jesus, the divine Savior, is important, not only to live confidently but also to do that which is pleasing to God. That is what Jesus means when He says, "If a man remains in Me and I in him, he will bear much fruit" (John 15:5).

When Christ rules our hearts and lives and our faith is focused on Him, His power will make us able to meet every situation in life and in death as God would have us meet it. We can say, "I can do everything through Him who gives me strength" (Philippians 4:13).

Blessed Lord Jesus, source of all goodness and strength, dwell in our hearts to make us strong forever. Amen.

Edwin P. Nerger

Revelation 22:1–5

I Am with You—for All Eternity

And He will reign for ever and ever. *Revelation 11:15*

Time and space are two mysteries no one can even hope to solve. We use the term *infinity*, but we cannot begin to visualize space without end. And when we consider eternity—time without beginning or end, or perhaps even the absence of time—our minds begin to reel.

Involved in these mysteries is the mystery of heaven. In this life we cannot hope to know where it is nor to understand it in terms of time. These are things that shall be revealed to us.

The Bible in glowing terms gives us a tiny glimpse of what heaven is like. We know that we shall live perfect lives of happiness there with perfect, glorified bodies, time without end. We know that there we shall meet again our loved ones who have gone before and that there we shall see God face to face. We know that there we shall forever experience the love of God in all its fullness.

In Christ Jesus, the Son of God, heaven itself has in one respect been brought down to this earth. For we have in Him already come to believe and to live in that love. In Him eternity has touched our world of time, for in Him we have been given, here and now, the gift of eternal life, which cannot be taken from us. And in this eternal life Christ Jesus is even now reigning in our hearts as Lord and King, even as He shall continue to reign for all eternity.

Lord Jesus, reign in our hearts, keep us in true faith, and be with us for all eternity. Amen.

Arnim Polster

Isaiah 41:10–13

It's a Matter of Priorities

Seek first His kingdom and His righteousness, and all these things will be given to you as well. *Matthew 6:33*

Here is a practical illustration to reinforce the idea that God's will, what He wants us to do, should take precedence. When it does, there will be time enough for all the activities that ordinarily mark our daily lives. It's a matter of priorities.

Take a jar and fill it three-quarters full of raw rice. Then fill a second jar with Ping-Pong balls. The rice represents all the daily activities that take so much of our time. The Ping-Pong balls represent those things our Lord would have us do. Try pouring the balls into the jar of rice. Not many will fit. There isn't room. Now reverse the process. Put all the balls into the jar and pour in the rice. Isn't it amazing that when we get our priorities straight, the Lord's business first, we have room for all the things we deem important?

When we confuse priorities, God's will so often comes up short. But when by God's grace we put His will and His desires first, there's room for those things that ordinarily constitute our lives. We need to ask the Holy Spirit to help us keep our priorities straight and put first things first.

Dear Lord, help us to put Your will before our own; in Jesus' name. Amen.

Irma S. Pinkerton

Philippians 1:1–11

....

Friends

We always thank God for you all mentioning you in our prayers. *1 Thessalonians 1:2*

It had been a long time since Paul left the little community of faithful believers in Thessalonica. He had come to introduce them to Jesus, about whom they knew nothing at all. He had led them to confess their sins and accept the forgiveness that Jesus, God's Son, and their Savior, had died to earn for them. And he had gone on to bring that same Gospel to other communities around his world.

Although Paul had traveled to other places, he never forgot the Thessalonians. They were good friends whom he remembered with fondness. They were an intimate part of his prayer life. He needed to thank God for them. He needed to pray God's continued blessing on them. Who knows what blessings were poured out on the believers in Thessalonica through their good friend's faithful prayers for them?

As you walk through life, you also leave behind a trail of Christian friends, many of whom you still think of often and remember with fondness. But do you include them in your prayers? Are there people for whom you need to thank God right now? Are there friends who could benefit from your prayers today?

Heavenly Father, I thank You for bringing _____ into my life. Please bring special blessings on them today; in Jesus' name. Amen.

Unknown

Luke 5:1–11

Facing Life's Changes Fearlessly

Don't be afraid; from now on you will catch men. *Luke 5:10*

There was a time when a person could choose a career and settle down secure for the rest of his or her working life. The fear of being uprooted seemed groundless.

How far this is from reality for most folks today! Even farmers, so traditionally stable, feel anxiety about losing their farms. Organized labor can be insecure. The fear of not being able to work is a reality to many. Does it cause you fear? Do potential life changes stir up in you fears about the future?

One wonders what fears the disciples experienced when Jesus called them from the security of good jobs as fishermen to a mid-life career change of catching men, a job they knew nothing about. But the one who called them calmed them. "Follow Me," He said. In the command was the promise of His presence.

Is it really any different for us? Hasn't Jesus promised that He would be with us "to the very end of the age" (Matthew 28:20)? Surely, we can trust His presence in our labors, in our changes in labor, and in our moves from one place to another. The one who loved us enough to die for us is going to be present in any life change. And that's enough.

Blessed Jesus, thank You for being present in all the changes of life and in my work as well. Amen.

Norbert C. Oesch

Matthew 28:16–20

....

God's Instruments

We are therefore Christ's ambassadors, as though God were making His appeal through us. *2 Corinthians 5:20*

A plane crashed at Idlewild Airport, New York, with many fatalities and injuries. A physician was thrown out of the plane on impact but, miraculously, was unscathed. He began to minister to the injured and the dying. He was heard to mutter: "If only I had my instruments."

The world is dying in its sins. The United States is the sixth-largest mission field in the world. Three out of every four people on earth do not believe in Jesus for their salvation.

God has chosen Christians to be His ambassadors, His messengers to share the story of Jesus and His love. We—personally and through our missionaries—must preach the Gospel to every creature (Mark 16:15) to carry out the Great Commission of our Lord: "Go and make disciples of all nations, baptizing … teaching …" (Matthew 28:19–20).

What a privilege to be His ambassadors! Not even the angels in heaven were chosen for this role! And the wonderful thing is that we, unlike that doctor at the airport, have the instrument to do this: the Gospel of Jesus Christ.

Dear Father in heaven, empower us through Your Word and sacraments with Your Spirit so we will be courageous ambassadors for Jesus, willing to share with all whom we meet; for His sake. Amen.

Andrew Simcak Jr.

Ephesians 4:11–16

The Holy Ministry

This is how one should regard us, as servants of Christ and stewards of the mysteries of God. *1 Corinthians 4:1 RSV*

What is a Christian pastor's task? It is this: He proclaims the Word of God so people will be aroused from their sin and need and will turn to Jesus Christ, their Savior and only hope. He pronounces God's forgiveness to all who repent of their sins. He shows them how to lead a life that matches their promises. He administers the sacraments so they may be strengthened and confirmed in this faith.

This is a daunting task! It takes more than human power. It takes Christ crucified, the power of God.

To do this job, the pastor has a divine call. He is called by God through a Christian congregation. In the Christian congregation, the pastor is a called and ordained servant of Christ. He is a redeemed sinner, even as his fellow members are. But he is also a spiritual leader who does his best to show others how the Christian Gospel must operate in their lives.

His people pray for him, encourage him, advise him, help him, and befriend him. They listen to him with open hearts, and they know that as they grow in faith and dedication they will also help their pastor grow. Thus the Lord Christ is honored and His Gospel does its saving work.

Lord Jesus, we thank You for Christian pastors. Help them, and help us to help them; for Jesus' sake. Amen.

David A. Preisinger

Matthew 6:5–13

Emergency Call Boxes

Pray without ceasing. *1 Thessalonians 5:17 KJV*

Emergency call boxes are located along remote stretches of some highways. If a motorist experiences car trouble or some other type of emergency, he or she can use this device to summon assistance.

Many people believe that prayer is for emergencies only, for communication with God in times of trouble. We may pray fervently in times of distress, but we forget to talk with God when our lives are going well.

Heartfelt prayer should be an integral part of our daily lives. God wants to hear from His children. He wants us to tell Him about our needs, desires, and hopes—everything that is on our mind. He wants us to thank Him for our blessings and praise His name. We receive great blessings by sharing everything in our lives with God. He hears and answers all of our prayers, and He has the power to solve every problem that we might face. Prayer is a time for us to listen to what God is telling us.

Prayer should not be reserved for emergencies. Rather, prayer is like calling home to chat with family and friends and catch up with good news, *the* Good News. It is the way we can live at peace. Prayer is the call box God has given us to stay in touch with Him.

Dear Lord, remind us to stay in touch with You by bringing all our cares to You, for You love to answer our prayers; in Jesus' name. Amen.

Henry E. Fuelberg

Matthew 27:15–18

Love Is Not Jealous or Boastful!

Love is patient, love is kind. It does not envy, it does not boast, it is not proud. *1 Corinthians 13:4*

In the Declaration of Independence we hold this truth to be self-evident: All men are created equal. Men may be created equal, but anyone can observe that there are obvious inequalities, obvious differences in talents, abilities, substance, and environment. The manner in which people use their gifts, whether industriously or indifferently, diligently or carelessly, can increase the difference.

In these differences are to be found the seeds of jealousy and pride, for humanity cannot refrain from making comparisons. Thinking of those who have more, a person can become envious; thinking of those who have less, one can become proud and arrogant.

Only a spirit of love can conquer both feelings—envy and pride. Love born of God recognizes the biblical truth that God does not play favorites. To God, every person is a sinner in need, and only His love can supply that need.

Only at Calvary's cross can these rough edges of envy and pride be chiseled from our heart. There we are confronted with the truth that all that we are and have is an undeserved gift of God.

The heart that understands this is stripped of all envy and pride, because it regards all fellow human beings as persons in need of Christ's love.

Lord, forgive us when we are proud and boastful or envious of others. Instead, fill us with Your Spirit of love and humility; for Jesus' sake. Amen.

William Kohn

Luke 6:46–49

Play It by Ear?

There was evening, and there was morning—the first day. *Genesis 1:5*

What shall I plan for today that I might fit it into the overall plan for my life? Or will I just take today and "play it by ear"? Planning the day can make for structured living. "Playing it by ear" can make for sloppy living. There is danger in both.

If we plan our day, we should never be so rigid that we become inflexible. Each day has its own surprises, and we must be ready for them because today's surprises are today's opportunities. They must be claimed for they may come our way only once. In keeping the goal of life before us, we must be open-ended enough to make an occasional detour to fill some special need. After all, we are in this world to serve, not to be served.

"Playing it by ear" can be risky and make life so loose that it has no direction or purpose. We need something to make life hang together and give it direction.

The apostle Paul wrote, "For to me, to live is Christ" (Philippians 1:21). He said this because Christ had lived and died for him. When, by God's grace, Christ is our goal, we will find that our plans are God's plans.

Lord Jesus, help me to be open to opportunities for service and love to others because of Your love for me. Amen.

Albert L. Neibacher

Philippians 2:5–11

The Telltale Mark of Maturity

Do nothing out of selfish ambition or vain conceit, but in humility consider others better than yourselves. *Philippians 2:3*

Note the day when you stopped thinking of yourself first and foremost. That day was the beginning of your maturity.

For the first years of life we are almost completely concerned about our own needs. We are insecure. We worry that we will not be taken care of. We grasp every chance to ensure our own rights. When the pie is divided, we want the biggest piece or, at least, as much as the next person. It takes a long time before our attitude changes. But gradually it does—when someone captures our heart. Soon that other person—the beloved—assumes first place in our attentions. We begin to make sacrifices for the loved one. We value the person more than his or her possessions. This turning point is reached at different times with each person. Some may reach it at a relatively young age; others, tragically, never.

With Christians it is the love of Jesus and their love for Him that triggers the turnaround. "He must become greater; I must become less" (John 3:30) becomes the Christian's way of life. At that moment maturity sets in—and a useful life begins.

Loving Savior, give me the mind that was in You so I may serve You and those whom You have redeemed. Amen.

Jaroslav J. Vajda

John 13:12–20

Greatness in Service

Whoever would be great among you must be your servant, and whoever would be first among you must be slave of all. *Mark 10:43–44 RSV*

In reading the New Testament, you may get the feeling at times that the kingdom of God is a topsy-turvy thing. It takes our human ideas and turns them upside down. God seems to have a very special kind of algebra in which every human plus becomes a minus and every human minus a plus.

For example, in the minds of many, greatness consists of power or wealth or fame. A great person is one who controls the affairs of people or nations, leads victorious armies, builds up a great fortune, displays scientific genius, or writes enduring literature.

But these human notions are exactly the opposite of God's standard of greatness. What must we do to measure up to the divine standard? We must become servants. That may seem strange, but it's exactly what our Lord says: "Whoever would be great among you must be your servant, and whoever would be first among you must be slave of all." And it all fits. For Christ Himself "came not to be served but to serve, and to give His life as a ransom for many" (Mark 10:45 RSV).

Holy Spirit, raise up faithful servants of Christ who glorify His name in all the earth; for Jesus' sake. Amen.

Frederick C. Hinz

Romans 10:8–18

The Church in All the World

Their voice has gone out into all the earth, their words to the ends of the world. Romans 10:18

Have we ever stopped to consider that the Christian religion may be summarized in just two one-syllable words: "Come" and "Go"? The first word is the Gospel invitation, "Come to Me, all you who are ... burdened, and I will give you rest" (Matthew 11:28). The second word is the missionary command, "Go into all the world and preach the good news to all creation" (Mark 16:15).

For 2,000 years the church has been listening to that command and, with the Spirit's active help in Word and sacrament, has been endeavoring to fulfill it. The results are evident. Of the heralds of the Gospel it may truly be said, "Their voice has gone out into all the earth, their words to the ends of the world."

The living church is a missionary church. If Christians feel no urge to carry the word of salvation to those, both at home and abroad, who are dying without hearing it, they may well lose that heritage themselves. By sharing its spiritual gifts with others, the church becomes ever stronger and more vital in its inner life.

The purpose of the church's missionary task is not to teach others to dress and act and live as we do. The great objective of Christian mission work is to proclaim the forgiveness of sins, life, and salvation through Christ to all people. To this end the church keeps praying the Lord's own missionary petition: "Thy kingdom come!"

Heavenly Father, give us the courage and the words to share Your love in Jesus with those who are lost so they too may have the joy of knowing You; for Jesus' sake. Amen.

Thomas Coates

Romans 5:1–11

In Jesus' Name

In that day you will ask in My name. I am not saying that I will ask the Father on your behalf. No, the Father Himself loves you because you have loved Me. *John 16:26–27*

"Just mention my name. Tell him I sent you." Sometimes the mention of a name gains admittance and the interest of people who otherwise would be unapproachable.

What comfort and power is ours, then, when the Son of God sends us to His Father and says, "Just mention My name!"

Timidly, we stand outside the door and say: "I cannot go in! God is God, and I am nothing but dust! How can God be concerned about me?" But Jesus urges: "Was I not born of flesh? Yet My Father loves Me! Just mention My name!"

Still we hesitate, "How dare I approach God? God is holy, and I have contradicted His will and deserved only His anger!" "Do not be afraid," says the Savior. "Has not the Father sent Me into the world to fulfill the Law you broke and then suffer the punishment you deserved? Just mention My name!"

"O Jesus," we cry, "*You* go in and ask the Father for me!" But He replies, "You can ask for yourself. He is your Father, and He loves you because you have loved Me! Just mention My name!" So as God's adopted children through Baptism, we go in boldly and speak the name of Jesus—and the arms of God open joyfully to receive us as His own!

We thank You, dear Father, that we need never again stand hesitantly outside Your door; for You have shown us the power of Your forgiving love in Your Son, Jesus. Amen.

Walter Troeger

Acts 27

God and the Travelers

Men, you should have taken my advice not to sail from Crete; then you would have spared yourselves this damage and loss. *Acts 27:21*

The apostle Paul was a traveling man, venturing far and wide by land and sea. He understood that not all journeys were safe and without danger (Acts 27:9–10).

Just think what Paul would say if he could see all the people on the move today. No doubt he would still predict danger and peril.

The problems of travel in Paul's day were mostly due to unmanageable weather elements and inadequate carriers. Today the major problem seems to be the travelers themselves. News reports of highway disasters and accident scenes are frequently attributed to driver negligence, alcoholism, road rage, and the like.

While alcohol, carelessness, speed, and fatigue are often causes of highway deaths, they are not excuses. Paul today would thunder against our violation of the commandment "You shall not kill." God, too, offers something to travelers as a basic rule for the road: "Love does no harm to its neighbor" (Romans 13:10).

But God also comforts travelers who face the unknown and events beyond their control. He says, "Do not be afraid, for I am with you."

Dear Lord, watch over us and those we love as we travel. Keep us from sudden death and injury, and help us always to put our trust in You; through Jesus Christ, our Lord, we pray. Amen.

Nicholas B. May

Deuteronomy 8:10–18

Total Dependence

O L**ORD**, you preserve both man and beast. How priceless is Your unfailing love! *Psalm 36:6–7*

If God withdrew from the universe, all life would come to an end, and nothing would be able to function. The world could not exist.

God's power governs, directs, and sustains all He has made. All created things function according to the powers and properties that He has implanted in them. God is actively preserving everything that exists.

Our next heartbeat depends on God. The smallest seed sprouts and grows because of His power. The sun rises and sets according to His ordinance. Much of what God does He does through His creation.

We are dependent on God for everything, especially for our salvation, for by His grace He made us spiritually alive in Christ through our Baptism and forgave us all our sins.

As we recognize that all our help comes from the Lord, we thank and praise Him as the source of all good. We also remember Moses' caution that if the children of Israel enjoyed many good things and flourished, they should not claim the credit. Rather, they should acknowledge that everything comes from the hand of the Lord. We too acknowledge: "O L**ORD**, You preserve both man and beast."

Gracious Lord, when we want to boast of what we can do, remind us that we are totally dependent on You; in Jesus' name we pray. Amen.

Oscar J. Klinkermann

Romans 8:28–34

Fortune

In all things God works for the good of those who love Him, who have been called according to His purpose. *Romans 8:28*

We sometimes say, "Some people have all the luck." But do they?

That person is not necessarily fortunate for whom everything seems to be going well. "Going well" means different things to different people. A millionaire who loses all of his fortune except $5,000 might think of himself as a pauper. A pauper who comes into unexpected possession of $5,000 might feel like a millionaire.

That person is fortunate whose life has solid moorings, who, in either good or evil fortune, lives by the sure hope that "in all things"—in good or evil alike—"God works for the good of those who love Him."

That person is fortunate who knows that as part of the family of God he is surrounded and upheld by God's unfailing love.

That person is fortunate who knows that in God's economy there is no such thing as "fate" or "luck" but that God is at work in and through everything that comes to us.

We can do all things through Christ who strengthens us. That doesn't mean we won't have bad days. It does mean that in the bad days we have Christ's strength to draw on.

Father, help us to live by faith, trusting that in all things You work for the good of those who love You; in Jesus' name we pray. Amen.

Wilbur J. Fields

Matthew 20:20–28

God's Design

They exchanged the truth of God for a lie. *Romans 1:25*

We miss the point of Paul's argument to the Romans if we don't sense that after his introduction (Romans 1:1–17) he then moved toward a radical but realistic statement about our natures: "All have sinned and fall short of the glory of God" (Romans 3:23).

This truth about ourselves is difficult for many today to accept, especially when used in reference to the way we live out our sexuality. Proponents of "gay rights" say that people who have the propensity toward being homosexual have the right to celebrate openly their sexual preference.

But thanks be to God, Paul states in the opening chapters of his letter that God has made us to function according to our biological natures.

To go counter to how He created us is unnatural to God's design. In the opening chapters of Romans, Paul states that there is another reason for not engaging in such practices. God has put in our conscience what is right. To go against this and to say good is bad and bad is good changes the truth of God into a lie.

But thanks be to God, Paul is willing to say just as assertively that all "are justified freely by His grace through … Christ Jesus" (Romans 3:24).

O God, make us willing participants in Your work of grace that through Christ we may see what is good. In Jesus' name we pray. Amen.

Gordon Beck

Psalm 100

Happiness in God's Vineyard

Whatever you did for one of the least of these brothers of Mine, you did for Me. *Matthew 25:40*

Jesus taught that happiness lies in servanthood, in being useful to somebody, in loving and serving another. You don't necessarily find happiness in a high-salaried position or getting married or acquiring property. You don't find it in what the modern world has come to think of as being independent—of meeting one's own needs first. Jesus thinks happiness is just the opposite of that: not being independent but being sympathetic and indispensable to someone.

Jesus Himself is the best example of the kind of happiness that makes itself useful to others. Because Jesus went about doing good, people flocked around Him, never leaving Him alone. This pursuit of happiness in life seeks day after day to give the best to someone who needs a lift. Despite His suffering, Jesus found the happiest moments of life going to the cross, carrying it for all of humanity.

Life is God's vineyard. Our purpose in it is to make an investment. When we take our eyes off ourselves, follow the example of Jesus, and gratefully do the Father's will, serving our heavenly Father by serving those around us, the result will be happiness.

Our Father in heaven, grant that we may find joy in serving others; for Jesus' sake. Amen.

Arnold G. Kuntz

Colossians 4:2–6

It's How You Say It

Let your conversation be always full of grace, seasoned with salt, so that you may know how to answer everyone. *Colossians 4:6*

There is an old saying, "Think three times before you speak." That rule would save us from saying many unkind, bitter, and harmful words.

We season food with salt to make it taste better. We need to learn to season the things we say with the salt of love, kindness, and helpfulness. Homes are much happier when we watch not only what we say but also how we say it.

According to an ancient story a king requested his wise men to interpret his dream. The first said: "Your dream has a sad meaning. All your relations—mother, brother, sister, and wife—will die and leave you alone" The king was displeased and had him lashed. A second wise man said: "Your dream promises you much happiness. You will be blessed with long life and health. You will live longer than any of your kindred." As a reward the king gave him 100 gold pieces. Both men said the same thing, but how they said it made the difference.

How do we speak to others about their soul, their need for the Savior from sin, or about their church attendance? Do we argue heatedly? That is what Paul warns against. Harsh words stir up anger. Instead, we need to cultivate a pleasant way of speaking and rely on the power of the Holy Spirit to help us season our answers and remarks with love, kindness, understanding, and concern.

Lord, help me to speak what is right and true. Help me to rely on the power of the Holy Spirit so my words will heal, comfort, and bless others; for the sake of Jesus, my Savior. Amen.

Herman A. Etzold

Philippians 4:4–8

Impressionable Minds

Think about such things. *Philippians 4:8*

We are all born with certain hereditary characteristics and a sinful nature. Yet our minds are also quite impressionable to the influences of our environment, ready to keep a record of everything we encounter along life's way. Stored there, many of our past experiences affect our present thoughts and actions.

We must marvel at God's design in providing us with this gray matter between our ears. Our minds and those of our children are our greatest stewardship responsibilities. We must be careful about what our minds receive.

So much is available to us that poisons our minds. That was true in Paul's day too. He exhorts the Christians at Philippi to watch what they feed their minds. He encourages whatever is true, noble, right, pure, lovely, admirable, excellent, or deserving praise, saying: "Think about such things."

The best nourishment for our minds is worship in the body of Christ with fellow Christians and a regular study of the Scriptures. Through them the Holy Spirit, having brought us to faith in Christ, works all good within us. And the promise holds true: "The peace of God, which transcends all understanding, will guard your hearts and your minds in Christ Jesus" (Philippians 4:7).

Heavenly Father, continue to nourish us with Your life-giving Word; in Jesus' name we pray. Amen.

Raymond L. Hartwig

Isaiah 44:1–5

Alive

This is what the LORD says—He who made you, who formed you in the womb, and who will help you. *Isaiah 44:2*

"Get a life!" is the contemporary reply we hear to rebut a whiny spirit or complaining tone. Usually spoken humorously, the phrase has considerable merit; carping or being disgruntled doesn't belong in the life of one who knows Jesus Christ.

But what is this life we are supposed to "get"? Is it a life filled with only good things? Is it a life where the way is always smooth? To be worthwhile, life should have more depth than that. It ought to include an inner composure that shows in the way we live, no matter our circumstance.

That's a life we don't have to work hard to "get." It is already ours. For God formed us in our mother's womb. God knew us before we were born. Our days are literally in His hands. We have His Word on it. And He will help us along the way because by His grace, He chose us to be His adopted children through Holy Baptism.

So the psalmist can sing that God knows everything about him (Psalm 119:168). How uplifting and sustaining that is! God's knowledge of us is nothing to be feared. Rather, we are led to praise God and to thank Him for His wonderful works by which we are alive in Christ and on the way to life everlasting.

Heavenly Father, we want to live all our days the life You have given us to live through Christ. Help us. Amen.

Leland Stevens

Ephesians 4:1–16

Designer of Unique People

We have different gifts, according to the grace given us.
Romans 12:6

Many of us are unhappy with ourselves. We have one or more features we wish we could change to be more like another person. When we are uncomfortable with who we are in comparison with others, we may have forgotten that our true goal is to be more like Christ.

In Christ, God redeemed us as His own. "In Christ we who are many form one body, and each member belongs to all the others" (Romans 12:5). Through His Spirit, poured out on us in Baptism, He endows each of us with special gifts and talents for rendering service to Him. God calls us to put our abilities to work for the good of the whole church—a labor of love that is a joy.

If we are experiencing a loss of creativity or enthusiasm in our service, it may be an indication that we have stepped out of the area for which God has uniquely equipped us. Spiritual maturity brings a self-awareness of where we function best. All God asks is that we express our uniqueness in Christian service. When we are the persons God has designed us to be—and we are doing the work for which He has equipped us—we will find satisfaction in our service again. It's a better way to live.

Heavenly Father, help us so employ Your gifts that we serve You with continual joy; for Jesus' sake. Amen.

Norman W. Stoppenhagen

John 3:25–30

The Direction of Life

Immediately the boy's father exclaimed, "I do believe; help me overcome my unbelief." *Mark 9:24.*

The above words, spoken by a frantic father, speak to the conflict in which Christians often find themselves. It is the struggle between belief and unbelief, between faith and doubt. So long as a person is able to pray, confessing his faith to God and asking Him for help to overcome unbelief, he is still a Christian. His faith, though shaken, is maintaining the upper hand. The direction our life takes, whether toward greater faith or toward unbelief, depends in large measure on whom we want to serve: the true God or ourselves. When we allow God to be central, grow in the Word, set Christian service as the goal of living, and in all things seek first the kingdom of God, then we are going the way of faith. This often involves a struggle, for going God's way takes us in an entirely different direction than what our sinful nature would take.

Our Lord Jesus Christ, completely obedient to His Father, gave Himself for us. Thanks to His atoning work, our sins of unbelief are forgiven. When we stumble because our faith is unsteady and we are not ready to place God first in our life, we need to pray what the distraught father prayed. God hears such a prayer.

Lord, increase my faith through Your Word and Spirit; for Jesus' sake. Amen.

Alfred M. Buls

Matthew 5

....

Flaws Are Dangerous

Forgive my hidden faults. *Psalm 19:12*

Comparatively few are guilty of glaring sins such as murder, robbery, adultery, or embezzlement. But what about the hidden sins, the so-called flaws, which many of us may deem unimportant?

Just how unimportant is a flaw? Is it unimportant in the giant steel cables that are designed to give strength to the bridge they support? in a balance sheet? in a precious stone?

Suppose there had been a flaw in Jesus. Would we have a Savior from sin? Would we have peace with God? Would we have the certain hope of life eternal? The answer is *no* to every question.

If we are honest with ourselves, we must admit there are flaws in us. Are they really unimportant to our families? Let husbands and wives answer that question. Let children be our judge. Do these flaws seem insignificant to those who work at our side? Let those who suffer from our impatience and stubbornness answer. Let those who put up with our thoughtlessness speak up. Do these flaws limit our usefulness and hurt our effectiveness?

It is little things that tear marriage to pieces. Talking and talking when there ought to be silence. Brutal silence when there ought to be words of encouragement and cheer. The pinpricks, the constant needling, the maddening irritations—these are dangerous flaws.

We certainly have a need to pray, "Forgive my hidden faults." In Jesus we have forgiveness through His death for sins such as these.

Lord, forgive us our flaws and by Your grace enable us to overcome them; through Jesus Christ, our Savior. Amen.

Elmer C. Kieninger

Sharing the Burden

Carry each other's burdens, and in this way you will fulfill the law of Christ. *Galatians 6:2*

You are carrying two bags of groceries home. Your arms ache, and your legs are rubbery. A friend meets you and carries one of the heavy bags for you. What a relief!

The Bible tells us to carry each other's burdens. What burdens? We may do this by sharing with others their sorrows, unrelieved problems, or ugly, inescapable situations. We sometimes forget that those who are alone need someone with whom they can talk. If we are willing to listen discreetly and respect the other person's confidence, we can help the lonely see things more clearly and help them in making decisions.

Christ told us to love one another as He loved us. We do that when we concern ourselves with the needs of others, easing their burdens by our words and deeds of love.

As we carry each other's burdens, we are mindful that Christ "took up our infirmities and carried our diseases" (Matthew 8:17). For Jesus' sake God lifts the burden of our sins from us. That's the greatest relief of all. Set free from this load, by God's grace we are both willing and able to help carry another's burden.

Gracious Lord, make us unselfish and loving so we may help others carry their burdens; in Jesus' name. Amen.

Oscar J. Klinkermann

Isaiah 55:6–11

Successful Failure

I planted the seed, Apollos watered it, but God made it grow.
1 Corinthians 3:6

It is praiseworthy that we like to be successful in all we do for the Lord, but sometimes we seem to fail utterly.

Jesus invited the people of Jerusalem to come to Him, but they would not. Paul did not win all to whom he preached the Gospel. In a parable that Jesus gave us, some of the good seed of God's Word fell on hard, shallow, and weedy soil and did not grow or produce a harvest.

God does not hold us responsible for success. He only asks that we work faithfully and to the best of our abilities.

God calls some of us to plant the seed, others to water it, but only He can make it grow. When a person believes in Jesus as Savior, that is entirely the work of God.

God can turn what looks like failure to us into success. What looks hopeless today may become God's great victory tomorrow. His ways are not our ways. We are sure that His Word will accomplish what He wants and our labors are not in vain in the Lord. In this confidence we serve faithfully—doing our sowing and watering—and leave the success in God's hands.

When things seem to go wrong, assure us, Lord, that the work we do in Your name will not fail; for Jesus' sake. Amen.

Oscar J. Klinkermann

Philippians 1:3–11

Growth and Progress

He who began a good work in you will carry it on to completion. *Philippians 1:6*

Spiritual progress is an objective of all dedicated Christians. We are living in a progressive age. Much is made of material, intellectual, and scientific growth and development. Why, then, not include the most important part of a person, the spiritual self?

As dedicated Christians we seek to grow in knowledge of God's Word. We want to know more about our great, wonderful God. What are God's glorious qualities? What are His infinite thoughts toward us?

We want to grow in faith. Where faith is weak and wavering, gloomy doubt and unbelief chill the soul. Confident faith brings to our possession and enjoyment all the priceless treasures for which Christ has purchased us. It lays its strong hand on the whole storehouse of God's promises. It makes for strong convictions, for bold and courageous Christian living.

The opportunities for personal growth and progress in the Christian faith are virtually unlimited. They are within easy reach—as close as your church for worship, as close as your Bible for reading, as close as your mind for meditation, as close as your heart for prayer.

Holy Spirit, help us grow in faith, knowledge, and Christian service; through Jesus Christ. Amen.

Edwin L. Wilson

Exodus 32:30–34

Children of God

Everyone who believes that Jesus is the Christ is born of God.
1 John 5:1

"God has no grandchildren, only children." Think about that quote for a moment.

Moses was willing to make the children of Israel God's "grandchildren" by taking the punishment for their sins on himself. But God said no —"Whoever has sinned against Me I will blot out of My book" (Exodus 32:33).

The religious leaders of Jesus' time thought they had a special "in" to heaven because they were Abraham's "grandchildren." Jesus let them know that their ancestry made no difference to Him.

No matter if we come from a long line of churchgoers, no matter if our grandparents were charter members and a stained-glass window in the church bears our family name, no matter if our relatives are missionaries and preachers—we have to believe in Jesus as our Savior ourselves to have peace with God. Nor can we believe for our children, and that lesson may be harder to learn. God has no grandchildren!

That puts the relationship between God and me where it belongs: between the two of us—person to person. Jesus takes away my sins. It is through God's grace and the faith given to me in my Baptism that I am saved—no one else gets in between. I am God's child—intimately, directly.

God, You are my Father. You have made me Your child. Your steadfast love keeps me forever. Keep me strong in You; for Jesus' sake. Amen.

Louise Mueller

Romans 15:9–13

Expressing One's Joy

At His tabernacle will I sacrifice with shouts of joy; I will sing and make music to the LORD. *Psalm 27:6*

Joy is one of God's great gifts. His kingdom, declares St. Paul, is "righteousness, peace, and joy in the Holy Spirit" (Romans 14:17). The same apostle prays in behalf of his readers that God may "fill you with all joy and peace as you trust in Him, so that you may overflow with hope by the power of the Holy Spirit" (Romans 15:13). The fruit of the Spirit is like a string of precious pearls, including these: "Love, joy, peace, patience ..." (Galatians 5:22).

The chief source of the joy of Christians is Jesus Christ, who, having completed our salvation, rose from the dead to put our joy on a firm and permanent footing.

Aside from the great gift of salvation, God grants other gifts, and these prompt our joy and thanks: the birth of a new baby, recovery from illness, doing well in school, better opportunities at one's work, enjoyable travel, visits with friends. Since it is from God that all blessings flow, it is only right that we thank Him. This is how the psalmist determined to express his joy: with sacrifices of thanksgiving, with shouts of joy, with singing and making music to God. We do this as well!

Lord Jesus, You are our priceless treasure, fount of purest pleasure, our truest friend. We thank You for bringing joy. Amen.

Unknown

Luke 12:22–31

Providing Love

"Your Father knows that you need them." *Luke 12:30*

"Your Father!" What a tender touch these words give to the reassuring words of Jesus. He had just pointed His disciples to the flowers of the field and the birds of the air as evidence of God's providing care and had cautioned them against anxiety over the inevitable needs of tomorrow.

The tired child at the end of day will often confide her wants and needs to her earthly father and then drift off to peaceful sleep. It is enough that Dad knows! He will find a way to meet his child's needs.

Our heavenly Father knows our every want and wish. And He is abundantly able and willing to provide. "He who did not spare His own Son, but gave Him up for us all—how will He not also, along with Him, graciously give us all things?" (Romans 8:32). There is no need in our life, however great or small, that God does not know and which He will not fill if it's necessary for our eternal happiness. "My God will meet all your needs according to His glorious riches in Christ Jesus," says Paul (Philippians 4:19).

In times of need let us remember that we are God's children. He is our living, loving, and almighty Father. Our welfare and happiness is a matter of His deep personal concern. He knows our names and our needs. It is enough that He knows, for could He know and withhold His help?

Heavenly Father, You know what we want and need. Help us to trust You to do what is best for us. In Jesus' name we pray. Amen.

H. W. Gockel

Philippians 4:1–3

Promoting Reconciliation

I ask you, loyal yokefellow, help these women who have contended at my side in the cause of the gospel. *Philippians 4:3*

The world is full of wonderful differences. Variety fills God's creation. He has gifted His children, too, with unique personal identities and perspectives. Differences are good.

Yet sometimes the differences develop into barriers. Sometimes people are unwilling to celebrate the differences and instead let them grow into hard feelings or hurt feelings, into resentment or quarrels.

Apparently this is what happened between two of Paul's fellow workers in spreading the Gospel in the city of Philippi: Eudoia and Syntyche. Sadly, it still happens among Christians today when people disagree.

The heavenly Father speaks to us through Paul as He did to the Philippians of that day. We dare not be a part of the problem. There is no room for taking sides or laying blame, no room for accusation or deceitful gossip. We must be a part of the solution by helping one another work out differences that rob us of closeness and unity. We dare not write others off as bickering troublemakers. We are *partners together* in sharing the Good News that God loves and forgives us in Jesus Christ.

Lord Jesus, heal our differences so we may, in partnership, share the Good News. Amen.

Daniel and Donna Streufert

1 Timothy 6:6–16

Youth for Christ

Remember your Creator in the days of your youth. *Ecclesiastes 12:1*

Our Creator has always placed a high value on the services of young people in His kingdom. There was Joseph, who at the age of 30 became the prime minister and food administrator of mighty Egypt. Samuel was a comparatively young man when he rose to leadership in Israel at a time of great political disturbance. David the youth turned the tide of the Philistine invasion when, by his sling, he conquered the bragging giant, Goliath. Paul put his young assistant, Timothy, in charge of the church at Ephesus and instructed him not to let anyone look down on him because he was young but to set an example for the believers in speech, in life, in love, in faith and in purity (1 Timothy 4:12).

We think also of the devotion of the faithful young women mentioned in the Bible. Ruth, as a young widow, showed a remarkable faith in God and devotion to God's people. Beautiful Esther was God's instrument in saving His people from annihilation. Many more loyal young men and women used their youthful energies to build God's kingdom.

God continues to want some of that enthusiasm, courage, endurance, and daring that is so characteristic of youth for His kingdom work. Now, who is willing to consecrate himself today to the Lord? (1 Chronicles 29:5)?

Dear Lord, raise up young people who will speak enthusiastically about You and work courageously to share Your love with others; for Jesus' sake. Amen.

T. A. Weinhold

Matthew 5:13-16

Caution—Saints at Work!

You are the light of the world. Matthew 5:14

As I drove down the highway, I saw a sign: "Caution—Men at Work." It meant, "Watch out. Things are happening here, men are working, and improvements are being made. Watch out for equipment."

And I thought: Could this be said about my church? Could we put up a sign on the front lawn that says, "Caution—Saints at Work"? Are things happening here? Are saints working? Are improvements being made? Could I put up a sign like that in front of my house?

And I asked myself: Would it be a good thing if every Christian were just like me? If all the members of my congregation were as strong or as weak as I am, where would we be? If I should drop out of life today, would there be any great difference in the holy Christian church or even in my congregation? How much do I help my fellow members to be better Christians? How much do I draw others to Christ by my good example day after day?

The things I say and do, the way I say and do them—this must give away the fact that I belong to God, that the living and saving Christ dwells in me. The kind of neighbor I am, the way I spend my time and money, the way I raise my children—all this shows God's light in me.

Lord, let Your light shine in me, as it has in all Your saints before me, so others may be drawn to You; for Jesus' sake. Amen.

David A. Preisinger

Mark 11:20–26

In the Picture

Come, you who are blessed by My Father, take your inheritance, the kingdom prepared for you. *Matthew 25:34*

Several youngsters playing at the seashore came across an artist painting a seascape. One of the children said to the artist, "Paint us into the picture, Mister." That is the major challenge for the church of the world today: Paint us into the picture. The Christian church has a great deal to offer: peace in the midst of surrounding turmoil, a purpose when everyone else seems to be devoted to self-service, forgiveness for all the times when we are less than what we ought to be, and always another chance. It's all wrapped up in the Savior, Jesus Christ.

But most of it seems so remote, so far removed, so much like "church." Does that have anything at all to do with us? Listen: All those things begin to live and move and have real meaning when you and I are in the picture. We need peace, purpose, forgiveness, and another chance. The echo of our need has sounded in the chambers of heaven, and God has addressed an answer to our need. In His great love He sent His Son, Jesus Christ, into the world to live and die for all people. That's the message of the church in our day. You and I are to be in the picture when it comes to believing and proclaiming it.

Help us to see that Your love, Lord, is for us; in Jesus' name. Amen.

Arnold G. Kuntz

John 21:15–23

Top-priority Question

Jesus said to Simon Peter, "Simon son of John, do you truly love Me more than these?" *John 21:15*

No question can match in importance the one Jesus asked Peter that early morning at the lakeside. Everyone who claims to be the Lord's disciple needs to make sure he or she has faced it and answered it honestly.

Jesus' question is simple and direct, and also personal, an indication perhaps that we should put our own name in place of Simon's: "Matthew, Emma, do *you* love Me?"

It is important to note, too, that He does not ask: "Do you love My church or My Word or My worship?" Of course we should and as fully as possible. But the prior question is: "Do you love Me, the one who came to earth for you, died for you, earned forgiveness of sins and life everlasting for you?"

Jesus desires above all that our relationship to Him be on a "you-Me" basis, joined by the greatest of all words: *Love.*

Thank You, Lord, for the love with which You have enriched my life. Enable me to respond always, "You know that I love You"; for Jesus' sake. Amen.

Albert W. Galen

1 Corinthians 6:12–20

Bought at a Price

Do you not know that your body is a temple of the Holy Spirit, who is in you, whom you have received from God? You are not your own; you were bought at a price. Therefore honor God with your body. *1 Corinthians 6:19–20*

It's my life. It's my body. I can do with them what I want. The Constitution guarantees my rights.

The Constitution, indeed, affirms human rights under God. But the law is not the only authority nor the highest one under which Christians live.

Your life and body are not yours alone. They are God's gifts. He expects you to care for them and use them to His glory. You should give your body proper nourishment, adequate rest, and protection against harm.

We're not free to use harmful drugs or to use alcohol or food in excess. Promiscuous sex, which includes all sex outside of marriage, directly violates God's Law and certainly does harm to our body and life.

The God who created us claims us as His own. He has made our body His dwellingplace. When Jesus gave His body into death on the cross to pay the price for our sins, He bought us, including our bodies, for God. He promises to raise our bodies to glory so we may honor Him for eternity.

Thank You, Lord, for Your indwelling Spirit. Help us to treat our bodies as Your temple; for Jesus' sake. Amen.

Edgar Walz

Deuteronomy 32:9–14

Born to Soar

Fan into flame the gift of God, which is in you. *2 Timothy 1:6*

Stirring up a fire and fanning the flame makes it burn brighter and hotter. Paul was reminding young Timothy to remain active in the Lord's cause.

Our God, who has declared us righteous through the merits of Christ, wants us also to be active in Christian service. He would do for us what the mother eagle does for her young, as stated in the suggested Bible reading.

The young eagles have a comfortable nest. The mother takes good care of them and carries food to them. They grow. But one day she comes with no food. Instead, she stirs up the nest, pulls the young eagles out, and drops them in space. Why does the mother eagle do this? Is she being cruel? Not at all. She dashes under them and bears them on her wings so they suffer no hurt. The mother eagle is teaching the young ones why they were born. They were born not to be coddled in a soft nest. They were born to soar and to fly high.

The Lord teaches us that we are not redeemed to pass our time in idleness but to do great and lofty things for Him and others. To this end He wants us to stir up the gift He has given us.

Lord, enable us to serve You in word and deed. We pray in Jesus' name. Amen.

Lewis Eickhoff

Matthew 18:21–35

Forgive One Another

Be kind and compassionate to one another, forgiving each other, just as in Christ God forgave you. *Ephesians 4:32*

How can we forgive the friend who now refuses to talk to us, the spouse who walks out on us, or the person who lies about us, burglarizes our home, or aggravates us day after day?

Nothing is harder or more necessary than to forgive from the heart. Forgiving us was the hardest thing God ever did. It cost His Son sweat, death, and hell. No matter what we have done, God forgives us when we pray sincerely, "Lord, forgive and renew me for Jesus' sake." As God forgives us, we forgive others.

Forgiving does not mean forgetting. It may be impossible to block certain painful memories out of our mind. Nor need we return to the same close relationship we once had with the one we have forgiven. Discretion is in place.

To forgive means we do not bear a grudge, and we do not try to get even or hurt the person who injured us. We pray for those who treat us badly and, when possible, do good to them. It may call for a personal contact or a letter to seek reconciliation. We are to forgive whether the other party wants our forgiveness or not. Is there someone we ought to forgive? If so, let us ask God for strength to forgive that person right now.

Merciful God, thank You for forgiving us; for Jesus' sake. Amen.

Herbert M. Kern

2 Thessalonians 3:6–13

Laziness

Go to the ant, you sluggard; consider its ways and be wise!
Proverbs 6:6

To be considered lazy is not a compliment. We don't have high opinions of people who refuse to provide for themselves.

It is striking that God uses the lowly ant as an example for us to follow. Just watch an ant. It is always on the go, a study of perpetual motion. The ant seems to be one of the busiest creatures God has put on this earth.

God does not want us to be lazy. It is His will that we should work and work hard. Our body is so constituted that it cannot remain healthy and strong unless it is engaged in some activity.

Jesus had work to do. He said that He must do the work of the one who sent Him (John 9:4). Thank God, Jesus fulfilled His work. He sacrificed His life for us—a labor of love on our behalf. We have forgiveness and life with God, now and forever.

"Idleness is the devil's workshop," it is said. As we make our way through life, let us remind ourselves to work while we have the opportunity, because "night is coming, when no one can work" (John 9:4).

May we diligently labor and live for our Lord, using all the opportunities in life that He gives us to love for Him.

Lord Jesus, help me to realize that there is so much work to do for You in and through my life. Amen.

Andrew Simcak Jr.

Matthew 17:1–9

Money Is Power

Command those who are rich …. to do good. … In this way they will lay up treasure for themselves as a firm foundation for the coming age. *1 Timothy 6:17–19*

It is not the amount of our assets that determines whether we shall be faithful or unfaithful in our stewardship. Only love and faith do that. To be faithful in our stewardship over one dollar is just as important as being faithful over thousands of dollars. "He who is faithful in a very little is faithful also in much" (Luke 16:10 RSV).

We do money an injustice when we say it is evil. It is evil only if it is under evil orders. Money has a tremendous power for good. It comes with the power of healing and mercy when it builds hospitals and nursing homes. When invested in seminaries to train pastors and teachers, in churches, and in schools, it has tremendous power to tell of God's love. Money given to produce Christian literature and radio and television programming spreads the Word around the world.

There is something wonderful about setting aside a good proportion of the Lord's gifts to support His good work. This method supplies a steady inflow of gifts to uphold the many good causes that every vitally alive Christian group chooses to support.

Dear Father, We give You but Your own. In any gifts we bring;
All that we have is Yours alone, a trust from You our King.
Amen.

Carl W. Berner

1 Corinthians 11:23–29

Spiritual Fuel

I worked … yet not I, but the grace of God that was with me. *1 Corinthians 15:10.*

Our cars need fuel to run. Our bodies need nutrients to function. Our spirits need power and nutrition to operate, the food only Jesus can provide.

Our Lord has furnished us with what we need to bring peace to the soul and vitality to our spirits. In the remarkable economy of His creativeness, that strength comes to us by the same avenue that gives us the certainty of our forgiveness. And more, it is the same means by which we are fortified for the hazards of day-to-day existence. Our lives are filled with troubles. We can be beaten down and depressed by our frailties and anxieties. But through Word and Sacrament we receive God's grace, the spiritual nourishment that comforts our troubled souls, strengthens our Christian walk, and first and foremost, forgives us all of our sins.

We need to avail ourselves of Jesus' spiritual food often and regularly so we can continue on life's journey. Cars do not run forever without regular refueling stops. Our bodies cannot go without daily, even three times daily, refreshment. And our spirits, too, need to be refueled, refreshed, and resupplied by regular and frequent stops for the Word and the Sacrament of Holy Communion. Then we can go on and on in peace and serve the Lord.

Lord Jesus, give me strength for the journey. Amen.

Henry E. Fuelberg

Psalm 5

Morning by Morning

He wakens me morning by morning, wakens my ear to listen like one being taught. *Isaiah 50:4*

Morning by morning the loving couple awakes. They greet the day together, watch the news, and have their breakfast. Morning by morning it's the same familiar routine. Lasting relationships are like that. They're built on routine. There are some exciting and sparkling moments maybe, but there is also lots of daily repetition.

Our relationship with God is daily, marked too by routine. Here and there, now and again, come high and holy moments. Maybe in some unique worship with thousands gathered to rally around the cross, sometimes in deeply moving moments of quiet, alone with our prayers in the middle of the night, we sense that we are in the presence of our God. But mostly our dealings with God are routine, built on repetition, the familiar, and even the droll.

The depth of a relationship is determined more often than not by what happens "morning by morning." That's true in our relationship with God. Waking with Him, facing the same old routine with Him, plodding step-by-step with Him over the long and sometimes tedious haul is how our relationship with our Lord is forged and deepened and strengthened. And over the long haul, step-by-step with Him, is how we come to the gates that usher us into eternal life.

Lord, with You I begin and with You I will end the day; in Jesus' name. Amen.

Barry J. Keurulainen

Matthew 6:2–25

No Time for Life

When you pray, say: "... Give us each day our daily bread."
Luke 11:2–3

The material gifts of God are the means by which we live and love. They are useful and desirable; we cannot live without them. Yet these things are only the provisions for living, not life itself. They are only the means, not the end. They are necessary tools for a job, not the job itself.

Life consists not in an abundance of things, but in an abundance of relationships. We are our brother's keeper. God gives us things to support us in our service to one another. Our primary goal in life is to love people, not gather things.

How easy it is to confuse the means of living with the meaning of life! We can become so busy storing up things for tomorrows that may never come that we have no time today for the needs of people. We can be too busy to listen to our children, too busy to see the needs of our family and friends, and too busy to serve our neighbors. We can be so busy collecting the provisions for living that we have little time left for the main business of life.

So Jesus wisely prompts us to narrow our concern over provisions to the needs of this day and to pray, "Give us today our daily bread" (Matthew 6:11). Keep the emphasis where it belongs. "Seek first His kingdom and His righteousness." Trust that "all these things will be given to you as well" (Matthew 6:33).

Good Lord, keep us from mistaking the provisions of life for life itself; for Jesus' sake. Amen.

Jack H. Ruff

Luke 9:46–50

God's Standard of Greatness

An argument started among the disciples as to which of them would be greatest. *Luke 9:46*

The desire to be somebody and to amount to something in life lurks in many human hearts. All of us desire, at least in some measure, to stand well with our fellow humans beings and to have them say a good word about us.

This desire is, in some respects, a good thing. It stimulates us to do our best in our activities. It prompts us to strive for excellence in all our efforts.

There is such a thing, however, as excessive ambition, false pride, and love of praise for its own sake. Even the disciples of Christ were at times filled with this false pride. In the gospels we read about the disciples debating among themselves who was the greatest. At such times Jesus took occasion to tell them what true greatness consists of in the sight of God and what it demands of a person.

God's standard of greatness is different from that of the world. The world lusts for power, wealth, knowledge, status, and extraordinary performances. However, in God's sight a person who has a trusting faith in Jesus, who obeys God's laws, and who humbly serves in the Lord's kingdom is truly great.

By our faith in the Savior, our obedience to the will of God, and our service to the Lord we can demonstrate that greatness that is the joy of God.

Lord, teach us to find delight in You and in Your Son. Amen.

Curtis C. Stephan

1 John 4:9–11

Real Love

This is love: not that we loved God, but that He loved us and sent His Son as an atoning sacrifice for our sins. *1 John 4:10*

If you look over the magazine displays, you will see that many of the magazines' feature articles are about love and people who are supposed to be in love or out of love. Love is a very popular subject in our American periodicals.

Love is also one of the foremost themes in the Christian religion, but Christian love is quite different from the love written about in many magazines. This is usually the emotional love between those of the opposite sex. We call it physical, or romantic, love.

The love of God and the love that Christians show to one another is something different. It is a sacrificial and unselfish love; a love that understands, that sympathizes, that plans, that works, that gives the very best for others. It is this kind of love that prompted God to send His own Son to suffer and die for people who did not deserve it.

Dear Lord, help us to show Your kind of love to all those around us; for Jesus' sake. Amen.

Howard W. Kramer

Luke 24:13–35

Long and Short Memories

We remember that while He was still alive that deceiver said, "After three days I will rise again." *Matthew 27:63*

Remember how He told you, while He was still with you in Galilee: "The Son of Man must ... be raised again." Then they remembered His words. *Luke 24:6–8*

When our Savior was crucified and rose again from the dead, His enemies seemed to have longer memories than did His followers. His enemies requested that His tomb be guarded because they were aware of a resurrection promise. His followers not only were surprised that the tomb was empty but had to be reminded that this was supposed to happen!

The enemies of Christianity to this day remember the promises of Jesus Christ concerning His church, the way its members are to live, and the power for good they are to be. From time to time they remind those in the body of Christ of their calling. "You are Christians," they will say. "Why don't you respond to this or that need? Aren't you supposed to love others?" We should not resent this but thank God that even through Satan's messengers we are reminded of God's promises and directives.

If God's enemies remember His promises, how much more should we, His children, trust in them and use them for our comfort and encouragement! Remember how He spoke to us while He walked this earth. If we live close to Him and His Word, we will never forget.

Lord, make our memories long for every good and perfect truth; for Jesus' sake. Amen.

Edward C. May

Psalm 1

Heroes of Faith

A student is not above his teacher, nor a servant above his master. *Matthew 10:24*

We dread few things more than standing alone. It requires a truly rare courage. We have in us an instinct that almost overwhelms us with the desire for companionship. To conform with groups of fellow humans beings, many renounce their beliefs and principles. They know that, unless they do so, the group will probably turn on them.

Part of the wonder of the growth of the early church is that it grew despite the certain knowledge that persecution would follow the adoption of Christianity. The rise of the church is plainly the triumph of God's power given to weak mortals.

Christians still pay a price for refusal to conform to the ways of the world. Because they conduct themselves as children of God, the world hates them. Non-Christians often talk a great deal about tolerance, but they do not always practice it. Long ago Christ warned of this hypocrisy.

The wonder is still that human beings will consent to pay the price. But Christians through the ages have shown this courage. Faith still makes heroes of frail men and women. We salute these unsung heroes.

Lord, when I shrink from paying the price of loyalty to You, let Your power triumph in me too; for Jesus' sake. Amen.

R. A. Jesse

Mark 6:30–44

New Strength from Silence

Be still, and know that I am God. *Psalm 46:10*

There is overwhelming noise created by modern technology. The deafening roar of jet airplanes, traffic, music systems, commerce, and even routine urban noises all merge together to assault our ears daily with increasing intensity. Even the Lord's Day is no longer totally exempt from this monstrous cacophony of sound.

But Sunday can still be used profitably to restore a measure of serenity and peace for our jangled nervous system. Quiet, prayerful visits to church, relaxed meals, and reflective walks in nature contribute wondrously to our inner well-being, giving new strength and incentives to us for beginning another busy week.

Jesus Himself valued solitude and often retreated to quiet places to escape the noises of His day. He refreshed Himself with prayer and meditation, speaking with His heavenly Father and receiving reassurances in return.

We need to learn from the example of Jesus. We must be quiet occasionally so God can speak with us and renew us. His message of love and forgiveness is sorely needed. He brings peace, confidence, and strength through His Word and sacraments. This message of renewal is available if we will listen in silence and receive it.

O Lord, communicate with us during moments of silence so our faith may be strengthened; for Jesus' sake. Amen.

Herbert G. Walther

Hebrews 12:1–4

Throw off What Entangles You

Let us throw off everything that hinders and the sin that so easily entangles, and let us run with perseverance the race marked out for us. *Hebrews 12:1*

Runners do not go to the starting line with their feet shackled or their coats on. To race well, runners must be prepared, and that means stripping off everything that might slow them, trip them up, or divert their attention from the finish line.

But how easy it is for believers to fool themselves into thinking that they can carry along some sin that turns their attention to themselves rather than to Christ and the goal that He has set for them! It is easy to forget the care of others, love for the loveless, and self-sacrificing for the suffering. We foolishly think that we can run the race with the shackles of greed, lust, or envy still binding us.

Jesus has come to be the coach and the trainer who will encourage us and stand by us as we run life's race. He empowers us to shift our gaze from ourselves to the goal, to take off the overcoat of sinful defensiveness and lay it on Him. He unshackles us from the insecurity that drives us into greed, lust, and envy. The forgiveness He gained for us and His presence enable us to run, alive and invigorated by faith in His promised victory.

Free us from our sin and all the evils that entangle us, Lord Jesus, and help us run life's race and reach You, our goal. Amen.

Robert A. Kolb

Luke 12:13–21

Fancy Cars

Do not store up for yourselves treasures on earth, where moth and rust destroy .... But lay up for yourselves treasures in heaven. *Matthew 6:19–20*

Nothing is more important on the journey of life than to define and understand its purpose. Many people believe that material possessions will provide happiness. They think that the "good life" can be achieved by owning fancy cars or a beautiful home.

Jesus encourages us to take a long-term perspective. He points out that possessions are temporary; they can rust away or be stolen. We can be rich today and poor tomorrow. Furthermore, the apostle Paul states that "the love of money is a root of all kinds of evil" (1 Timothy 6:10). It is easy to become so preoccupied with acquiring things that we resort to sinful means to get them. Have we profited if we gain the world but lose our soul (Matthew 16:26)?

We must be vigilant to maintain the right priorities in our lives. Loving God and others should rank far above acquiring material possessions. When we seek the kingdom of God first and His righteousness, everything else we need will be supplied (Matthew 6:33). The Christian life will provide an inner happiness that is unmatched by anything we can get through what we purchase. Our journey through life with Jesus at our side will lead to our eternal happiness.

Jesus, You are my priceless treasure, my source of purest pleasure. Amen.

Henry E. Fuelberg

Matthew 9:1–8

He Knows What Is Best

"But so that you may know that the Son of Man has authority on earth to forgive sins. ..." Then He said to the paralytic, "Get up, take your mat and go home." *Matthew 9:6*

The teachers of the Law constantly questioned Jesus' methods. They found fault with Him because He didn't do things in ways they found acceptable. But the miracle in our text proved to the crowd that Jesus did have the authority to forgive sins and to do things His way. It was the teachers who were wrong, not Jesus.

Someone becomes ill. We know instinctively what God should do, but He doesn't do it. Problems arise, and Jesus fails to remove them. We expect Jesus to do things according to our scheme and schedule. But Jesus is above our plans, and in His wisdom He does things in ways that we cannot begin to comprehend. Those ways are wiser; those ways are better; those ways are far superior to anything we might devise. Christ's plan is such an improvement over ours that we cannot comprehend the mind of Christ. His ways are beyond our finding out.

Jesus is Lord, and He knows what He is doing. We have neither the right nor the wisdom to second-guess His plan for us. Ours is not to question but to trust His Word. Ours is to place ourselves into His everlasting arms and depend on Him to carry us all the way to our eternal home.

Lord, teach me to trust Your guidance for my life; in Jesus' name. Amen.

Mark R. Etter

Romans 15:1–7

The Benefit of the Doubt

A man's wisdom gives him patience; it is to his glory to overlook an offense. *Proverbs 19:11*

There are two words we use interchangeably that Scripture uses in specific ways. The first is perseverance: the ability God gives to deal with difficult circumstances or situations. The second word is patience: the ability God gives to deal with difficult people. If you are in a difficult situation, pray for perseverance. When faced with a difficult person, pray for patience.

It is the wise person who can patiently overlook an offense. We call this "giving others the benefit of the doubt." Instead of assuming every offense is a deliberate act meant to cause harm, be patient. Instead of trying to judge her actions, give your neighbor time to demonstrate her good intentions.

Parents would do well to take this proverb to heart. So often our children do foolish things. In those moments we are tempted to rush in to discipline only to realize later the offense was not that serious. Children deserve patience as much as anyone. Remember God is long-suffering with us, His children. He chose to overlook our sin until the day it was placed on the shoulders of our Lord, Jesus Christ. God's discipline is always carefully and thoughtfully applied. He is patient with us and treats us with forgiving love.

Father, teach us to be patient with each other; for Jesus' sake. Amen.

Ronald C. Moritz

Proverbs 12:9–28

The Value of Work

Make it your aim to … earn your own living, just as we told you before. *1 Thessalonians 4:11 TEV*

Christians in Thessalonica and in our world today need to understand the value of work. Our Lord holds us accountable to support ourselves and our families, to earn our own living. Paul isn't telling us that we ought to be driven by our work. In fact he's not really making a statement at all about work attitudes beyond simply telling us that God created us to take responsibility for our own welfare in this world—to earn our own way.

Some big questions remain: In modern society, do we make it possible for everyone to earn his or her own way in life? How do we best provide every human being the dignity of a job? What are we prepared to do to provide for those who can't work or can't find work?

Paul worked in Thessalonica, probably making tents, to earn his own way. Jesus learned the carpenter's trade, and then He left that work to carry another piece of wood—the cross—to Calvary for us. He dignified our lives by granting us forgiveness and eternal life. He asks us to dignify everyone's life by providing the opportunity for all to work.

Lord Jesus, thanks for Your work that gave us our salvation. Bless us in our daily work. Use us to provide the dignity of work for everyone. Amen.

Unknown

Matthew 5:43–48

The Offering of Prayer

I urge, then, first of all, that requests, prayers, intercession and thanksgiving be made for everyone. *1 Timothy 2:1*

Prayer can be an offering to God on behalf of others. It is so easy to forget this in our concern for our work, our family, and our health. It is reassuring to know that we can bring such personal needs to God in prayer. "We can cast all [our] anxiety on Him because He cares for [us]" (1 Peter 5:7).

But let us not, lost in self-concern, fail to follow the instruction to offer prayers "for everyone." Remember that we are part of the church universal, united in Christ with believers the world over, many of whom are facing keen hostility toward the faith and even harsh persecution. Let us pray for them and for the work of pastors, teachers, missionaries, and Christian congregations around the globe.

Let us also remember our leaders in government. Daily they wrestle with problems of staggering dimension. Their decisions will affect the future of the world and its people.

We are likewise to remember our enemies. Christ tells us to pray for them. They do not need our revenge, our hatred; they need our prayers.

Christ died for our sins. By faith in Him we have access to God. Let us use this open door to offer prayers for the suffering and needy world around us.

Father in heaven, use us to relieve the world's needs; through Christ, our Lord. Amen.

Robert Howard Clausen

Psalm 122

I Was Glad

Remember the Sabbath day by keeping it holy. *Exodus 20:8*

I heard someone say, "I was bored in the house of the Lord." Another said, "I was insulted in the house of the Lord." But a great many people say with all sincerity, "I rejoiced with those who said to me, 'Let us go to the house of the LORD' " (Psalm 122:1).

I am glad to go to the house of the Lord because there God speaks to me. It is not merely the pastor's voice I hear, or the voices of the choir, or my neighbor's voice singing in my ear. But it is the voice of God Himself, speaking to me through His Word. And without His Word about Christ, my living Savior, I cannot live in the grace of His forgiving love.

I am glad to go to the house of the Lord because there I worship in fellowship with other Christians. In God's house I remember that we are brothers and sisters in Christ, children of the heavenly Father, temples of the Holy Spirit—all of us needing and receiving His grace and forgiveness through His Word and the sacraments of Baptism and Communion as we worship Him in spirit and in truth.

I am truly glad as I look forward to going to the house of the Lord!

My Lord, grant that I may always worship You in spirit and in truth; in the name of Jesus. Amen.

David A. Preisinger

John 15:4–10

His Presence

Surely I am with you always, to the very end of the age.
Matthew 28:20

Is it really possible to live and walk with Jesus in this day and age? Can we walk with Him in the shop, in the office, in the household, in the street? When trouble comes and work wears on us and our best-laid plans fall to pieces, can we then walk with God?

The answer is a confident yes. It is not necessary to flee behind stained-glass windows or into a quiet corner to have Jesus' continuing presence. He who knew the streets and shops of Nazareth and carried the cross of our salvation up a street in Jerusalem knows the streets of our cities and towns as well as we do. He knows the temptations they offer. He hears their noise and confusion. He sees the problems they bring. Our faith brings Him near through His Word and Sacraments.

Our faith is not everything it should be if it fails us in the everyday experiences and troubles in life. For great trials and sorrows our Lord gives great strength. But He also gives the steady power to bear the little problems of life, the daily annoyances, and the small difficulties in office, shop, or household. He is always present, a powerful Savior, a warmhearted friend, a loving companion in business and at home.

Lord Jesus, we thank You that You are always near and ready to help in every need. Help us to realize Your continual presence so that by Your gracious power we may always walk with You. Amen.

O. P. Kretzmann

1 Corinthians 16:1–2

It Is Rather Stupid!

Do not store up for yourselves treasures on earth. *Matthew 6:19*

"Riches have wings" is a saying understood in every age. People in their search for security find that nothing is forever. Money spent for pleasure or for daily needs is soon gone. Men put their money into sound investments, such as stocks, bonds, banks, or real estate, or they fill their safety-deposit boxes with jewelry or cash. However, no investment, no safety-deposit place on earth is safe. The stock market goes down and business firms fail. Obligations of corporations and of governments are annulled by inflation and refinancing. Banks close their doors, and fire and flood wipe away the value of land and buildings.

One man, afraid of a clothing shortage, bought several expensive suits. He placed them in mothproof vaults. Six months later he found that he had gained so much weight he could not wear even one of them! We may lock our investments in banks and make them burglarproof, but time and death—the cleverest thief of all—take away the owners. We end our days as we began them—with nothing!

How much wiser is the Christian who, through the love of Christ, is generous toward the Lord and invests time, talents, and treasures in that which will bring eternal dividends!

Lord Jesus, help us to see that our investments for eternity are the only investments we shall keep. Amen.

Elmer C. Kieninger

2 Corinthians 9:6–15

God Is Able

God is able to give you more than you need, so that you will always have all you need for yourselves and more than enough for every good cause. *2 Corinthians 9:8 TEV*

Words that aptly describe our entries in life's daily diary read something like this: "Project unfulfilled," "Objective not achieved," "We were unable to reach our goal." Even when the day began in high hope, it usually ends with these footnotes. Each person has limitations. No one is able to do all he or she would like to, and so we tend to scale down our ambitions to fit our abilities.

In contrast to human shortcomings, God is able to state His purposes confidently. What He promises, He also does. He does not have to first prove His capacity. Most people concede that God is able.

How does that help us? God has found a way to bridge the gap between His ability and our inability, and that is the way of grace. In grace He understands our incapacity, and by grace He takes measures to help. In love He did what were unable to do. He sent His Son to redeem us.

Because God loves us, He makes His ability available to us in life's many situations. In Paul's words, "God is able to give you more than you need." The same God who was able to do this in Paul's day is still able to multiply His grace to and through us.

Inspire us, dear Lord, to seek the good and great things You are able to accomplish through us; for Jesus' sake. Amen.

Arnold A. Wessler

Ephesians 4:29–32

Every Christian a Caring Person

Carry each other's burdens, and in this way you will fulfill the law of Christ. *Galatians 6:2*

"Mind your own business" is not a biblical maxim. "Carry each other's burdens" is.

The apostle Peter advises, "Cast all your anxiety on Him because He cares for you" (1 Peter 5:7). We have a caring God. He cared enough to send His Son for our redemption. His Spirit moves us to express His care. If we want to be like Him, it is essential that we care for one another.

God has put us into the church—a community of faith—so we may help each other stay on the path to heaven. The principle given the ancient church applies to us today as well: "Brothers, if someone is caught in a sin, you who are spiritual should restore him gently" (Galatians 6:1).

"It's none of my business" is almost never true. What others do affects us, and what we do affects others. We have the responsibility to speak and act on behalf of Jesus Christ for the benefit of others. God has made it our business to do that.

We need the care of other loving Christians, and they need our care. God directs, "Above all, love each other deeply, because love covers over a multitude of sins" (1 Peter 4:8).

Dear Lord, heavenly Father, let every contact with every human being be an opportunity for me to communicate the love of Christ. Amen.

Carl W. Berner Sr.

John 15:1–8

The Godly Man Is Creative

He is like a tree … which yields its fruit in season. *Psalm 1:3*

A man, to be a man, must also "yield fruit." Created in God's image, he was meant to "subdue" the earth, to "rule over" things: to ferret out the secrets of nature and harness them to his life under God (Genesis 1:28).

Because he is "planted by streams of water," he has life in abundance and so can yield "fruit in season." In all realms of human endeavor—science, economics, politics, education, social betterment—he is on the side of God, creative, concerned, dedicated to serving rather than exploiting human need. As a man of God he is working with God the provider: providing, not exploiting; he is on the side of God the preserver: preserving, not destroying.

But beyond all this he is on the side of God the Redeemer. With all his gifts and talents, his energies and his resources, he is busy about God's purpose of saving the world. By his life he shows the glory of God. With his tongue he proclaims the Good News of God's redemption in Jesus Christ, who on Calvary's cross gave His life that all people might live forever. Such a man is blessed, not only because he has life in abundance but also because through him this life flows abundantly to others.

Heavenly Father, grant me grace and strength in every area of life to confess Christ and show Your glory. Amen.

Henry C. Duwe

Matthew 10:17–20

The Spirit Bestows Endurance

Whenever you are arrested and brought to trial, do not worry beforehand about what to say. Just say whatever is given you at the time, for it is not you speaking, but the Holy Spirit. *Mark 13:11*

Writing this piece in the comfort of my study, I feel that if I were threatened with persecution at this moment I would cave in. I do not feel bold enough to confess the faith to the point of death. But as certain as I am that I do not have courage such as Jesus describes here, so certain am I that when the persecution comes, the Holy Spirit will enable me—and you—to confess and endure.

Endurance in Christ's name is a gift. The Holy Spirit, who began His work of richly giving me all that I need for life on my baptismal day, will freely bestow the gift of endurance when kings and governors want to talk to us about denying our Lord. Jesus is indeed the Lord, the one who conquered death itself. He will banish fear of death when that becomes necessary so we can freely confess His name. That confession is His instrument to bring life to His children and to strengthen His people in the faith that frees them from fear of the hatred of kings and governors. The life that He gives endures, and by His grace, our confession of His name shall endure with it to the end.

Lord Jesus, comfort us with the assurance that You provide us with courage and strength through Your Holy Spirit. Amen.

Robert A. Kolb

2 Corinthians 8:1–9

Giving Is Worshiping

Ascribe to the LORD the glory due His name; bring an offering and come into His courts. *Psalm 96:8*

Today is another special Lord's day. Again we have an opportunity to gather with our fellow believers in God's house to receive a blessing and to offer Him our worship and praise.

Part of our worship is the bringing of our regular offerings to the Lord. For God's people this is a privilege and a joy. Christian giving is not simply a duty that we perform in connection with the worship service. It's a very important act of worship. We bring our tithes and offerings, not just because funds are needed to keep the church going, but as a joyful response to the grace of God in our lives. It's part of our stewardship—the way we use the gifts of God for His glory.

The Macedonian Christians give us the key to worshipful Christian giving. They knew the grace of our Lord Jesus Christ, and so they "gave themselves first to the Lord." As we come into His courts with our offerings, let us also do it joyfully, willingly, and as God has prospered us. Paul refers to our willing giving as a gracious gift of God. Having received His love, we too can give to the Lord the glory due His name.

Lord God, help us to bring our offerings as a true act of joyful and thankful worship; in Jesus' name. Amen.

August T. Mennicke

Hebrews 3:12–19

The Most Important Day

This is the day the LORD has made; let us rejoice and be glad in it. … Give thanks to the LORD, for He is good; His love endures forever. *Psalm 118:24, 29*

Which is the most important day of my life? The day I was born? The last day of my school years? The day I got my first job?

This is the day says the psalmist. My red-letter day is today. Because of what I do and say today, the world and I will not be quite the same as yesterday.

This is the day the Lord has made. To me it may be a miserable day, yet all is happening according to His divine plan. The day may seem full of confusion, yet God is fulfilling promises each hour of this day. Everything may appear to be going wrong, yet "in all things God works for the good of those who love Him" (Romans 8:28).

Therefore I can rejoice today and be glad. This day is a day of hope. God promises His presence in the midst of discouragement. This day is a day of peace. Jesus is still the Savior. His forgiveness and mercy are mine. This is a day of prayer. God is not "out." He is on call day and night.

This day, then, is the most important because it is now that I live, work, serve, and speak of God's wondrous love through Christ who saved me.

Lord, enrich each hour with opportunities to make this day worthwhile and well remembered. Then Yours shall be the praise and the honor from this time on; in Jesus' name. Amen.

Alfred Doerffler

Luke 12:13–21

No Fooling!

God said to him, "You fool!" … This is how it will be with anyone who stores up things for himself but is not rich toward God. *Luke 12:20–21*

The pitiable character of the parable is a rich man. He could be anyone. In the story that Jesus told, the rich man was a farmer. Life was going so well that he planned to build more and better barns to hold his burgeoning crops. But these could have been other things. Instead of barns, he might have gathered cars or boats or real estate. It really doesn't matter.

Jesus was warning us that what we can see and collect seems to be the real world. We like to gather and accumulate what we can see and count and touch. We begin focusing on the gifts and forget all about the giver.

Jesus wants us to think about the giver and have a right relationship with Him. The great thing about God the giver is that His giving went right to the heart of the matter. His greatest gift came as His Son, the Savior. God not only requires a right relationship with Himself but also makes it possible in Jesus Christ.

Jesus calls us to Himself and in Him we find the true treasures of life: grace, peace, and eternal life. Through faith in the Gospel we are spiritually enriched and are sustained in fellowship with God.

God, giver of all good things, give us above all a believing mind and a thankful heart; for Jesus' sake. Amen.

Richard T. Hinz

Ephesians 3:8–21

Above All That We Ask or Think

"Now to him who is able to do immeasurable more than all we ask or imagine … be glory." *Ephesians 3:20–21*

There is little danger that we are expecting too much of our Christian faith and hope and love. The real danger lies in expecting too little or the wrong things. The Scripture passage for today declares that our prayers and our thoughts are always far below that which our God is able to do. Because we are human, our thinking about God and our speaking to Him are human and, therefore, limited. Our minds simply cannot grasp the vastness of divine power or the infinite capacity of God to do His gracious will in our life, in His kingdom, and in the world. We ask too little of God because we cannot even imagine what is within His power and within the capacity of His love. The well-known missionary William Carey stressed this truth when he said: "Expect great things from God."

Perhaps our relationship to God in Christ often means comparatively little to us because we do not expect enough from it. It may be that we are not looking for great manifestations of His glory. Our worship in church and at home may not have the value for us which it could have, and our prayers may be asking far too little because we have forgotten that our God "is able to do immeasurably more than all we ask or imagine."

God, however, knows our limitations and has promised us His Holy Spirit given to us in God's Word and sacraments both when we pray and when we think of Him.

Eternal Lord, fill us with the wisdom that comes from You; in Jesus' name we pray. Amen.

Otto H. Theiss

James 3:1–12

Watch Your Words!

Likewise the tongue is a small part of the body, but it makes great boasts. *James 3:5*

Someone has estimated that the average individual has as many as 700 occasions to speak during a busy day. In the course of these conversations a talkative person might speak as many as 100,000 words, using 12,000 sentences!

What destruction can be wrought in a single day by just one person with that many words! But also what blessing! It all depends on how words are used. Although damaging consequences can result from the tongue's misuse, much good can be accomplished if it is used properly.

How will your tongue be used today? To speak words that bless the Lord, encourage others, and witness for Christ? Or will it be involved in gossiping, judging, and criticizing? If during a 24-hour period everything said were recorded and then played back to us, would we be shocked?

So watch what you say! Whether you are a talkative person using 100,000 words or the silent type using less than 10,000, make them count for good! Penitently seek divine pardon for past misuses of the tongue, through the merits of the Savior, then let Him control your speech and conversation.

Lord, let the words of my mouth be acceptable in Your sight, for You are my strength and my Redeemer; in Jesus' name. Amen.

Dennis A. Kastens

Acts 27:22–31

God's Limits

On the seventh day God rested from all His work. *Hebrews 4:4*

God does not want our days to be filled with restless endeavor. He urges us to put down our work and find rest in Him. He has put the laws of the universe beyond our reach, but He assures proper momentum, equilibrium, and harmony. That is God's pattern of creation.

Likewise He has set a definite pattern for our lives, limiting our capacities. Man's life is not to be constant striving. It is to be an interchange of labor and rest, using the day for labor and the night for rest. When our Lord came as the Son of Man, His work had its limits. As the time for His arrest and crucifixion drew near, Jesus prayed to His Father, "I have brought You glory on earth by completing the work You gave Me to do" (John 17:4). Jesus knew what His life purpose was and when it was near completion. Likewise, all that is required of us is the work which He gives us to do. We must learn to pray, "Teach me Your will," knowing that in the discovery of God's will we will find rest.

The closing day impresses such thoughts upon us. So much remains to be done. We may be inclined to reproach ourselves because we have accomplished so little. But is there not as much sinning on one side as on the other? Some have been lazy, but others have burned themselves out, neglecting time for rest and Sabbaths ordained for man's blessing.

Dear Jesus, we are often weary and burdened. Draw us back to You, for in You alone do we find rest for our souls. Amen.

Bernard H. Hemmeter

Colossians 4:5–6

Windows of Opportunity

Be wise in the way you act toward outsiders; make the most of every opportunity. *Colossians 4:5*

It happened at the Sea of Galilee just a few years ago. I was up early to photograph the sunrise over Galilee. It was magnificent. I snapped pictures, one after another. Soon I ran out of film.

Just then, coming into view on the lake was a fishing boat with a fisherman, casting his nets out just the way people did in New Testament times. I frantically looked for more film. The sunrise had been beautiful, but I had missed the richer moment because I wasn't ready for it.

In our role as witnesses of Jesus Christ, we are blessed with such rich moments. The Lord makes it clear that we are to be ready. They come as windows of opportunity, opened to us for just the right word, just the appropriate response. The window opens, then it is shut. We have time to say what's on our heart, give the answer to a question, speak the caring word of witness, and then the time is gone.

We must be ready, equipped with the Word, motivated by the redeeming love of Jesus Christ, full of compassion for the lost, and able to recognize an open window. We thank God for His Spirit, who guides our witness and reminds us of Christ's words.

Lord, train me and keep me ready for the open windows of opportunity for witness; in Jesus' name. Amen.

Dean W. Nadasdy

Titus 3:3–8

One Baptism

Be baptized, every one of you, in the name of Jesus Christ for the forgiveness of your sins. *Acts 2:38*

Martin Luther suggested that a Christian ought to frame his baptismal certificate, hang it on a wall in his bedroom, and so be reminded of his Baptism every morning upon arising.

In Baptism God adopted us as His children. A child in a courtroom does not understand the significance of adoption proceedings. It is the same with an infant in God's house for Baptism. She is oblivious of the goings-on, but that doesn't detract from the importance of the occasion. Baptism is God's way of adopting us as His own. When we are baptized, Christ becomes our Brother. We become members of His family.

Our Baptism says our Father's arms are ever open toward us. This does not mean that salvation is automatic because we can go back on Him. But He'll never go back on us. We can run away from home and disown Him, but He will never run away from us or disown us. As far as He is concerned, His love and forgiveness is always available to us.

Lord, help me to remain in my baptismal grace; for Jesus' sake. Amen.

Bertwin L. Frey

Romans 10:1–17

Moments of Meditation

Faith comes from hearing the message, and the message is heard through the word of Christ. *Romans 10:17*

Amid the stress and strain of daily life—amid the hustle and bustle of this hurried, hectic work-a-day world—we need these quiet moments of meditation. We need these quiet times for communing with Jesus. It is good for us to dwell on God's Word and let the Holy Spirit lead us.

Paul tells us that the Holy Spirit works faith in our heart through the power of the Word. We need power so we can grow in faith and find forgiveness and peace in life.

Are you troubled by pet sins? Too often we hang onto our bad habits, hang-ups, and wounded pride. We struggle with our inclinations to gossip and be greedy. Often our nerves are frayed, and our tempers are short.

Does your conscience haunt you? Are you homesick? Does the tension at work get to you? Do you shudder at the thought of death? Then listen to Jesus and His Word. Jesus, our ever-living, ever-loving Savior, is our refuge and strength. Jesus, speaking to us through the Word, is our guide through life. We trust Him for forgiveness and for our eternal salvation. We hear Him say: "Blessed rather are those who hear the word of God and obey it" (Luke 11:28). Through that Word comes faith.

Our heavenly Father, we thank You for these moments of meditation. We thank You for the good news of Your Gospel. Amen.

Victor F. Halboth Jr.

Ephesians 3:14–21

To Him Be Glory in the Church

We are surrounded by such a great a cloud of witnesses. *Hebrews 12:1*

It would not take long to list all kinds of things to be thankful for: food and clothing, home and country, peace and health.

More important in my thankfulness are the gifts God gives by which I have His life: His Spirit dwelling in me, making life out of my mere existence; His Son, who died and rose again so I might have life instead of death; His Gospel, the message by which He gives me this new life; His church, my fellow Christians, some living on earth, some in heaven, who share this Gospel and this faith with me.

Such a great cloud of witnesses surround us: Christian parents, who started me on this Christian walk; a spouse, who by her example is a living gospel for me; Christian children, who also reflect the love of Christ; Christian friends, who by their Christlike lives are speaking Christ to me; a Christian pastor, who shows me how to speak God's Word with power.

Such a great cloud of witnesses surround us: The glorious company of the apostles, the fellowship of the prophets, the noble army of martyrs, the holy church throughout the world!

> For all the saints who from their labors rest,
> All who by faith before the world confessed,
> Your name, O Jesus, be forever blest. Alleluia!

I thank You, Lord Jesus, that this Christian road I walk is no uncharted path. Amen.

David A. Preisinger

265

1 Kings 3:9–14

Making the Right Decision

Teach me knowledge and good judgment, for I believe in Your command. *Psalm 119:66*

Life would be so much easier if we had perfect judgment. Solomon has a reputation for the wise decisions he made. It is specifically wisdom that he sought when he became king.

The fact is that we too have to make decisions daily, and many times we make choices almost blindly, without any real assurance or even a hint of what the outcome will be.

All of us want to act decisively. No one appreciates a person who can't make up his mind. If the decision is ours to make, we should do so, with concern for the well-being of others as well as ourselves.

Probably the most important virtue in decision making is humility, the humble recognition that we do at times make poor decisions that may be wrong. Human frailty in matters of judgment is universal. No one is exempt, though some may be endowed with a better sense of judgment than others. Above all, we know: If we have erred in our judgments, if we have tried to do what is right and in keeping with God's will, and if we seek forgiveness, we can be sure that for Christ's sake our mistaken judgments are forgiven. That assurance and that acceptance is most important.

O God, Your judgments are perfect. By Your Word and Holy Spirit guide us in all our decisions; in Jesus' name. Amen.

Dorothy Rosin

Deuteronomy 1:26–46

The Problem with Complaining

Do everything without complaining or arguing. *Philippians 2:14*

Complaining! We hear it wherever we go—in our families, among our co-workers, from our friends, and even in our churches. It is one of our most popular pastimes. Yet the apostle Paul admonishes us to do everything without complaining.

God knows that constant complaining is not good for us and usually ends up making us unhappy. When the children of Israel got caught up in constant grumbling, the results were tragic. Only Joshua and Caleb were allowed to enter the Promised Land.

What do we do when something irritates or concerns us? Paul wrote, "Do not let any unwholesome talk come out of your mouths, but only what is helpful for building others up according to their needs, that it may benefit those who listen" (Ephesians 4:29). Instead of grumbling, we are able to go to people and speak to them directly, firmly, and gracefully, trusting that Jesus Christ will help us to bring contentment to others. Through the Spirit's power we can replace the word of complaint with a word of grace. We demonstrate with our lips as well as with our lifestyle that we depend on the power of Jesus Christ, our Savior.

Lord Jesus, replace my words of grumbling with words of grace. Amen.

Luther C. Brunette

Malachi 3:1–6

Me, a Living Sacrifice

Therefore, I urge you, brothers, in view of God's mercy, to offer your bodies as living sacrifices, holy and pleasing to God—this is your spiritual act of worship. *Romans 12:1*

"It's my body. I can do whatever I want with it. I can eat too much, smoke, have an abortion, use drugs, or get drunk!" Have you heard comments like these? They state a popular philosophy.

But God teaches something different. He tells us to present our bodies as a living and holy sacrifice to Him. How can we present our bodies to God? One way is to take care of our bodies and not abuse them. Another way is to serve God and our fellow human beings by using the energy, skill, and special talent He has given us.

With your hands you can prepare and serve meals. With your time you can baby-sit. With your energy you can help those who are in desperate need of help. There is no end of things we can do in service to God and others. Indeed, Christ expects us to serve. He Himself came not to be served but to serve (Matthew 20:28).

Jesus offered His body as a living and holy sacrifice for us. That is the supreme act of service. Our bodies are not ours to do with as we please. Like the body of Christ Himself, our bodies are tools with which to serve.

Jesus, help us use our bodies in service to You and to others; in Your name. Amen.

Kay L. Meyer

Luke 13:18–30

Faith as Small as a Mustard Seed

If you have faith as small as a mustard seed ... nothing will be impossible to you. Matthew 17:20

Jesus calls our attention to a tiny mustard seed. If you were to place a grain of sand and a grain of mustard on the palm of your hand, you would almost need a magnifying glass to tell the difference. God's marvelous wisdom and power are in that small object. The mustard seed has life in it. Put it into the ground, Jesus is telling us, and it will take root and grow into a plant that is the largest of the herbs—a treelike plant with stalk, branches, leaves, and blossoms, a plant large enough for birds to perch in it and to build their nests.

This parable tells us how a small nucleus of believers, such as the group that followed Jesus, will under God's blessing grow into a strong congregation. And it keeps growing because, together with other congregations, it sends out mission workers to add other people to Christ's church. Many thriving church bodies in various parts of the world were begun in this way. The gospel of Jesus Christ, the Savior from sin, is God's power unto salvation to all who believe it. What we need is stronger faith, being fully convinced that for Christ's people nothing is impossible.

Almighty God, heavenly Father, we pray for a faith as small as a mustard seed so we may do Your work. Amen.

Walter H. Ellwanger

Matthew 18:1–10

A Child's Faith

Let the little children come to Me, and do not hinder them, for the kingdom of heaven belongs to such as these. *Matthew 19:14*

Our homes are the best schools of Christian living. What children learn in the home from the example of their parents will be woven into their character and the design of their later years. This places a tremendous responsibility on parents.

From the time Jesus said, "Let the little children come to Me," He destroyed the blindness of the world to the glory and meaning of childhood. Christianity took note of children from the beginning and never deserted them. Jesus never used harsher words than when He warned against the abuse and neglect of children. To offend a child in his or her faith is to tamper with eternity.

There is no better way to serve Christ than to serve Him through service to children. Those who faithfully instruct their children in the home and church are making one of the greatest contributions to the kingdom of God and of man. "And whoever welcomes a little child like this in My name welcomes Me."

Heavenly Father, help me model and speak of Your love to the children around me; for Jesus' sake. Amen.

C. W. Berner

Matthew 4:18–22

A Disciple's Education

Follow my example, as I follow the example of Christ. *1 Corinthians 11:1.*

Disciples of learned men in Jesus' day received intense hands-on education. Studying under great teachers meant that disciples lived with their teacher. Students not only learned the master's philosophies but also observed their master's daily life. Disciples studied to become like their teachers.

Jesus' disciples followed Him everywhere. They heard His words. They went fishing with Him and took walks together. They saw Him heal the sick, restore sight, and feed the hungry. These disciples not only knew Jesus' teachings, they knew Jesus, the teacher. They went beyond just knowing what He knew. They imitated what He did.

Jesus calls us to discipleship. We hear Him loud and clear in the Holy Scriptures and follow where He leads. He sits at our table, if we take the time to visit with Him. He walks with us, if we don't become too busy to sense Him there. He performs miracles all around us, if we stop to recognize Him.

Following Jesus is not just knowing about His teachings. By God's grace, it is knowing the teacher. It is getting to know the one who taught humble servanthood by dying on a cross for the salvation of all sinners. Once we know Him, with His help we strive to become like Him.

Let us ever walk with Jesus; follow His example pure. Amen.

Gloria K. Lessmann

Romans 8:28–39

They Can't Take It Away from You

I am convinced that neither death nor life, neither angels nor demons, neither the present nor the future, nor any powers, neither height nor depth, nor anything else in all creation, will be able to separate us from the love of God that is in Christ Jesus our Lord. *Romans 8:38–39*

Wow! What an assurance. Nothing can take the love of God away from us.

There are many forces around us that try. One is the love we have for ourselves. We may value our life, our body, our job, our rights, or our possessions more than God's love. We may pursue earthly goals rather than heavenly gains.

The world around us is a second force that competes with God's love in Christ. The world tempts us to desire more money, more power, more recognition, and more prestige. And the love of God in Christ doesn't even get a thought in the rat race around us.

My, how the devil loves those Godless forces! He uses every opportunity he can to egg us on to claim our rights and satisfy our needs, to get with it and do as the world does.

But hang in there. God is not only with you in the struggle of life but also fighting for you. His forgiving love will support you through all of life, into eternity. Trust Him and His Word.

Thank You, God. Stay with us always; for Jesus' sake. Amen.

Edgar Walz

Exodus 20:8–11

Using Our Time

Then, because so many people were coming and going that they did not even have a chance to eat, He said to them, "Come with Me by yourselves to a quiet place and get some rest." *Mark 6:31*

A management company in Pittsburgh computes that in a life span of 75 years the average amount of time spent sleeping is 23 years; working, 19 years; in amusement activities, 9 years; traveling, 6 years; eating, 6 years; waiting in line, 5 years; cleaning the house, 4 years; preparing meals, 3 years; returning telephone calls, 2 years; searching for misplaced items, 1 year; opening junk mail, 8 months; sitting at red lights, 6 months; worshiping, 6 months; and praying, 19 days.

Our Lord set a day aside for us to rest and to spend time in His presence, giving Him thanks and praise. Christ took time to separate Himself from the daily routine for rest and prayer. Look again at the list of how we spend a life's worth of time. Prayer comes out at the bottom and Bible study not at all. We don't have time, we complain. We have time, it would seem, for less important activities. And if we followed Christ's example, we would make time by carving out a space for prayer and study and by arranging a significant time to be in the Word.

After all, time spent in prayer and with our Bibles is when we come face-to-face with our Redeemer.

Dear Christ, lead us to spend our time with You. Amen.

Irma S. Pinkerton

Thessalonians 4:1–8

Sex in the Christian Perspective

The man and his wife were both naked, and they felt no shame. Genesis 2:25

These straightforward words from Scripture tell us that God is in favor of sex. He made it. There is nothing inherently dirty or evil about sex. Adam and Eve were naked in each other's presence, and they were not embarrassed. Before there was sin, there was sex. God Himself pronounced it good. Sexual thoughts and drives are therefore not in and of themselves something to be ashamed of.

These words also tell us that God made sex for marriage. "For this reason a man will leave his father and mother and be united to his wife, and they will become one flesh" (Genesis 2:24). To this union the Creator God gives the command and the blessing: "Be fruitful and increase in number; fill the earth and subdue it" (Genesis 1:28).

Through the gift of sex God has provided for the creation of new human life. In His wisdom the Creator has made this necessary part of existence a thing of pleasure and satisfaction within the state of marriage.

To be sure, our sexuality has been affected by the fall into sin. But how comforting it is to know that Jesus died on the cross to atone also for our misuse of His good gift of sex.

Dear Lord, thank You for creating us male and female. Help us to use this precious gift of our sexuality in accordance with Your will; for the sake of Jesus Christ, our Savior. Amen.

Samuel H. Nafzger

Respectful

Submit to one another out of reverence for Christ. *Ephesians 5:21*

A well-known comedian constantly complains that he "gets no respect." Lack of respect for one another is really not a laughing matter. Once again Jesus is our role model. He had great respect for everyone, especially for those whom others failed to respect.

This attitude of Christ, respect for others, Paul expresses in our text as submission to each other. It consists of putting others and their interests before ourselves or our ambitions. There is no place in the Christian's life for "lording it over" someone else.

Jesus gave His life as a ransom for all. That gives everyone priceless worth. This high regard for all people, regardless of their station in life, is what lies behind the establishment of Christian hospitals and agencies that give care to those in need. This respect for others erases the lines of privilege and seeks to abolish inequity, unfairness, and injustice in our dealings with people.

It begins at home. The home is the basic training camp where we pick up our Christian attitudes, not simply by what we are told, but by what we observe. In our homes we learn to forget ourselves and to be alert to the needs and wishes of others.

Lord God, help us to build and bolster one another; for the sake of our Lord and Savior, Jesus. Amen.

Leland Stevens

Luke 5:1–11

Discipleship Test

Simon answered, "Master, we've worked hard all night and haven't caught anything. But because You say so, I will let down the nets." *Luke 5:5*

Simon couldn't believe his ears. Did Jesus really expect him to go out there and start throwing his nets again? Right after he had finished the messy job of cleaning them up? And after a whole night of tough work—all for nothing? We can almost picture Simon's face clouding up for a retort like: "Nothing doing! I'm no fool."

Had he done so, quite likely we never would have heard of fisherman Simon, who became Peter, the heroic disciple. He would have missed the chance of his life. This was a crucial turning point. Jesus was giving a discipleship test. Was Simon's faith up to it? His answer proved it was.

Our Lord still poses such discipleship tests. The tasks He assigns are not always to our liking—to be His witnesses when we fear we'll be rejected, to attend church services instead of sleeping in, to teach a fidgety Sunday school class, to take a big percentage off the top of each paycheck for the Lord's work, and so on. Frankly, we'd rather not.

But not doing so may mean missing the chance of a lifetime. Peter did not lose a thing that day by taking the Lord at His word. Neither shall we.

Give us humble hearts and alert minds, dear Lord, ready for our discipleship tests to act upon Your Word; in Jesus' name. Amen.

Albert W. Galen

Ecclesiastes 3:9–14

Standing in Awe

I know that everything God does will endure forever; nothing can be added to it and nothing taken from it. God does it so that men will revere Him. *Ecclesiastes 3:14*

Be careful! The week can get so full of activities that we fail to take in our wonderful world. All around us are the things God in His good pleasure has given us. We stand in awe of Him and His power, beauty, and wisdom.

Let your mind soar for a moment! At the speed of light (186,273 miles per second), one could travel around the earth seven times in one second, but it would take five and one-half hours to reach Pluto, and 100,000 years to cross the diameter of the Milky Way.

Our God has created a spectacular universe! Why? So that, recognizing Him as creator and provider, we would stand in awe of Him!

But God's greatest act is not found in the stars or in a beautiful sunset, but in the cross of Christ on Calvary, where salvation and eternal life were gained for us sinners. While His universe is awesome, one day it will pass away. But His greatest act, forgiving our sins through the cross and the empty tomb, will endure forever.

In awe and joy we stand before Him in prayer and worship and let Him know how great He is.

Dearest heavenly Father, I stand in awe of Your power and great love. All praise and honor to You alone! Amen.

Barry J. Keurulainen

Matthew 25:31–46

The Church on Monday Morning

Do it all for the glory of God. *1 Corinthians 10:31*

The church that gathers to pray, praise, and give thanks on Sunday should be no different from the church on Monday. The speaking and hearing of the Word of God in church should equip and strengthen us to be the church during the week while we are scattered throughout the community.

What is the church to do? We, the church, are to do all things to the glory of God, even personal things, such as eating and drinking. With the spiritual welfare of others as our aim, we shall avoid giving offense or seeking our own advantage selfishly. We have been called by God's grace as His redeemed children to minister to each other. As Christian citizens we shall be law-abiding and work for the good of the community. As parents we shall bring up our children in the discipline and instruction of the Lord. As children we shall love our parents and not dishonor them by our behavior. As employees we shall do our job honestly and render services to the best of our ability. As employers we shall reward services with fair wages. As members of the Christian church we shall give of our time, money, and abilities to further the church's work and to build up our fellow Christians in the saving faith of Christ. In everything we shall radiate Christian love. Our Sunday religion is for Monday also.

Lord, purify our motives so our daily activities may glorify You, our only Savior. Amen.

Herman A. Etzold

1 Corinthians 6:9–20

My Body

I praise You because I am fearfully and wonderfully made.
Psalm 139:14

I praise God for the gift of my body.

It is not what it might be or ought to be. I have inherited from a long line of ancestors, stretching all the way back to Adam, flaws and weaknesses and susceptibilities that have weakened and maimed it. I have also inherited that fatal sickness of sin that leads to death. Yet it is a wonderful machine I inhabit—this body of mine—while I live.

With no conscious effort on my part, my heart keeps beating, my lungs breathe, my glands secrete, food is digested, and my body is kept in constant repair.

But greatest of all natural gifts is the gift of reason. My body may not have the sight of an eagle, the strength of a horse, or the speed of an antelope, but it has something none of these has—a superior brain. No computer can match it in its ability to learn, remember, reformulate, verbalize, communicate, and create.

To what greater purpose can I put this, my body, than to use it wisely, keep it healthy, increase its strength and ability, and above all give it back to Him to become a dwellingplace, a temple, for His Holy Spirit?

Thank You, heavenly Father, for the wonderful gift of my body. Let me use it to serve You and give You glory; for Jesus' sake. Amen.

Walter E. Kraemer

Romans 8:28–39

It's a Boy! It's a Girl!

"My thoughts are not your thoughts" … declares the LORD.
Isaiah 55:8

It's a boy! It's a girl! Which did we have our heart set on? After the passing of time, we say: "It's a good thing that God decides." We pray—and our prayer is not answered our way. Time passes. Then the day comes when we say: "I'm glad that it wasn't my decision to make!"

In our Christian life there are situations that we cannot explain. Things go contrary to what we want. Seemingly everything goes wrong. Many, as we know, then become bitter and cynical, or they even despair.

We Christians have a different outlook. It is based on God's promises, nothing less. He says that He makes the decisions in our lives, including those major decisions concerning health, economics, success, or loss.

God says that His decisions are often different from ours. However, this need not disturb us, for He turns everything to the good of those who love Him. "My ways are higher than your ways" (Isaiah 55:9).

This all-powerful, all-wise God loves us. He is in control. He promises that in every decision He seeks to benefit us.

Dear Father, You are the potter; we are the clay! Form us into a vessel fit for Your use; for the sake of our Lord Jesus. Amen.

George Beiderwieden Jr.

Matthew 5:38–48

Pray for My Enemies?

But I tell you: Love your enemies and pray for those who persecute you, that you may be sons of your Father in heaven. *Matthew 5:44–45*

Enemy—the very word conjures up feelings of anger and hatred. Surely Christ must be joking. The only prayers we'd want to offer for our enemies have to do with retribution and revenge.

Yet Jesus prayed for His enemies. He laments their rejection of God (Matthew 23:37–39) and forgives them from the cross (Luke 23:34). It would have been easy to bring punishment down on those who failed Him. Yet even Judas is loved and called "friend" at the very moment he would betray Jesus (Matthew 26:50).

What good things would follow were you to pray for your enemies? What if you were to pray that your enemies might know the Lord better and become more loving like Him? What if you asked the Lord to help you understand what your enemies are going through? As you bring them before the Lord in prayer, you might find His power working in your heart, softening your feelings toward them.

Are there people right now whom you would call enemies? Talk about them with the Lord in prayer. Call for the power and forgiveness of the Lord to transform their lives. You might end up with a Christian friend instead of an enemy.

Lord, bless my enemies that they may be Your friends and mine; in Jesus' name I pray. Amen.

Mark R. Etter

1 Peter 3:8–17

Burdens for Blessings

If someone forces you to go one mile, go with him two miles.
Matthew 5:41

Under Roman law a soldier could require you to carry his baggage one mile, but no farther. "To go the extra mile" means to do more than is required.

Jesus encourages us to do much more than the bare minimum. We help others not grudgingly because we have to, but freely and gladly out of love for our Savior.

Jesus did infinitely more for us than we deserved. He obeyed His heavenly Father perfectly to fulfill the Law for us. He willingly accepted the death penalty on the cross for our sins. He went the extra mile for us to provide us with forgiveness and eternal life.

Jesus calls us to respond in faith and love by bearing the burdens of others and going that extra mile. We resist the temptation to take revenge on those who have offended us and, instead, repay evil with good, just as Christ has loved us despite our offenses against God. We assist the undeserving, knowing that we too do not deserve the numerous blessings that are ours through the grace of our Lord Jesus Christ. And instead of bearing grudges, we forgive those who may seem unforgivable because God in Christ has forgiven us all our sins.

Help me, Lord Jesus, to walk the extra mile with others because You have gone the extra mile for my salvation. Amen.

Michael C. Trinklein

Romans 8:28–39

The Uncompromising Lord

To him who overcomes, I will give the right to sit with Me on My throne. *Revelation 3:21*

Many have said that to live in this world a person must give and take, come to terms, split the difference, strike a balance—in other words, compromise. Whether in business, the political arena, or our social life, we seem to be constantly hedging a bet.

The Lord Jesus, on the other hand, calls us to be uncompromising when it comes to our Christianity and the way we live out our faith in our daily encounters with family, friends, business associates, and the strangers we meet on the street. He tells the church of Laodicea that He would prefer for it to be either hot or cold. Then He could at least tell where it stands. Unfortunately, the church was neither hot nor cold; it was luke-warm toward the claims of Christ and His promises to it.

Even so, in His love, the Lord promised to those who repented and were willing to confess Him unashamedly the right to sit on His throne. He makes the same promise to you and to me. He does not want us to compromise His person or His work but rather to give bold witness to the unbounded love He displayed for us on the cross.

Help me, Lord Jesus, to speak clearly at all times and in all places about Your love for me. Amen.

Carlos H. Puig

1 Kings 18:20–39

The One Way to Heaven

Jesus answered, "I am the way and the truth and the life. No one comes to the Father except through Me." *John 14:6*

According to an opinion poll, 65 percent of the people surveyed say that Christians, Jews, Muslims, and Buddhists all pray to the same God, although called by a different name.

The devil has been highly successful in convincing people that it does not really matter what God one believes in. The world thinks the important thing is belief in a higher being. If you believe sincerely, you will be rewarded by your "God."

The Bible clearly teaches that there is only one God, the God revealed in Holy Scripture. In this one God are three distinct persons: God the Father, who created the world; God the Son, who redeemed the world; and God the Holy Spirit, who sanctifies us and keeps us in the true faith. There is no other God and no other Savior than His Son, Jesus. "Salvation is found in no one else, for there is no other name under heaven … by which we must be saved" (Acts 4:12).

Jesus has revealed the true God to us. He has through His death saved us from God's righteous anger because of our sins. He has given us peace, life, and salvation.

Jesus, You are my way, my truth, and my life. Amen.

Andrew Simcak Jr.

Matthew 5:33–37

Out of the Same Mouth

Out of the same mouth come praise and cursing. My brothers, this should not be. *James 3:10*

During the first years of our lives, we do an amazing thing. We learn how to talk.

A child learning to talk is able to make any of the thousands of sounds used by all the languages of the world. But as the child learns the language of his or her people, unused sounds disappear. Few English speakers can copy the sound of a Spanish-speaking person pronouncing a rolling *r.* Had they learned it as children, it would be easy.

How we make sounds, however, is not as important as what we do with the sounds we make. A lifetime spent uttering silly oaths and vile curses, of speaking the name of our God in anger rather than in prayer, builds a pattern. Prayer becomes a foreign language to the tongue trained to curse.

A lifetime spent in praising God with our tongues, however, equips us with a language of worship. Our mouths stutter at anything foul. Unclean words are no longer part of our vocabulary.

To avoid the dilemma described by James in the text, we do well to practice the language of praise. When we do, we find no lack of words to say or hymns to sing in praise of our loving God.

O Lord, open my lips, and my mouth will declare Your praise; in Jesus' name. Amen.

John W. Oberdeck

Matthew 25:14–30

Hidden Talents

To one he gave five talents of money, to another two talents, and to another one talent. *Matthew 25:15*

Many of us try our best to stay mentally and physically fit. Exercise should be regular and within our limits. To keep our minds sharp, we read or solve problems. The subtle message that lies behind our efforts is, "If you don't use it, you lose it."

All of us have received from God various gifts and abilities. Christian artists and musicians produce beauty that we can see and hear. But some talents are hidden. God has given each person some gift that can enhance His kingdom. Romans 12:6–8 lists serving, teaching, encouraging, contributing to the needs of others, leadership, and showing mercy.

Reflect on these gifts. You may discover one or more hidden talents that you can exercise for the benefit of others. In 1 Corinthians 13, Paul describes the greatest gift: love. We Christians received this gift while we were yet sinners, when Christ died for us. Love for others is our response to God's great love for us. With the Spirit's help, all of us can use this gift to enlarge His kingdom. Investing in these talents guarantees the highest dividends for God's kingdom and to His glory.

Forgive us for not using our gifts as we could, Lord. Help us to find ways to show more love; for the sake of our Savior, Jesus. Amen.

Lynn C. Hoy

Matthew 5:1–16

Dare to Be Different

Do not conform any longer to the pattern of this world.
Romans 12:2

A rebellion is in progress today against moral standards that have been handed down to us from previous times and cultures. The tragedy is that the standards to which the nonconformists eventually conform tend to be worse than those against which they rebel. The modern sexual revolution is a case in point.

Christianity also challenges us to be different. It asks us to consider who we are and what God wants us to become. It points to the mercies of God by which He became our Father and we became His children. It asks us to probe the good, acceptable, and perfect will of God as the standard for our morality, actions, and ambitions. It begs us to differ from the standards and principles accepted by Godless society, not to let the world squeeze us into its mold or pattern, but to let God remold our minds from within.

A real change takes place in a person when Jesus is worshiped as Lord and Savior. A silent, steady change takes place in society too when people look to Christ as their life and hope, turn to His character as their pattern, and are inspired with His Spirit as their motivation. In Jesus' name, dare to be different from the world!

Help me to choose, O Lord, not the easy way of self-gratification and conformity to the world, but the way of self-sacrifice and service to You, in Christ Jesus. Amen.

Herman A. Etzold

Mark 10:13–16

Managing Our Children

Let the little children come to Me ... for the kingdom of God belongs to such as these. *Mark 10:14*

One of the greatest responsibilities in any of our lives is the care of the children God gives us. What a special privilege is ours to bring new lives into this world, and what a tremendous responsibility accompanies this blessing!

Never, it would appear, have the challenges to this extremely important responsibility been greater. Families are under siege by a host of contrary forces, threatening to estrange children from parents, endeavoring to pollute their minds and bodies with sinister forces and substances from television tube or street corner. Pressures on marriage and resulting parental separations create havoc and emotional confusion in children's minds.

Our text highlights the greatest need of children, which is also the greatest need of us all: to come to Jesus Christ. In Holy Baptism His love is poured out on us, bringing us to faith and salvation and making us members of His kingdom. And throughout life we grow in faith through His Word, and we experience His love through the care of Christian parents and others—love that is manifest in both words and deeds, love that overflows into prayer.

Help us, O Lord Jesus Christ, to bring others, especially the children, closer to You. Amen.

Raymond L. Hartwig

Luke 22:24–34

We Offer Our Prayers

Simon, Satan has asked to sift you as wheat. But I have prayed for you. *Luke 22:31–32*

In Psalm 50:15 God says, "Call upon Me in the day of trouble; I will deliver You and You will honor Me." Here God tells us to pray. He promises to hear us. And He says plainly that He expects us to acknowledge His help. This we do when we give Him honor and glory.

The "Our Father" of the Lord's prayer is a daily reminder that we are to pray with and for each other. Actually, we are to offer prayers for all people, not only for the good and gentle but also for all who are in need of prayer: the weak and the strong, the oppressor and the oppressed.

In our text we find that Jesus prayed for His disciple Peter, who had a wavering faith. We too should offer our prayers for the weak, whether the weakness is spiritual, mental, moral, physical, or economic. The fervent prayers of one who is right with God by faith in Christ are effective. Christians are people who give. We offer prayers for the criminal and his victims, for the predator and the prey, for those who feel that they are undeservedly the outcasts of the world, for the unemployed and underemployed, for the overemployed and underpaid, and even for those who, because of injustice, are underemployed yet overpaid.

Lord God, forgive our sins and heal the wounds we cause; in Jesus' name. Amen.

Clemonce Sabourin

John 17:18–23

On a Mission

As You sent Me into the world, I have sent them. *John 17:18*

From the Latin word for "send" we derive the word *mission.* Depending on our experience, we may get various pictures in our minds from that word. Some will think of the space shuttle missions. Others will envision a courier bearing secret messages, bombers on a seek-and-destroy mission, or perhaps a physician on a mission of mercy.

In any case, *mission* brings to mind someone going out to do an important task. Jesus was the greatest missionary because He was sent by His Father to redeem the world. He completed His task on Good Friday and announced it by saying, "It is finished."

Jesus honors Christians by sending them to proclaim the benefits of His divine work. We are invited to take part in His great work. Not all can or need go to faraway places. We can have a part in Christ's mission in many ways. With our own talents and means and opportunities, we can respond to Jesus' sending.

Our Lord calls us to Himself that we may believe and be saved. But He does not coddle us forever. He sends us out that others may be saved.

When You send us out, Lord Jesus, grant that we may be willing and eager to carry out Your mission. Amen.

Richard J. Schultz

2 Timothy 3:14–17

Shifting Winds

We will no longer be infants, tossed back and forth by the waves, and blown here and there by every wind of teaching and by ... men in their deceitful scheming. *Ephesians 4:14*

Wind direction and speed are important parts of weather observations. The wind can change abruptly, and some manmade religious doctrines change about as often as the wind. Many churches abandon biblical teachings. We hear about religious cults and novel religions, such as the New Age Movement. Some of these messages are tempting because they are more appealing to our sinful nature than the doctrines found in God's Word.

How can we distinguish the true Christian religion from all the false claims? The answer is to study the Scriptures. The Bible is the Word of God, against which we compare every human teaching. Jesus said, "Search the Scriptures" (John 5:39). Paul told Timothy to learn the Scriptures so he might be "wise for salvation through faith in Christ Jesus" and be "thoroughly equipped for every good work" (2 Timothy 3:15–17).

Our Bibles should not be gathering dust on shelves. They should be well-worn and full of notes and underlining. A thorough knowledge of the Bible will help us withstand all of the shifting winds of life.

O God, Your Word is a lamp to my feet and a light to guide my way. Help me to understand its message better and to apply it in my daily life; in Jesus' name. Amen.

Henry E. Fuelberg

Matthew 6:25–34

This Is My Father's World

Your heavenly Father knows that you need them. *Matthew 6:32*

What a different world this world becomes when we remember that this is our Father's world! No blind force, no blind fate, but our Father's love still guides and shapes the destiny of all His children in things both great and small.

He who guides the flight of the sparrow and traces its final fall has promised to guide us safely through all dangers in life and to bring us safely to heaven.

What a wonderful thought with which to open each new day and with which to go to sleep at night! Through Christ, the God of the trackless universe has become my Father, and the unspeakably marvelous world in which I live, whose air I breathe and whose life I share, is forever bright with promise—His promise!

He has promised to uphold, sustain, and guide not only the celestial spheres of the firmament but also the single sparrow in its solitary flight—and me, His precious child, redeemed by Jesus Christ, His Son. The world in which I shall go to sleep tonight and to which, He wills, I shall awake tomorrow is still my Father's world—His world to govern, guide, and keep for me and for all His trusting children. In Him my faith abides!

Lord, keep me ever mindful: This is my Father's world; in Jesus' name. Amen.

Herman W. Gockel

1 Timothy 6:3–10

Illusiveness of Riches

Cast but a glance at riches, and they are gone, for they will surely sprout wings and fly off to the sky like an eagle. *Proverbs 23:5*

One of the quickest ways to lose money is to get into a "shell game." A shell game has one pea hidden under one of three shells. After they've been shifted around as fast as the hand can move, the contestant must pick the shell that hides the pea. In most cases the contestant loses. The premise is, "The hand is quicker than the eye." The human eye, as complex as it is, can't keep up with hands that are even quicker.

More basic than this principle is one that draws people into shell games in the first place. It's the principle of human greed. Greed is defined as always wanting more. Greed is the underlying compulsion behind every form of gambling, from shell games to casinos. The human heart is not satisfied with the blessings God provides, so we risk what we have in vain attempts to get more. Yet, as Proverbs declares, "Cast but a glance at riches, and they are gone."

The opposite of greed and the endless pursuit of riches is contentment. Paul writes, "Godliness with contentment is great gain" (1 Timothy 6:6). Two words come together: Godliness and contentment. When we are Godly, confessing Jesus as Savior and Lord and trusting Him for the gift of eternal life, we learn how to be content with the worldly blessings God gives.

Father, teach us Godliness with contentment; for Jesus' sake. Amen.

Ronald C. Moritz

Psalm 19:7–14

Listen—then Speak

This, then, is how you should pray … Your will be done on earth as it is in heaven. *Matthew 6:9–10*

True prayer is always a person's answer to God's Word. Prayer is half a conversation—the last half. How important that we see our prayers in this way—as our part in a conversation with God that was begun when God called us through His Word.

A good conversation requires patient listening as well as talking. When one ceases to listen and does all the talking, that person is no longer taking part in a conversation, but is making a speech. If we see our prayers as our part of a conversation initiated by God, we shall understand how important listening is to prayer.

In our life with God we need to alternately talk and listen. Both activities are essential for a healthy relationship with God. To pray and then not meditate on God's Word is to ask a question and then fail to listen for the answer.

We pray, "Your will be done." In answer to this prayer, God will give us the strength to follow His direction. But the knowledge of His will is to be gotten from His Word. He has given us His Word to serve as "a lamp to [our] feet and a light for [our] path" (Psalm 119:105). "Let the Word of Christ dwell in you richly" (Colossians 3:16) and "pray without ceasing" (1 Thessalonians 5:17 KJV). The Christian life is the outcome of this two-way conversation between God and His trusting child.

Good Lord, help us to listen to You as patiently as You listen to us; in Jesus' name. Amen.

Jack H. Ruff

Matthew 19:1–9

Marriage on the Rocks

What God has joined together, let man not separate.
Matthew 19:6

Someone has said that the most popular cocktail today is "marriage on the rocks." How sad, but how true! In our present society, including the church, the Christian marriage vow is being taken less and less seriously.

The clear words of Christ make marriage a lifelong union: No one is to separate the couple that God has joined. The solemn pledge "until death do us part" is watered down by many to mean simply "until our love dies." The tragic result is "marriage on the rocks."

Let us remember that it was God who instituted marriage (Genesis 2:24). It was God who pronounced the married man and woman "one flesh," clearly indicating a lifelong union. And according to Jesus Christ, it is still God who joins a man and woman in marriage today. No one is to break this bond, except for reasons God Himself has given (Matthew 19:9 and 1 Corinthians 7:15).

God grant us grace that we may maintain the sanctity of Christian marriage! With His help, our marriages can reflect the pure, selfless love that Jesus Christ has for His bride, the Christian church.

Lord, preserve the sacredness of the Christian marriage vow and help us all conform to the image of Christ; for Jesus' sake. Amen.

Herman W. Gockel

Hebrews 10:1–18

Today

Each day has enough trouble of its own. *Matthew 6:34*

Someone has said, "Today was tomorrow yesterday." Indeed it was. And it is just as true too that today will be yesterday tomorrow. Yesterday is past; we cannot change that. Tomorrow is not yet here. We cannot yet live in that. Today is all we have as the day to live in.

Many of us are behind in today's tasks because we are catching up with what we should have done yesterday. Some of us are hampered from doing our best today because we are worried about what might happen tomorrow. Others of us are frustrated because we are not meeting the responsibilities that lie before us today. Procrastination is the word for it. Most of us are inclined to do what we like to do and postpone what we don't like. Today can easily slip by without our having brought to it our very best.

It is a part of the Christian life that we do with vigor the task set before us. Paul told the Colossians: "Whatever you do, work at it with all your heart, as working for the Lord, not for men. … It is the Lord Christ you are serving" (Colossians 3:23–24). Serve the Lord heartily, that is, with all your heart—today! It is this moment, this hour that God gave us to serve Him. It is all we have.

Help us to do well the tasks that lie before us today, O Lord. Keep us from worrying about yesterday or tomorrow; we ask this in Jesus' name. Amen.

Wilbert J. Fields

Exodus 18:13–26

You Can't Do it All

Select capable men from all the people—men who fear God … and appoint them as officials. *Exodus 18:21*

Moses had to learn what to do. He had to learn what not to do. It was harder to learn what to have others do. Learning to delegate is a hard lesson. Bookstores are filled with books offering help. A recent fad book portrayed such insights to be learned in one minute.

In one minute you can read Exodus 18:17–23. It is the word of Jethro to his son-in-law, Moses. Jethro outlined the art of delegation. He said that Moses should get others to help so the objectives would be met. When studying administration at the University of Nebraska, I was surprised to see this Bible story in secular textbooks. Dwight L. Moody, an evangelist of a bygone day, said: "It is better to train ten people to work than to do the work of ten people."

Jesus trained the Twelve. He also trained the 70, then 120 more. He knew that He was returning to heaven. Others would carry on the mission of proclaiming salvation. He enlisted and equipped people for ministry, then sent them out. The principle still applies. Jesus still gives pastors, teachers, and other workers "to equip the saints for the work of ministry" (Ephesians 4:12 RSV).

Help us, Lord, to do Your work as best we can and to enlist others to help. Amen.

Marcus T. Zill

Matthew 26:6–13

Why the Waste?

When the disciples saw this, they were indignant. "Why this waste?" they asked. *Matthew 26:8*

It's easy to understand the disciples' reaction. Made aware of the needs of people by their ministry with Christ, they could not understand pouring costly, aromatic ointment on the Savior's head. This woman was wrong. The hungry needed food. The sick needed medicine. That ointment could buy a lot of help for human beings.

Jesus didn't stop the woman. He let her pour the perfume on His head and chided the disciples: "The poor you will always have with you, but you will not always have Me."

Many Christian actions fall under the same judgment as the woman's. "It's a waste," some say. "Who needs bells and steeples? Who needs organs and altars? Who needs youth programs and recreational activity?" Maybe the critics are right, but maybe they are wrong. The way to tell is by checking the reason for any given action or activity. That which is dedicated to God, shows His glory, and reveals His intent for life is not wasted. Only what expresses duty without love, help without concern, art without divine honor is wasted.

Our values are under God's judgment. He sees both action and motive. That which does not respond to His love is waste. Ointment poured in appreciation of Christ's sacrifice is not waste.

O Lord, we worry about what is not wasted and waste much without any worry. Help us see the difference; we pray in Jesus' name. Amen.

Charles S. Mueller

Hebrews 12:1–13

Life's Flat Tires

We also rejoice in our sufferings, because we know that suffering produces perseverance; perseverance, character; and character, hope. *Romans 5:3–4*

Car trouble is a serious matter, especially on a long trip. Whether it is a flat tire, a dead battery, or something more complicated (and more expensive), these unexpected events disrupt our journey. They can alter our plans drastically.

Our lives are filled with "flat tires." We may become seriously ill, lose our job, or have financial problems or marital difficulties. God has not promised us carefree lives. However, He has promised to be with us at all times and to give us strength to handle any situation, no matter how serious or hopeless it might seem.

Tribulations are not pleasant; however, "we know that in all things God works for the good of those who love Him" (Romans 8:28). Our tribulations should strengthen our faith (James 1:2–3). They also can assist us in being better witnesses for Christ. They allow us to speak from personal experience about God's love.

Jesus through His Word and sacraments is the mechanic for all the breakdowns along our journey through life. He can repair all our problems and make us stronger than ever. Most important, His death on the cross has repaired our broken relationship with God. Our bill? Paid in full—we owe nothing.

Holy Spirit, increase my faith as I experience the "flat tires" of life; in Jesus' name. Amen.

Henry E. Fuelberg

Romans 14:1–12

Giving Account

Each of us will give account of himself to God. *Romans 14:12*

All of us, whoever we are and whatever our station in life, will have to give an account of ourselves to God. That means that we will have to answer to God for our conduct as well as the use we have made of the time and the other things that He has given us.

This does not apply only to the rich or those who have received special talents. All of us have some possessions, gifts, and abilities that we can use in the service of God or our fellow human beings. How we do this is of concern to God. He requires us to give an account to Him of how we are using what we have.

Are we using those precious eyes, which He has given us to behold things that are good and beautiful, to read His holy Word? Are we using our ears to listen to Him and to respond to the cries of the needy? Are we using our mouths to witness to Christ, to speak words of kindness, to pray, and to praise? Are we using our hands to help and our feet to rescue the troubled? Are we sharing our blessings with the less fortunate? Are we following God's commandments?

Our loving Father, help us to remember that we must give account to You of how well we have done our duty in serving You. Grant us faithfulness always, using our gifts and talents to Your glory and to the welfare of our fellow human beings; for Jesus' sake. Amen.

William A. Lauterbach

Acts 5:17–32

Your Highest Authority

We must obey God rather than men! *Acts 5:29*

Many people give orders—bosses, parents, and government representatives. God commands us to obey those in authority (Romans 13:1–7).

But Peter and the apostles were in an unusual situation. The authorities commanded them to stop preaching the Good News of Jesus Christ. Peter replied with conviction, "We must obey God rather than men!"

When human authorities contradict the authority of God, we have no choice but to obey God. God is our Creator. His Son is our Redeemer, who willingly suffered and died to take away our sins and rose again as Lord of all. His Spirit moves us to dedicate ourselves wholeheartedly to serving God. The triune God is our highest authority; there is none higher.

When we perceive a conflict between God's will and human commands, we must obey God. But we must be absolutely certain that we are acting according to God's Word. We can delude ourselves into thinking that our own desires are the desires of God. Through prayerful study of Scripture, the Spirit will enable us to know whether we are struggling against unchristian directives, or whether the human authorities are to be obeyed as God's representatives.

When I am in conflict, Lord God, help me discern Your will according to Your Word and act accordingly; for Jesus' sake. Amen.

Michael C. Trinklein

Romans 8:32–39

Speak Up!

Speak up for those who cannot speak for themselves. *Proverbs 31:8*

We're all pleased when we hear that someone has put in a good word for us, especially when we didn't expect it. Having someone defend us or plead our cause means a lot. At times people find it necessary to hire lawyers, specialists in the law. They have the expertise, the knowledge, and the ability to speak on our behalf.

Jesus is also an expert in the Law—God's Law. He kept the Ten Commandments for us and took upon Himself our punishment for breaking them. He knows both sides of the Law, including our inability to keep it, and pleads for us before the heavenly Father, offering proof of our salvation through His life, death, and resurrection. Scripture assures us that He continually puts in a good word for us.

How about us? Can we put in a "good word" for someone unfairly accused or for one who is not there to defend himself? How about the unborn, those "speechless" infants whose lives may be snuffed out before they can take their first breath? Loving our neighbor includes going to bat for him and defending his good name, even as Jesus has given us His good name, "Christian." Can we say something kind about another, even someone in our own family?

Help us, dear Savior, to speak kindly and in truth about others and to others; in Your name we pray. Amen.

J. Barclay Brown

Matthew 25:31–40

An Unexpected Return

Cast your bread upon the waters, for after many days you will find it again. *Ecclesiastes 11:1*

Sometimes people don't appreciate your acts of Christian love. But human approval is not our motivation—the love of Christ prompts our love for others. Jesus descended from heaven to take upon Himself the sin that separated us from God. He carried it to His cross and left it in the grave when He rose again.

Jesus' grace toward us remains constant. Though we all disobey His will and fail to appreciate God's generous gifts, He still loves us.

In thankfulness we serve Him with our lives, especially by performing acts of Christian generosity. We do so without a thought of reward and often without receiving a word of thanks.

But today's reading says that the bread of compassion you cast upon the waters of others' lives does indeed return to you. The reading from Matthew 25 describes how the Lord Himself will acknowledge our works of love on the Last Day. He sees what is done in secret, and He knows the thoughts and motivation of our hearts. He appreciates the service we render Him, even if no one else seems to notice. Eternal life awaits those who serve Christ in faith.

There are days when I get tired of doing good. Lift my spirit, gracious Lord, and renew my enthusiasm for honoring Your holy name through deeds of love; for Jesus' sake. Amen.

Michael C. Trinklein

Matthew 27:24–31

The Joy of Being a Witness

Blessed are those who are persecuted because of righteousness, for theirs is the kingdom of heaven. *Matthew 5:10*

Throughout the ages, martyrs have been thrown to the lions, boiled in caldrons by pagan tribes, or imprisoned in totalitarian nations for worshiping Christ. The death of Jesus Christ for our sin and His resurrection to life again has given Christians the courage to suffer all, knowing that for those in Christ, death is but the door to eternal life.

The word *martyr* comes from the same Greek word as *witness*. In New Testament times, a witness to Christ stood a good chance of becoming a martyr. Today, too, even though our society officially guarantees freedom of worship, Christians increasingly face persecution. There are many subtle and overt pressures to deny Christ.

Our role is to imitate the saints and martyrs who have gone before us. We witness to the truth of Jesus Christ, who alone can save us from our sins and grant eternal life.

Christians always face opposition from the world (unless they compromise their faith) because they are not of this world. The world takes out its anger at God on those who represent Jesus. But despite insults, hatred, and rejection, Christ promises that the kingdom of heaven is ours.

O Lord, may we be faithful Christian witnesses until death, knowing that the kingdom is ours by Your promise; for the sake of Your Son, our Lord Jesus. Amen.

Frederick G. Boden

Revelation 5:6–14

The Vast Company of Saints

In Christ we who are many form one body, and each member belongs to all the others. *Romans 12:5*

Imagine this: You are the only Christian on the face of the earth. All others have left the faith. Consider the problems this would raise. You are the last of the believers. Your spirit would soon sag. You might even start questioning your faith, for if everybody else had rejected it, you would wonder how you can be sure of what you believe yourself.

If the Good News you wanted to share fell on the deaf ears of others while it was bursting within you, and you could not find anybody to share it with, it would tear you up inside.

Such probing can possibly help you appreciate how good it is to be surrounded by a vast company of saints. They help you know that people have testified to that same faith through the ages. They keep your spirits high as you gather with them, talking about the faith and worshiping together. They strengthen you for daily living as you engage in the struggle of life together. The many members of Christ's body are joined into one great company of saints through the ages.

That helps you keep going day by day!

Help me to appreciate the company of saints with which I am surrounded, Lord, and help me, in turn, to enrich the lives of others. In the name of Jesus, my Savior, I pray. Amen.

Hubert F. Beck

John 1:14–17

Law and Gospel

For the law was given through Moses, grace and truth came through Jesus Christ. *John 1:17*

The Bible contains two distinctively different messages. For instance:

Have you ever felt depressed, desolate, on the verge of despair because of some wrong you had done—a deliberate lie? a dishonest business deal? a deliberate sin of sex? Did you feel miserable, worthless, guilty before God?

That was the condemning message of God's Law. His Law demands perfection; it passes judgment; it pronounces the inexorable verdict of guilt and the punishment of death.

On the other hand, did you ever feel free as a bird, completely at peace with God, fully forgiven through faith in Christ, consciously living in His grace? That was because you had heard and believed the message of His Gospel.

The Law, after all, can only demand, condemn, and ultimately kill. But the Gospel, the good news of God's love in Christ, assures us of forgiveness, peace, and joy. It is important that in our Christian faith and life we distinguish clearly between these two. When God's Law threatens to destroy us, we must always flee to Jesus' open arms and hear His Gospel: "Your sins are forgiven. ... Go in peace" (Luke 7:48–50).

Lord, forgive me for Jesus' sake. Amen.

Herman W. Gockel

Colossians 3:1–4, 17

First Things First

I consider my life worth nothing to me if only I may finish the race and complete the task the Lord Jesus has given me—the task of testifying to the gospel of God's grace. *Acts 20:24*

Everywhere around us people are busy. Conversations with people of all ages and occupations reveal that most people have hurried schedules and jam-packed lives. And why? With improved communication, transportation, and technology, we should be more efficient and have more time, right? No, the more quickly we can do things, the more we cram into our lives.

What takes up our time? When there seems to be more to do than time and energy to do it, then Christian stewards must reassess what is important. God tells us that what is important is testifying to the Gospel of Jesus. Our testimonial is the same, but each of us has been chosen to testify to the Gospel in different ways, using differing gifts (1 Corinthians 12:4). Our first priority is to use our gifts and accomplish our task of witnessing to Jesus, whether in our home, our workplace, our school, our church, or our community. In so doing, we have our priorities in order and are fixed "on things above" (Colossians 3:2).

The gift of salvation sets up a new set of priorities for the investment of our time and the use of our talents as we testify to Him, for Jesus' sake.

Dear Father, set our priorities on things above; for Jesus' sake. Amen.

Gloria K. Lessmann

1 Corinthians 9:24–27

Trophies

They do it to get a crown that will not last; but we do it to get a crown that will last forever. *1 Corinthians 9:25*

I have some trophies on my bookshelves. I worked hard to win them and displayed them proudly. Now they seem merely a fleeting memory of a triumphant hour.

How avidly we collect trophies, not just those that stand on bookshelves but houses, cars, jewelry, and club memberships. We work hard, look for opportunities, take risks, and savor the victories.

Paul writes about athletes training rigorously to win a coveted garland crown. "They do it," he says, "to get a crown that will not last." And only one gets the prize. How futile the pursuit of fading crowns or trophies that will gather dust.

Paul goes on to describe a more worthwhile pursuit for "a crown that will last forever." He sees the Christian life as a race or boxing match. Rugged training and self-discipline are needed for a life of service to God. But the crown of eternal life comes only by God's grace. His Son came to earth, obeyed the Father's will, and endured suffering, pain, and death on the cross for our sins. Risen from the grave, He freely offers the crown of life. We respond by living for Him, never taking our eyes off Jesus Christ and our crown of life. Our trophies gather dust. His trophy shines forever.

Lord Jesus, help us to value only Your crown of eternal life; in Your name. Amen.

Stephen J. Carter

Genesis 2:18–24

Adam's Rib

The LORD God said, "It is not good for the man to be alone. I will make a helper suitable for him." *Genesis 2:18*

The Lord caused a deep sleep to come over the man. While he slept, the Lord took from his side a bit of bone, and from it He fashioned a delightful person. In so many ways she was like Adam, yet totally different.

A rib is strange building material for the Lord to choose. It was as if God intended for the woman always to be at man's side, to share both joys and sorrows of life with him, to be, in that quaint old English word, a "helpmeet" for him.

She stands by his side in the spring of life, as the world is filled with hope, looking forward with him to what life will have in store for both of them. She labors at his side through the summer of life, sharing the sweat of his work and laughing with him through the long, warm evenings. She stands by him in the autumn of life when the first frost lies on the ground, and she remembers with him all that they have accomplished. In the winter of life, she stays by his side, drawing strength from his strength and sharing in turn hers with him.

They love each other as Christ loved the church and gave Himself up for it.

We thank You, Lord Jesus, for letting us see Your constant love working in each other. Amen.

Alston S. Kirk

Romans 13:1–1:7

Pray for Our Elected Leaders

I urge … that requests, prayers, intercession, and thanksgiving be made for everyone—for kings and all those in authority.
1 Timothy 2:1–2

God commands us to pray for those who rule over us. The rulers are really God's representatives over His people. We are to view them as ministers of God who are "appointed" by Him for our good and to punish evil.

Our rulers are in need of our prayers. They need them first of all because they are human and are subject to the same human frailties and sins as we are. Therefore, we are commanded by God to pray for them. We pray that God will give them wisdom in making their decisions because many of these decisions have worldwide implications. We also pray for their physical safety. It seems that our rulers' lives are in constant danger, and assassination has always been a part of our world history.

All of us have to confess that we often forget to pray for those who rule over us. We are very quick in criticism of them. While we have the right to be critical of our leaders, we also have the responsibility to pray for them. We ask God's forgiveness for our failure to pray for our rulers. Jesus died and rose again to redeem us from this sin also.

Father in heaven, we pray for those in authority over us. Cause them to be guided by Your Spirit; for Jesus' sake. Amen.

William H. Griffen

Romans 5:15–17

The Lord's Addition

And the Lord added to their number daily those who were being saved. *Acts 2:47*

Sometimes we fall into the trap of supposing that there is something we can do to save ourselves. If we pray enough, or attend church services, or live good lives, we can rectify the wrongs we do and earn God's approval. That's the way we may be tempted to think from time to time.

Or we may conclude that others are saved because of our activity. Perhaps God used us as the instrument to bring the Gospel to someone who believes and is saved. But we may confuse the instrument with the cause and conclude that we were the reason why another is brought to Christ.

We are reminded in Acts that it was the Lord who added to the number of believers those who were saved. Actually, only God can do that. Salvation is too gigantic a task for a human being to accomplish. Only Christ's death on the cross was sufficient for our salvation. Only He had the power to defeat death and Satan. Only He could convince us of the truth of the Gospel message and bring us to faith through His Word and Baptism.

This is God's work alone. We can only humbly accept His mercy and rejoice that He uses us to make Christ known to others.

Lord Jesus, our Savior, make us Your instruments as through the Word You add believers to the church. Amen.

Paul A. Boecler

John 4:19–26

When the Heart Goes to Church

God is spirit, and His worshipers must worship in Spirit and in truth. *John 4:24*

It was Sunday morning, we may imagine, and the church was filled with people. Yet, throughout the service, the house of worship was strangely silent. The organist played, but there was no music. The minister preached, but no words came from his lips. The choir and the congregation sang and prayed, but not a sound was heard—none except the lone voice of a little child.

A dream? Perhaps, and yet, this is certainly true: All our worship is meaningless motion and voiceless sound, going nowhere, unable to penetrate to the ear of God—all except that which comes from the heart of the child of God.

That is what Jesus means when He says that "God is spirit" and that we must worship God "in Spirit and in truth." It is our heart that must go to church, not merely our well-dressed body. And our heart will go to church if, so to speak, our heart is a church, a temple of the Holy Spirit. As Jesus lives in our heart by faith, His Holy Spirit will work through Word and sacraments to spiritualize our worship. He will move us to repent of our mechanical worship and make our singing and praying a childlike "Abba, Father." And that is worship.

O Holy Spirit, grant me grace to worship my Father, in the name of my Savior, Jesus Christ, with all my heart; in Jesus' name. Amen.

Oswald G. Riess

Jeremiah 18:1–11

In God's Hand

Like clay in the hand of the potter, so are you in My hand, O house of Israel. *Jeremiah 18:6*

It was a familiar sight—a scene common to the bustling city of Jerusalem. Jeremiah had seen it hundreds of times—a craftsman fashioning a clay pot with a practiced, gentle touch. But on this day God impressed on Jeremiah an important lesson. God was like the potter, and His people were like the clay. "O house of Israel, can I not do with you as this potter?"

There is no greater illustration in all of the Bible of God's care and patience. When the ancient potter discovered a flaw in the vessel he made, he did not throw it away. He went to work on it and reshaped it.

When we fail to carry out God's purposes, when we sin against His Law, when we put self first, God does not give up on us. We can still feel the hand of the divine craftsman working in the secret places of our lives. He still pursues us with His grace and love. We are in God's hand. What a picture of God's eternal patience in action—working our salvation in Jesus Christ! For the sake of Jesus He erases our sinfulness. The Holy Spirit through the Gospel in Word and sacraments gives us new life.

Lord, how often we spurn Your love! Yet You continually offer us love and forgiveness. For this we praise and thank You; in Jesus' name. Amen.

John F. Johnson

Matthew 20:20–28

Choices

One thing I ask of the LORD. *Psalm 27:4*

David was pretty sure of himself. He could specify just one desire, and to him it was everything. All he wanted was to "dwell in the house of the LORD" all the days of his life.

Perhaps it was easier for him to isolate his big desire. He was alone, driven out by his enemies, under attack. The prospect of a peaceful return to the Lord's house and the opportunity to behold the beauty of the Lord and to inquire in His temple—this could be a fairly easy choice!

But I, Lord, have so many desires—and I find it hard to choose. I love Your house, but I love mine too. I desire to behold Your beauty, but I cherish the beauty of my family too. I long to inquire about You, but there are so many daily things to look into.

Will you help me satisfy my desires by fulfilling them all in Yourself? May I love my house because I love Yours. May I cherish the beauties of my life because You are the fairest in my life? May I search for substance in my daily routine because You are the final meaning to all of life.

O Father, I believe I may, for You have given me Christ to satisfy every desire, both Yours and mine. "In Him all things hold together" (Colossians 1:17).

Dearest Jesus, keep my eyes of faith focused on You, for then all of my life stays in proper perspective; in Your name. Amen.

Nicholas B. May

2 Thessalonians 1:11–12

Surrender or Demand?

We constantly pray for you. *2 Thessalonians 1:11*

Prayer is never the first word in a conversation. Prayer is always an answer, the answer of faith to the Word God has spoken.

The very first premise of prayer demands that we listen to God's Word about Himself. We take the time to pray because God has revealed Himself to us as the Father who cares for us. We mention our cares to Him because we know He is concerned.

For the Christian, prayer is not just an emergency call, nor is it a way of getting what we want when all the usual means have been tried in vain. Prayer is bringing our needs, plans, and proposals before our Father. It is sharing the burden of our hearts and our ideas with Him, asking that we may have His blessing, bounty, and guidance.

Our prayers are sometimes demanding but only because our Father invites us to make demands of Him. Our prayers are never just demands but always, at the same time, the surrender of our will to His. Because we know Him as Father, our will is to do His good and gracious will. We parade our plans before Him for approval. We pray because we value His will more highly than our own. Our prayer is confidently requesting what He promises to give; it is submitting our will for His approval and correction.

Good Lord, may our will always be to do Your good and gracious will. In Jesus' name. Amen.

Jack H. Ruff

Romans 1:8–10

Special People

I have not stopped giving thanks for you, remembering you in my prayers. *Ephesians 1:16*

You may need a pencil for this devotion. Make a list of people who have touched your life in a special way. Perhaps your list will begin with the name of a pastor or teacher, a parent or grandparent, a friend or co-worker. Think about the people on your list. What made or makes them so special to you? Have you ever told them about the influence they have had on your life? This might be just the time to send a note or card that expresses your gratitude for what some special person has done for you. Take time to offer a prayer of thanksgiving that the Lord has brought each of these special people into your life.

Are you making a difference in someone's life? Add to your list the names of those persons you will strive to influence for good. Pray that opportunities will be opened to bring that influence to bear.

Add a prayer of thanksgiving for the person of Jesus Christ. He comes into our lives without us asking. "While we were still sinners" (Romans 5:8), He chose you to be His special person.

Keep your list before you. Use it to prompt your prayers for special people.

Dear Father, we lift to You our words of praise for all the special people in our lives; in Jesus' name. Amen.

Irma S. Pinkerton

Isaiah 58:6–12

A Question for the Angry

The LORD replied, "Have you any right to be angry?" *Jonah 4:4*

Jonah was angry because a shading plant withered, but he had no feeling about the lives of more than 120,000 Ninevites.

Today many express impatience and anger over those who are poor and ill-equipped for gainful employment. Such angry reactions usually have to do with government programs of relief at taxpayers' expense. We are tempted to easily dismiss feelings of sympathy for the plight of the poor and disadvantaged by judging them en masse as undeserving of social welfare.

God's question to Jonah can also be directed to us. It's a question that stimulates self-examination and directs attention to God's mercy and compassion for all people. Are the poor in our society in need of God's mercy and our compassion? Are not the sins of greed, prejudice, racism, unfairness, and injustice largely responsible for these problems?

Are we justified in our anger over the failures and troubles of our fellow human beings? Our anger does not help them or us. How much better for us all if we express a Christlike compassion and dedicate ourselves to constructive action to bring deliverance to people ensnared in such dehumanizing situations! What a joy then to also share with them the saving Gospel of forgiveness in Christ!

Father, in Christ strengthen our ministry to the poor; in Jesus' name. Amen.

Carl A. Gaertner

1 Corinthians 12:1–11

An Awesome Task from an Awesome God

Each one should use whatever gift he has received to serve others, faithfully administering God's grace. *1 Peter 4:10*

The church exists that we, its members, may carry out the Great Commission: "Go and make disciples of all nations" (Matthew 28:19). Have you ever considered how awesome a task that is—making disciples of all nations? It's not just our family, our community, or our country, but all nations. That translates into bringing the Good News to over five billion people scattered throughout the world and speaking thousands of different languages. And it means bringing the Good News to those who are members of our own family.

But for such a task God gives the awesome power and guidance of the Holy Spirit. He gives us the power of the Gospel and the promise that His Word will not return void. God gives us resources for the task at hand. And in addition to that, the Lord gives each of us at least one spiritual gift to be used in carrying out the Great Commission.

Our Lord challenges us as good stewards to use our gifts to make disciples of all nations. It is an awesome task, but we also have awesome help from an awesome God, whose Son died that we might live, paying the price that we might have forgiveness. The awesomeness of God's power translates into saving love.

Lord Jesus, use me and my gifts in serving others. Amen.

David W. Hoover

1 John 4:7–12

An Oasis of Love

As I have loved you, so you must love one another. *John 13:34*

A new church member wrote to the pastor: "The first thing that struck me when I came to your church was the people. They were warm, friendly, and caring. They care about you every day of the week as well as on Sunday. They help not only each other but everyone who comes to the church. They love." That's the way it should be. In a world full of selfishness and hate, the church is to be an oasis of love in the community.

Martin Luther said that Jesus' followers are to be little Christs. Jesus helped and healed people. We are to be a healing influence—to encourage one another, help the needy, and visit the sick. Jesus taught people. We are to listen to His Word and study it. We are to teach the faith in the home and church. Our Lord came to seek and save the lost. We are to strive to bring others into the church. We are to support generously and pray earnestly for our church's missionary efforts.

Jesus loves the church and gave Himself up for it. We show love for the church by being good representatives of Jesus wherever we are. We strengthen fellow believers by sharing the Good News of Jesus. We ask God to give our pastor love, wisdom, strength, and zeal and to give our congregation a spirit of unity and love.

Spirit of God, make our congregation strong and united in Your Holy Word. Move us to reach out to the unchurched; for Jesus' sake. Amen.

Herbert and Alma Kern

Hebrews 12:1–6

Understanding and Wisdom

He who walks with the wise grows wise. *Proverbs 13:20*

To live abundantly, each of us needs to see the world around us, not only through our own eyes but also through the eyes of many others. I often think that God gave us four gospels instead of one that we might see Jesus through more than one pair of eyes and thus see Him more clearly and meaningfully.

Each new generation stands on the shoulders of the last generation. Using our predecessors' experiences and failures, we reach new, never-before-reached heights. One of the magnificent ways we have learned to profit from the experience of others is through reading. In the pages of books we share great minds and gather new insights and inspiration for our own lives.

Beginning with the Book of books, the Bible, Christians in their reading seek to be alive to what God wants them to know to enjoy a full life in Jesus, their Savior and Lord. In biography, history, poetry, novels, and Christian literature we find food for growth in understanding and wisdom. Make it a part of your abundant life to read good books and to share their thoughts with others. This is the secret of being twice blessed.

Enrich our minds, heavenly Father, through Your gift of the written Word and the printed page; in Jesus' name we pray. Amen.

Harold Midtbo

Romans 12

Remember Your Creator

Remember your Creator in the days of your youth.
Ecclesiastes 12:1

While it is true that, humanly speaking, we are never too old to repent and turn to God, it is equally true that we are never too young to do so. God, our Creator, is to be remembered in the days of our youth.

When Martin Luther starts to recount the great blessings we have received by creation, he does not begin with trees or flowers or sunsets. He does not give priority to gold, silver, copper, or iron. He says, "God has given me my body and soul, eyes, ears, and all my members, my reason and all my senses." What profound insight! These are the things with which the Creator has endowed us and which are at their keenest in the days of our youth. Too frequently, there are days and days when we express little appreciation for them. We will begin to understand their value only when our strength wanes and the powers of our senses fail.

We must realize that our bodies are temples of the Holy Spirit, who dwells in us. Because God in Christ invaded human flesh to redeem us from sin and restore us to holiness, we should remember our Creator and thank Him for every good and perfect gift in the world.

Praise to You, O Lord, the Almighty, the king of creation;
through Jesus Christ, Your Son. Amen.

Edward C. May

Luke 9:59–62

Looking Forward

Let us fix our eyes on Jesus, the author and perfecter of our faith, who for the joy set before Him endured the cross, scorning its shame, and sat down at the right hand of the throne of God. *Hebrews 12:2*

It is said that in order to plow in a straight line you have to look ahead. If you focus on a post or building and head for it, you will make a straight furrow. If you look back to see where you have been, you are bound to swerve, and there will be a bend in the row.

We, as Christians, are called on to keep our eyes focused on the everlasting victory that Jesus won for us at Calvary. This is not an easy task. We are tempted to look back. Maybe we want to admire all we have done or see how bad our mistakes have been. Both are futile activities. We cannot change or undo the mistakes we have made. The Bible says that the Lord has forgotten them. "As far as the east is from the west, so far has He removed our transgressions from us" (Psalm 103:12). If God will "remember [our] sins no more" (Hebrews 8:12), we should put them behind us and focus on the future.

Nor can we focus on our future goal if we are looking back to see our past accomplishments. To move forward in a straight line, we must keep our eyes focused on the landmarks of eternal life, which Jesus has won for us through the cross.

We ask You, Lord, to help us keep our focus on You; in Your name, Jesus, and for Your sake. Amen.

Irma S. Pinkerton

Ephesians 4:1–16

We're All in This Together

Let us do good to all people, especially to those who belong to the family of believers. *Galatians 6:10*

Preservation of the family gets a lot of attention these days. We read much about dysfunctional families, where members' roles have become confused. Family relationships become strained and sometimes break down.

God is also concerned about preserving the family—His family of believers. God sacrificed His only Son so that, by His sacrifice and glorious resurrection, we all could be part of His family. While "there is one body and one Spirit" (Ephesians 4:4), there is not always unity in the family of believers. Because of our sinful nature, family members bicker, criticize, belittle, complain, and blame. And the devil loves it.

God's command and plan for family unity is clear. "Be completely humble and gentle; be patient, bearing with one another in love" (Ephesians 4:2). Only with God's help can we swallow our pride and make peace when we would rather make a point. Only with the patience of our Lord can we wait for a fellow family member to grow spiritually. Only with the indwelling of the Spirit can we show forbearance with others, as God does with us, and make allowances for the mistakes of those who are "heirs" with us of eternal life. God's family is united in Christ and is called to function together in love.

Father of all, enable Your family of believers to live in peace and accomplish Your will. Amen.

Gloria K. Lessmann

1 Peter 4:7–11

Whom Are You Serving?

The Son of Man did not come to be served, but to serve. *Matthew 20:28*

Serving in church or reaching out to those in need can be frustrating, especially when we forget who it is we serve. We serve one another but not only and not primarily. We are called to serve God. If our service is devoted solely to people, we will soon be disillusioned and frustrated when we are met with ingratitude and selfishness.

Paul was willing to "become all things to all men" (1 Corinthians 9:22), but he did so as the bondservant of Christ. He said, "Christ's love compels us" (2 Corinthians 5:14). When Paul was rejected, challenged, and even hated by the very people he sought to serve, he remained secure because he knew he was serving God. His satisfaction came from being faithful to God's calling.

Where does your satisfaction in service come from? When you sing in the church choir or give assistance to a sick neighbor, whom are you serving? If you are serving people only, you are setting yourself up to be frustrated. When our service is rendered to Christ in response to what He did and still does to serve and save us, then no one and nothing will dampen our enthusiasm for serving people for His sake.

Father, thank You for giving me the privilege and satisfaction of serving You; for Jesus' sake. Amen.

Barry J. Keurulainen

Philippians 2:25–30

Longing for Home

For he longs for all of you and is distressed because you heard he was ill. *Philippians 2:26*

When the church at Philippi heard that Paul was in prison, they gathered an offering for him. Epaphroditus was selected to deliver the gift. He stayed on and served Paul with complete devotion. He became ill but was spared by God's grace. No matter how exciting it was to be with Paul and how greatly Epaphroditus desired to serve this man of God, there were times when he longed for home.

Separation from home and loved ones seems quite commonplace today. Families are separated by educational needs, by military service, and by occupations and services that take some family members far from home. The church also separates families by sending people to serve in distant lands all over the world.

Although absorbed in the services they render and in the needs they desire to meet, there are still moments when missionaries think of home and family. There is only one who spans the miles, to whom the mountains and rivers, the jungles and oceans are no obstacles. He will never leave nor forsake them.

These, our friends, represent us, our families, our nation and our church in faraway places! It is our privilege to pray to the Lord on their behalf.

Dear Lord, we want to be like faithful Aaron, holding up the prophet's hands. Help us always to support Your missionaries with our prayers and gifts; for Jesus' sake. Amen.

William H. Kohn

2 Timothy 3:10–17

What a Book!

All scripture is given by inspiration of God. *2 Timothy 3:16 KJV*

There is no other book in the world like the Bible. Why? It alone was "given by inspiration of God." Two Greek words describe the inspiration of the Bible. One is *graphe*, "writing," and the other is *theopneustos*, "breathed out by God."

The original manuscripts were written in Hebrew, Aramaic, or Greek. Every word of every sentence was put there through the guidance of God. The apostle Peter described it this way: "Holy men of God spoke as they were moved by the Holy Spirit" (2 Peter 1:21 NKJV). St. Paul said, "This is what we speak, not in words taught us by human wisdom but in words taught by the Spirit" (1 Corinthians 2:13).

Jesus regarded Scripture as the divinely inspired Word of God, saying, "The Scripture cannot be broken" (John 10:35). Jesus said He did not come to abolish the law and the prophets but to fulfill them, upholding their divine authority.

The purpose of Scripture is to make us "wise for salvation through faith in Christ Jesus" (2 Timothy 3:16) because "there is no other name under heaven given to men by which we must be saved" (Acts 4:12).

Lord Jesus, help us cherish the Scriptures because they testify to You as our dear Savior. Amen.

Leonard H. Aurich

Matthew 6:25–34

How to Ruin a Day

[Jesus said,] "Therefore I tell you, do not worry about your life." *Matthew 6:25*

Want to ruin a perfectly good day? Start worrying. Dwelling on the past or worrying about the future is a sure way to put yourself into an unhealthy and unproductive funk.

A counselor once analyzed the problems of people seeking his advice. He found that 40 percent worried about things that never happened. Another 30 percent worried about decisions already made and not changeable. Another 12 percent worried about sickness that never came, and 10 percent worried about children and friends who actually were fine. That left but 8 percent with worries about real problems. His conclusion was that 92 percent of our worries are needless.

There is no need to worry about three kinds of troubles—those we have had, those we may have now, and those we think we might have in the future. Wisdom includes the realization that the things you are anxious about today may very well seem unimportant tomorrow.

Satan seeks to fill our hearts with worry and gloom. Faith in Jesus, our Savior, is the source of a cheerful Christian outlook on life. He supplies all we truly need: the forgiveness of our sins, eternal life, and the comfort that God is with us each day.

Lord Jesus, replace my needless worry with confident trust in You. Amen.

William Wagner

Malachi 3:6–12

Honoring God with Thank Offerings

Sacrifice thank offerings to God. *Psalm 50:14*

Christians are God's stewards, doing God's work with what He has given them. They are to do it gratefully and honestly. And so we bring our thank offerings. It is not that God needs them, for He owns everything. But we need to bring them for our own good.

Our thank offerings are to be in keeping with our God-given blessings; they are to be our best. God censured some in Israel who brought defective animals for "sacrifice." The whole idea of sacrifice is to give up something valued, not something we can easily do without. God gave His best, His Son, Jesus Christ, for our salvation. He asks for our best.

In the Old Testament God set the tithe—10 percent of income—as the rule for giving. With it He challenged Israel: "Test Me in this ... and see if I will not throw open the floodgates of heaven and pour out so much blessing that you will not have room enough for it" (Malachi 3:10). In Luke 6:38 He promises: "Give, and it will be given to you." We cannot out-give God. Many Christians can testify to the truth of God's promises.

Lord, help us to remember that You don't need our money, time, or talents but that we should give them in thankfulness for Your mercy in Jesus Christ. Amen.

William A. Kramer

Luke 22:39–46

Prayer and Action

We receive from Him anything we ask, because we obey His commands and do what pleases Him. *1 John 3:22*

"Give us today our daily bread." Do we expect God to deliver three meals a day at our doorstep? God answers our prayer for daily bread, but He expects us to use the strength and skill He gives us. True prayer commits us to action. Prayer without doing God's will is insincere. It displeases God.

When we pray for good health, we should do our part: get the proper rest, food, and exercise. If we ask God to improve our marriage, we should forgive and be patient and considerate. If we ask God to overcome our loneliness, we should be friendly and look for ways to help others. If we pray for world peace, we should be peacemakers wherever we are.

Jesus offers an excellent example of the connection between prayer and action. The night before His death Jesus prayed, "Not My will, but Yours be done" (Luke 22:42). The Father answered Jesus' prayer. Jesus acted out the Father's will. Our Lord did this extremely hard thing because He loves us in an extreme way. As our love for Jesus grows through God's grace given us in Word and sacrament, so will our obedience to God's will and our willingness to be part of God's answer to our prayers.

Our Father, enable us to take whatever action is needed to receive what we ask of You, knowing also that without You we can do nothing. In Jesus' name we pray. Amen.

Herbert M. Kern

Genesis 39:6–23

Moral

How then could I do such a wicked thing and sin against God? *Genesis 39:9*

To be moral is to know the difference between right and wrong and to choose what is right.

It may seem that today there are few moral absolutes. The shades of behavioral gray are increasing. But God still speaks to all human beings. Paul, describing the wickedness of the first century, underscored the awareness and accountability of everyone to the Law of God through conscience (Romans 2:15).

Immorality ignores conscience. Rationalizations abound to justify what's wrong. "Everyone's doing it" is a favorite, whether "it" refers to cheating on one's income tax or on one's spouse.

In the Old Testament story out of which we lift today's text, Potiphar's wife expected Joseph to rationalize that the safe thing to do was to accept her invitation to sin. After all, she was the authority; he, the slave. If he refused her invitation, would that bring him harm? He did, and it did. Joseph responded to temptation with an answer so classic that it has inspired unknown numbers to say throughout the centuries, "How then could I do such a wicked thing and sin against God?" Joseph's action landed him in prison.

The criterion is not what I want, not even what is expedient or safe. Rather, it is what God wants.

Lord, help me find pleasure in doing what You want; for Jesus' sake. Amen.

Leland Stevens

Acts 9:36–42

How to Serve

[She] was always doing good and helping the poor. *Acts 9:36*

This is the description of a woman whose name was Tabitha in Aramaic and Dorcas in Greek. She was a disciple, that is, a follower of Jesus in the early church. She lived at Joppa, a port city. Tabitha made it her special concern to sew coats and garments for the poor. It happened that she became ill and died. There was much sorrow in the church. When the Christians heard that Peter was at a nearby city, they sent for him. In a miraculous way Tabitha was brought back to life in answer to Peter's earnest prayers.

What we want to notice in the life of Tabitha was the way in which she translated her faith in Jesus into very practical and simple ways of meeting the needs of the people around her. Today we might ask, "How many coats and dresses did she sew? Could it not have been done more efficiently if a society had been formed to do more?" Maybe so. Sometimes we need that also. But the point is that Tabitha didn't wait for that to happen. She started where she was—with what she had—because her love and concern for the poor, which she had received from her Lord, was heartfelt and needed to be expressed.

Dear Lord Jesus, remind us again of the truth that when we show love to those in need it is shown to You; in Your name. Amen.

Martin L. Kretzmann

Matthew 24:36–44

Be Alert!

No one knows about that day or hour, not even the angels in heaven, nor the Son, but only the Father. Be on guard! Be alert! You do not know when that time will come. *Mark 13:32–33*

You are alert, for you are waiting for someone—a special someone. At first each approaching person is scanned to be sure he or she is not the one. Time goes on. Ways and means are discovered to pass the time. Each glance at the clock makes one marvel that minutes can pass so slowly. When will this person come?

Perhaps you have experienced this as you've waited for the doctor to return with a report or waited for a friend or a soon-to-come guest. The arrival seems to take forever.

We are warned that it is so with Christ's final coming. No one knows just when He will return. We are told to be alert, to be ready. When we least expect it, Christ will return to claim His own.

Christ gives us directions on how to pass the time until He returns. As we wait and watch, we are to share with others the glorious message of our Savior. We are to enlist other guards in the watch. We are to make disciples of all nations so they too may be ready and join us in the great celebration when our Savior returns.

Lord Jesus, keep me alert for Your coming. Help me share Your Word as I wait for You. Amen.

Jeanette L. Groth

Exodus 12:21–27

Days of Remembrance

I will remember the deeds of the LORD; yes, I will remember Your miracles of long ago. *Psalm 77:11*

National holidays mark great events in history. Anniversaries and birthdays remind us of special times in our families. Annual days of remembrance help us better appreciate the past and bring us closer to those we love.

God gave His Old Testament people specific holy days and feasts to observe; even the rituals were prescribed. They had a purpose: to remind the people of God's deliverance, care, and blessing.

Christmas, Easter, and other church festivals are days of remembrance of the great events of our salvation—the events that saved us from sin and death and brought us into God's people, God's family. Every Sunday is a Christian holiday. We remember Jesus' resurrection on the first day of the week; Word and sacraments bring His forgiveness and presence into our lives.

Observances disregarded are too soon forgotten. We need this day of remembrance. We need to gather with fellow Christians to receive the blessings of Word and Sacrament. Today's remembrance prepares us for the week ahead.

Happy holiday! Happy holy day!

As I call to mind Your deeds, O Lord, I remember the wonders You worked for the redemption of Your people; in Jesus' name. Amen.

Louise Mueller

Luke 22:39–46

Time Out

He withdrew about a stone's throw beyond them ... and prayed. *Luke 22:41*

For the hard-running athletes, for tired parents, for exhausted executives, for all of us the wise word is "Time out!" We take "time out" from work for relaxation and from routine for recreation. We take "time out" for a coffee break in the morning and a nap in the afternoon. Above all, we need to take "time out" from everything else in life to pray.

How often our life is taken up with big plans that turn into small accomplishments because we did not take "time out" to pray for guidance! How easy it is for us to become so dazed by success in our efforts that we forget to take "time out" to pray in thanksgiving! How heavy our life all too often becomes when we are weighed down by the burden of guilt and do not take "time out" to pray for forgiveness.

As we hurry from home in the morning, as we rush through a busy schedule at work, as we fill up the hours with all sorts of activities, as we return to our home where things must be done, we need to take "time out" for personal communication with Him whose will is: "Call upon Me!" (Psalm 50:15). Every day we need to catch our spiritual breath and take "time out" to pray.

Lord, remind us that when we are too busy to pray, we are too busy; in Jesus' name. Amen.

Theodore A. Daniel

Philippians 4:4–9

Attitude More Than Aptitude

Finally, brothers, whatever is true, whatever is noble, whatever is right, whatever is pure, whatever is lovely, whatever is admirable ... think about such things. *Philippians 4:8*

Charles Swindoll has said, "I am convinced that life is 10 percent what happens to me, and 90 percent how I react to it."

The story is told of two young girls who delighted in paging through their "wish book," a mail-order catalog. The six-year-old, as she paged, said, "I want this; I'd like to have that." Turning the pages, she came to one thing after the other that she was certain she needed. Her four-year-old sister opened to the first pages and said, "I have this and I have that." The sisters were looking at the same book, but they saw things differently.

What is your overriding attitude? Are you, like the four-year-old, conscious of all the blessings God has lavished on you? Or do you, like the older sister, perhaps, see everything as something you want and need?

Let us be grateful for all God has given us, beginning and ending with the gift of forgiveness and everlasting life in Jesus. Let God attend to what we need. We will focus on what we have and give thanks for that.

Help us, Jesus, to be thankful for all You have given us. Amen.

Irma S. Pinkerton

Acts 22:3-13

A Question about Life's Direction

"What shall I do, Lord?" I asked. *Acts 22:10*

When Saul, an enemy of the church, asked Jesus the question above, he had been struck down and made blind by the light from heaven. He realized he had been persecuting the Lord of glory and that his life was in Jesus' hands. Christ changed him from Saul to Paul and made him history's greatest missionary.

Probably not many of us have had the course of our lives changed so suddenly and dramatically. Yet life's problems may drive us to our knees as we seek direction from God.

Instead of waiting for a crisis, we do better to live each day with the inquiring attitude, "What shall I do today, Lord?" We seek God's direction in the smaller things of life, yes, but especially at times of decision: "What shall I do about career, job, marriage, retirement?"

God does not disappoint us when we ask trustingly for His guidance. For Paul it was a life of joyful missionary service. Even the beatings and imprisonments did not cause him to regret following the Lord's directions. We have the confidence: "He who did not spare His own Son, but gave Him up for us all—how will He not also, along with Him, graciously give us all things?" (Romans 8:32).

Gracious God, grant us direction for our lives, trusting in Your merciful goodness; for the sake of Jesus Christ, our Lord. Amen.

Norbert V. Becker

Philippians 2:1–11

True Humility

Remind the people ... to be peaceable and considerate, and to show true humility. *Titus 3:1–2*

A country tune whimsically notes, "It's hard to be humble when you're perfect in every way!" Although not many would be so arrogant as to claim perfection, the song does illustrate our reluctance to recognize our sin. We may call a falsehood "just a little white lie." When we are rude to others, we may excuse ourselves by saying we are "having a bad day." When men and women break the marriage vows they made before God, we say they simply "were incompatible." We like to sugarcoat the evil that we perform. But the fact is that the evil we do, including our words and deeds of pride, constitute sin against God.

True humility begins with a personal confession. It does no good to compare ourselves with other people, for God's yardstick of holiness and perfection reveals that we all fall short of the glory of God.

Jesus Christ humbled Himself for us, becoming a servant and dying for us on the shameful cross, to forgive all our sins, including those of pride. Our response in faith includes showing true humility by treating others with respect, defending them, speaking well of them, and living peaceably with them.

Lord Jesus, teach us to be considerate and loving toward others as Your humble servants. Amen.

William R. A. Ney

Acts 10:34–43

Nothing Unusual

So you also, when you have done everything you were told to do, should say, "We are unworthy servants; we have only done our duty." *Luke 17:10*

How pleased we often are with ourselves when we have carried out an assignment in a better than the usual way, when we have extended ourselves—gone the extra mile, as it were! We are thrilled because it seems so out of the ordinary. We seem to be saying, "Look, we didn't have to do all this, but we did it! Applause, please!"

Our Lord interrupts: "When you have done everything you were told to do [not only some of the things but *everything*], say, 'We are unworthy servants; we have only done our duty.' " We are servants and deserve no credit; we only did our duty. What a blow to pride!

What we may consider unusual in the performance of our duty ought to be the usual. That is what Jesus wants. The good we do from time to time is something He wants to see happen all the time. That much goodness God gives us richly. His Son provided it with His suffering, death, and resurrection. The merits of His goodness are conveyed to us through Word and sacraments. Our Lord urges us to use His goodness. That's why He was so lavish in giving it to us.

Lord, help us to do our duty and to think nothing of it; in Jesus' name we pray. Amen.

Paul W. F. Harms

Luke 1:35–38

"Once upon a Time"

For nothing is impossible with God. *Luke 1:37*

Is it fact or fiction? Often we cannot tell the one from the other. Parents read fairy tales to their children because these stories stimulate the imagination. They read them so often the stories become real to the children.

In our day Santa Claus has become so real and commercially successful that he has all but eased the baby Jesus out of His manger. Bunnies and colored eggs at Easter have for many all but replaced the empty tomb of the risen Lord. Is it not strange how "once upon a time" fairy tales are accepted as real and true stories from the Bible are looked upon as fairy tales?

"Once upon a time" Jesus was truly born, lived, died, and rose again. All this was truly God's wonderful way of giving to all people a Savior from sin and a Lord for life. What a true story to tell and tell and tell again!

"Once upon a time!" They may not begin with just those words, but there are many true stories in the Bible, interesting to read, challenging to consider, essential to believe. As we read and meditate on the "once upon a time" stories of the Bible and the eternal truths of God of which they speak, let us make the prayer of the Virgin Mary our own prayer and expression of faith: "Let it be to me according to your word" (Luke 1:38).

Dear Lord Jesus, increase in us the desire to study the Scriptures, for they testify about You, our Savior; in Your name we ask it. Amen.

Theodore A. Daniel

Luke 11:5–13

The Miracle of Prayer

If you remain in Me and My words remain in you, ask whatever you wish, and it will be given you. John 15:7

Prayer is to be thought of as a miracle. In the twinkling of an eye we can be in the presence of God. The channel is always open for us through the name of our Savior. We never get the "busy signal." The answer to our prayer is also a miracle. Perhaps there are myriads of details that will have to be ordered to work together for an answer to our prayer. God wants us to come with large petitions. He wants us to submit our case to Him even when it seems hopeless. He loves the faith that ascribes to Him the power to overcome seemingly insurmountable problems.

We may also think of prayer as worship. God Himself has taught us in the Lord's Prayer to seek His honor first. Prayer is more than just asking for things. It is bringing our sins to Him for forgiveness. It is telling Him how much we love Him, how much He means to us, and how earnestly we desire to serve Him.

We should also regard prayer as a ministry. Through prayer we can ask God to bless others. We invite God's blessing on people in our family, congregation, neighborhood, and in all the world.

Does God answer every prayer of His children? Yes, every prayer that is for our good and that achieves God's honor is answered.

Lord, give us the faith to come to You in the worship and ministry of prayer. Teach us to pray; for Jesus' sake. Amen.

Carl W. Berner

Philippians 4:4–7

Joy beyond All Telling

I say these things while I am still in the world, so that they may have the full measure of My joy within them. *John 17:13*

Christianity is a religion of joy. It was born in a song and has been singing ever since. Pagan religions have no song because they have no genuine joy. They have no joy because they have no peace or hope. They have no peace or hope because they have no Savior.

The Bible is resonant with good news. Put your ear to it and listen to the "glad tidings of great joy." The Lord Jesus Christ has solved our basic problems: sin and its curse, death and its darkness, hell and its terrors. These enemies lie at His feet. He has adopted us into His family. He cares for us, intercedes for us, and fights for us. He is preparing a place for us, and He is preparing us for that place in the Father's house.

If that doesn't fill us with laughter and song, something is dreadfully wrong with us. God wants us to be happy and confident. "God hates heavy and sorrowful minds. He loves cheerful hearts. Therefore has He sent His Son to cheer up our souls in Him. God commands us to rejoice and be glad." So wrote Martin Luther. Many of his hymns reflect this joy and arouse it in those who sing them.

Lord Jesus, fill my life with the joy of salvation in You, and let my joy be contagious. Amen.

Carl W. Berner

Luke 12:16–21

Where Is Your Treasure?

Do not store up for yourselves treasures on earth .... But store up for yourselves treasures in heaven. *Matthew 6:19–20*

Perhaps you have seen the bumper sticker that says, "He who dies with the most toys wins." In our society today the accumulation of wealth and creature comforts seems to be the measure of a person's success and the goal for which many live.

Jesus warns us of the danger of spending our lives seeking earthly treasures that do not last. A farmer may spend his entire life building bigger and better barns and purchasing larger machinery. A professional person may acquire expensive cars and luxurious homes. But the truth is that all of these things will eventually be gone. There is wisdom in the old saying that you never see a U-Haul truck following a hearse. Physical possessions will not give a person lasting comfort or hope.

Jesus tells us to seek first His kingdom and righteousness; God will supply all that we need. Our real treasure is Jesus Himself, who redeemed us by His blood, which is more precious than silver or gold. The forgiveness of sins and life everlasting in heaven surpass the entirety of the world's wealth. Our lives are well spent with a strong and abiding faith in Jesus, serving Him and our neighbor to the glory of God.

Heavenly Father, help us focus on what is eternal that we may receive Your spiritual treasure. Amen.

William R. A. Ney

Colossians 1:1–6a

Destination Shapes Attitude

We have heard of your faith in Christ Jesus and of the love you have for all the saints—the faith and love that spring from the hope that is stored up for you in heaven. *Colossians 1:4–5*

Destination shapes attitude. It was that way when our family made the long, 14-hour drive to visit Grandma and Grandpa. Loaded into the car were five people and a dog. The potential of an ordeal was high. I'll always believe, though, that our *destination* made those trips not just bearable, but even celebrative. We knew that waiting for us were two great people who loved us and the best chocolate chiffon cake on earth.

In the Christian life on earth, destination shapes attitude. The Bible has given us the ending of our life story, and the ending is happy indeed. At the end of our journey—after all the bumps and scrapes and disappointments—is Christ. He has lived for us and died for us, and He is waiting for us.

We are aware of our destination. We have set our hearts on the things that are above. With such a destination, we approach life with confidence and with the kind of love we have come to know in Christ. We find this true: Where there is faith, there is also love and hope. Destination shapes attitude.

Lord Jesus Christ, when my faith and love are stretched, shape my attitude with the certain hope of heaven. Amen.

Dean W. Nadasdy

Genesis 18:1–10; Hebrews 13:2

Way of Hospitality

And one more thing: Prepare a guest room for me, because I hope to be restored to you in answer to your prayers. *Philemon 22*

Paul must have been on close terms with Philemon not only to have asked for a guest room at his house but also to have assumed that Philemon and his family would pray for Paul's liberation.

Hospitality in that day, when Christians often had to flee persecution, was both necessary and hazardous. Harboring hunted people exposed the host to the same treatment as his guests.

Hospitality is a declining virtue, partly because many of us live so much to ourselves, partly because many homes are not built for guests, and partly because motels and hotels are so convenient.

But hospitality takes forms other than putting up people in our home. It includes greeting visitors at church, welcoming newcomers to the neighborhood, inviting others to dinner even though they are not close associates.

Whatever form Christian hospitality takes, it gets its inspiration from our heavenly Father, who for the sake of Christ welcomes all penitent sinners. Our Lord Jesus assures us: "In My Father's house are many rooms …. I am going there to prepare a place for you" (John 14:2).

Knowing that we serve You by serving those who need our love, we pray: Come, Lord Jesus, be our guest. Amen.

Ernest R. Drews

Galatians 2:8–10

Somebody Forgot

We should continue to remember the poor. *Galatians 2:10*

An atheist once asked a poorly dressed boy coming home from Sunday school what he had learned that morning. The boy replied, "God is love." He was asked: "If God is love, why didn't He tell someone to give you clothes and shoes?" After a few moments' pause the boy sadly replied: "I guess God told somebody, and somebody forgot."

Time and time again the Lord in His Word reminds Christians to have a heart for those in need, to look for opportunities to help others in His name and for His sake. He would have all of us remember—and true love is especially good at remembering—that every cup of water, and every piece of bread or clothing given to the poor in His name is given to Him. He reminds us that whoever loves God loves his brother also and that if we do not help those in actual need God's love is not in us. Our Lord told us about the Good Samaritan, but how little we have learned.

"Somebody forgot," said the boy. Do we always remember? What things await our remembering today? Perhaps if we loved others more, we would remember them more. It is the very nature of love not to forget.

Lord Jesus, because You gave Your life to save us, teach us to remember the needy in their distress. Amen.

John E. Herrmann

Matthew 5:1–16

Let Your Light Shine

But now you are light in the Lord. Live as children of light. *Ephesians 5:8*

Rudyard Kipling told the story of how he suddenly found himself a guiding light to an old woman living by herself on a hillside opposite his home. He had purchased an old farmhouse on a mountain slope in an unsettled part of Vermont. One day he and his wife tramped down through the valley to the tiny house on the other side. There he met the old woman. "Be you the windows with the light across the valley?" she asked. She told them how much their light meant to her. Then suddenly in apparent concern she asked: "Be you going to stay and keep your light burning or maybe not?" After that day, Kipling remarked, they always kept the light burning in their window and even removed the curtains so more light would shine out.

We Christians must always remember that we are light in the Lord and that, whether we are conscious of it or not, someone is being guided by our light. It is this truth that Jesus wanted to impress on His disciples when He reminded them that they were the light of the world. Only eternity will tell the full story of how others were guided by our light and depended on it. This light is revealed in our smile, our lips, our life, our sympathies, our simple confession of faith, our charities, our evident love, in the things we shun, in the things we pursue, in the helping hand, in the willing foot—in fact, in our total life.

Lord Jesus, so direct my lips and life that I remain a light to others. Keep me ever in Your light. Amen.

Erdmann W. Frenk

Romans 15:7–13

Music to God's Ears

Let everything that has breath praise the LORD. Praise the LORD. *Psalm 150:6*

"That's music to my ears," says the mechanic as the once-silent engine whirs into action without a cough or a sputter.

"That's music to my ears," says the construction foreman as pounding hammers work rhythmically to erect a new structure.

"That's music to my ears," says the teacher as a struggling student reads a story flawlessly.

As Christians we believe that everything we do in faith brings glory to Christ's name. Everything done to His glory brings praise and thanksgiving to our God. Surely then all the sounds of the working Christian are beautiful music to God, for He rejoices in the multitudinous ways His people praise Him by what they think, say, and do.

"But I'm no musician," you say. Yet Christians across the world make beautiful music as they unite their talents and abilities to praise God. How can we add to the symphony? By sharing the Good News of Jesus with others. As we do this, we add new dimensions to the praise and worship of our God.

Listen to those around you. Join your song to theirs in one great chorus. "Let everything that has breath praise the LORD!"

Dear God, I dedicate all that I do to Your name. May it add new sounds to glorify You; for Jesus' sake. Amen.

Jeanette L. Groth

Isaiah 60

Floodlights

Arise, shine, for your light has come, and the glory of the LORD rises upon you. *Isaiah 60:1*

Have you ever seen lights in the distance as you drove along an interstate at night? For miles you try to guess what they are, what they illuminate—a shopping mall, a used-car agency, the parking lot of an all-night diner. Finally, you come close enough to make out what purpose the lights are serving. In the light it all becomes clear. Little is hidden in floodlights, and much is revealed.

Jesus Christ is the light of the world. He has the ability to flood our lives with a revealing light of truth in His Holy Word so intense that nothing remains hidden. Everything is revealed. His light illumines our poor choices and rationalizations. His Gospel light drives away all fear and makes us feel secure. When we are caught by the results of our own regrettable decisions or paralyzed by anxiety, the light of the world shows us the way and reveals to us our Savior. In this light, we play and work, live and die with confidence and courage. Above all we discover, as we draw closer to the light of the world, that our sins have been forgiven and we have received through Holy Baptism the adoption of sons and daughters of the most high God. It is a light *that no darkness can overcome.*

O Jesus, let Your light so flood our world that Your love and goodness is revealed to all. Amen.

Donald C. Schaefer

Psalm 100

....

We Are Stewards

Turn in the account of your stewardship. *Luke 16:2 RSV*

All that we are and all that we have is a trust from God. "We brought nothing into the world, and we can take nothing out" (1 Timothy 6:7). Yet God lends to us many wonderful gifts to use while we are here on earth. God retains ownership of these gifts, and we are the managers of them. We are stewards.

As Christians we gladly acknowledge that we are only stewards. Thankfully we admit that not only the gift of salvation but also "every good and perfect gift is from above" (James 1:17). With John the Baptist we confess, "A man can receive only what is given him from heaven" (John 3:27). It does not surprise us, then, that God, the owner, expects us, the stewards, to manage His property first and foremost for Him.

As stewards we know that God will demand an account of our stewardship. Therefore we will not say to ourselves, "My body, my mind, my time, my talents, my treasure are mine to use as I please." Rather, we will say, "Lord, what will You have me do?" We know that health and wealth, skill and will, brain and brawn, work and wages, income and profit, honor and success all come from God and are to be used in the manner that pleases Him. We want to give a good account. And we can, if we live Christ-centered lives.

O God, You loan us so many wonderful gifts. Help us to be good and faithful stewards of them; for Jesus' sake. Amen.

William S. Graumann

Romans 13:1–14

Why Me, Lord?

God did not appoint us to suffer wrath but to receive salvation through our Lord Jesus Christ. *1 Thessalonians 5:9*

In one of my favorite cartoons, the first frame shows a man sitting in a rowboat in the middle of a flood asking, "Why me, Lord?" The next frame shows the man with an expression of surprise on his face and a voice from heaven saying, "Do you want a list?"

In a way we are like the man in the boat. We have a hard time accepting the unpleasant things in life. We invariably ask "Why me?" as if God's punishment is the reason for our lost job, illness, or financial problems. Our text makes it clear that our hard times are not to be regarded as God's ultimate goal. God does not want us to suffer wrath but, on the contrary, to have a joyful life overflowing with abundant blessings, the greatest of which is eternity in heaven. He will finally bring us to the salvation He planned from the beginning. To that end Jesus came into the world, suffered, died, and rose again. His blood washes away all our sin so we may enter God's presence as His forgiven children.

We need not ask "Why me, Lord?" in fear or anger. In Christ Jesus, God's purposes for us are only good. Let us praise Him for appointing us to a salvation that will never end!

Thank You, Lord, for Your mercy. Amen.

Carlos H. Puig

Ephesians 2:19–22

Home Is Where the Heart Is

[Jesus said] to the disciple, "Here is your mother." From that time on, this disciple took her into his own home. *John 19:27*

If you want to see what a person is really like, spend some time in the home. We can put on an air of kindness at work or school and lead others to believe that we are the kind of people they want us to be. But at home we let our hair down. Our family members see us as we really are. Our selfishness shows; our lack of concern for others comes out. Where we live and what we do at home reflect on what is in our hearts.

At home we also reflect Christ's love in us. By His enabling power we show patience. We forgive over and over again. We sacrifice personal advantage to see someone through a crisis. Together we grow in faith into Him who is the head, that is, Christ. Home is a place of refuge. Home is a place of refreshing rest. Home is where we gain the strength to face the world, which seeks to tear us away from Christ. Home is where others help us to stay close to Him who gave His life for us.

Building a Christian home requires effort. Together in our home we daily seek God's will for our lives and pray earnestly for His blessings.

Thank You, dear Lord, for giving us a home in which to grow in faith. Bless our home today and every day. Amen.

Norris G. Patschke

Rachel Weeps Again

A voice was heard in Ramah, weeping and great mourning, Rachel weeping for her children and refusing to be comforted, because they are no more. Matthew 2:18

The prophet Jeremiah (31:15) poetically portrays the sorrow of the children of Israel as they were being deported into captivity. He pictures Rachel, Jacob's favorite wife, who so longed for children, as weeping in her grave. This is the way Matthew describes the grief caused by Herod's senseless slaughter of infants at the time of our Savior's birth.

Rachel must be weeping again. If she could be described as grieving over the death of perhaps 25 babies at the hand of a jealous despot, what uncontrollable sobs must fill her tomb now at the report of well over a million legal abortions annually in the United States alone! How can she be consoled?

The death of the innocents at the time of Christ's birth reminds us that God's Son Himself took on our flesh in the Virgin Mary's womb. Through His death on the cross He gives us the will to seek the alleviation of those circumstances that make the killing of the unborn appear to be justified by economic and social needs. He strengthens our resolve not to rest until all human beings have the protection of the law of the land. Not until then will Rachel's weeping be quieted.

Gracious Lord Jesus, forgive our sins of failing to act to defend our defenseless neighbors in the womb. Amen.

Samuel H. Nafzger

Matthew 13:44–46

Switched Labels

Seek first His kingdom and His righteousness. *Matthew 6:33*

"The world, as we live in it," said Dr. Temple, the late Archbishop of Canterbury, to a group of Oxford students, "is like a shop window in which some mischievous person has got in overnight and shifted all the price labels around so that the cheap things have the high-price labels on them. And we let ourselves be taken in."

Really there are only two things that rate high-price labels. When we shall stand, as we soon will, before the great white throne, there will be only two things that will everlastingly matter: first, whether we are standing at Christ's right hand with the number of those who have "washed their robes and made them white in the blood of the Lamb"; second, whether there will be someone standing beside us who is there because of what we said or did and were while here below. Jesus combines these two things and says, "Seek first His kingdom."

First! The trouble is that for many of us the kingdom comes far down in the list and is not even a poor second. As Temple said, "We let ourselves be taken in." It is high time that we get labels—and priorities—straight. It is time to seek first God's kingdom.

Our Father who art in heaven, hallowed be Thy name; Thy kingdom come. Amen.

Oswald G. Reiss

Revelation 19:6–10

A Banquet

He has taken me to the banquet hall, and His banner over me is love. *Song of Songs 2:4*

Who among us does not like to attend a banquet, especially a wedding banquet? The food is delicious; the atmosphere is exuberant; the fellowship is unmatched. We wish it would never end.

Our Lord has prepared a banquet for us. In Holy Communion, the Lord's Supper, we eat and drink Christ's body and blood for the forgiveness of sins and the strengthening of our faith. Through Holy Communion our Lord fulfills a promise He gave to His disciples at His ascension and gives us a foretaste of life everlasting in His presence. In Holy Communion we see the fulfillment of His promise and sample the glory of His never-failing presence. Our Lord is physically with us in, with, and under the bread and wine.

He gives us a foretaste of an even more glorious meal, a meal at His banquet table in heaven. Jesus is often referred to as the bridegroom and we, His church, as the bride. The day will come when our Lord will lead His bride, the church, to her eternal home.

Until that day, we are assured, strengthened, and forgiven in the Lord's Supper.

Gracious heavenly Father, thanks and praise to You for so great a blessing as the Lord's Supper. Keep us strong in faith until we feast forever at the table You set for us in heaven; in Jesus' name. Amen.

James Freese

Luke 1:26–38

....

God's Holy Angels Protect Us

He will command His angels concerning you to guard you in all your ways; they will lift you up in their hands, so that you will not strike your foot against a stone. *Psalm 91:11–12*

God created the holy angels to praise Him and to serve humanity. The Bible speaks eloquently of their services.

At the creation the angels shouted for joy (Job 38:7). An angel delivered Daniel in the lions' den. An angel announced the birth of Jesus to the shepherds. Then multitudes of angels sang, "Glory to God in the highest, and on earth peace to men on whom His favor rests" (Luke 2:4). An angel freed Peter from prison (Acts 12:8–9). An angel ministered to Jesus in His suffering in the Garden of Gethsemane (Luke 22:43).

There are also evil angels—demons—who seek our harm. But the good angels are our guardians, God's helpers, who stand by us. With them we sing creation's story and proclaim the Messiah's birth. They protect us as they have protected God's people since the beginning of time.

We do not pray to the angels because they are not God. But we praise God with them and for them as we enjoy their protection and unseen presence among us.

Dear Lord, "Let Your holy angel be with me that the evil foe may have no power over me"; in Jesus' name. Amen.

William A. Kramer

1 Corinthians 12:1–11

Many Gifts, but One Spirit

There are different kinds of gifts, but the same Spirit.
1 Corinthians 12:4

It is Paul's aim here to stress the unity of the church. We know that the congregation in Corinth had factions in it and that there was quarreling among the members. One reason for this spirit may have been the envy and jealousy some had toward others. Paul says that there are many kinds of gifts in the church, just as there are many kinds of service.

The point to remember, Paul says, is that all these gifts are from the same Spirit. Therefore there is no reason for them to be the cause of division in the church. The same God inspires the "varieties of working" in everyone.

We should not define the word *gift* too narrowly, as if it referred only to some spectacular and unusual performance or to such intellectual gifts as speaking, praying, teaching, and writing. If we look on the whole of the Christian life as a service to God, as we should, then the special gifts of the mason, the carpenter, the electrician, the painter, the engineer, and the plumber are to be used to glorify God and witness to Him just as much as the gifts of preaching and teaching. The same Spirit gives them all.

Lord, help us to appreciate and give thanks for all the gifts You have given to Your children; in Jesus' name. Amen.

Martin L. Kretzmann

Galatians 4:4–7

The Glory of Fulfillment

When the time had fully come, God sent His Son. *Galatians 4:4*

Only God decided when the hour had come for which the world had been waiting. When in His judgment all the conditions were right, when time had woven all the threads of the centuries into the pattern of His design, when the events in the history of the nations had reached the point that He had predetermined—then, not before and not after, the fullness of time was come, and then God sent forth His Son.

There is a glorious majesty in the thought of God's timing of His acts. He is not to be pressed into hasty action. Until His hour has come, humankind must wait. Nor can He be persuaded to postpone His plans. When His measure of the days and years is filled, there is no more delay. The Lord is His own counselor, and He acts when He decides.

This is most significant for our own life and experience. Because our judgments are clouded as a result of sin, we can so easily become impatient and demand premature action that would distort the balance of our lives. Or we can be slow and late in our timing and again disable the mechanism of events in which each part must mesh perfectly with all the rest. There is a readiness for all things that is known only to God and the determination of which must be His alone.

Grant us, O Lord, patience to wait for Your fullness of time and a confident trust in Your judgment; for Jesus' sake. Amen.

Daniel E. Poellot

Matthew 15:1–9

"Behold, Your Mother!"

When Jesus saw His mother, and the disciple whom He loved standing near, He said to His mother, "Woman, behold, your son!" Then He said to the disciple, "Behold, your mother!" *John 19:26–27 RSV*

Jesus not only died on the cross for our sins, He also exhibited the kind of life God wants us to live. There is no better demonstration of the meaning of the Fourth Commandment than the touching example of Jesus' love and respect for His mother just moments before His death. Seeing her there before Him, He commended her into the care and keeping of His beloved friend and disciple, John, who cared for her from them on.

All of us have parents. There comes a time, to be sure, when "a man will leave his father and mother and be united to his wife" (Genesis 2:24). But we don't stop being our parents' children when we grow up and leave home. Nor does God's command that we honor our parents have any time limit on it.

Today God blesses us by letting us have our parents with us longer and longer. May the example of Jesus' concern for His mother, even while dying for us, motivate us not to forget but to honor our parents and elders in their declining years with our love and respect. God has added a special promise to those keeping this commandment.

Lord Jesus, forgive me for not being sensitive to the needs of my parents. Help me to follow Your example. Amen.

Samuel H. Nafzger

Matthew 6:1–4

Jesus Needs You

Andrew, Simon Peter's brother, spoke up, "Here is a boy with five small barley loaves and two small fish." *John 6:8–9*

Jesus was forever borrowing. He borrowed a stable—probably a cave—in which to be born, a boat to be used as a pulpit, five loaves and two fish to feed 5,000, a donkey for His triumphal procession into Jerusalem, the Upper Room to institute the Sacrament of Holy Communion, the back of Simon of Cyrene to help Him carry the cross, and the tomb of Joseph in which to be buried.

Jesus, of course, did not have to borrow anything because all things belong to Him. He borrowed to show us that today He needs us.

Jesus needs us! How flattering! How thought provoking! How awesome! Jesus needs us—that is why we are who we are, what we are, and where we are. Jesus needs us to fill some special assignment or to touch some life that no one else can do.

There is purpose to our lives. We are here not just to fill space, not just to accumulate an estate. We are here to be a credit to God and to serve Him and our fellow human beings. To this end Jesus Christ redeemed us.

O Lord, take me. Use me wherever and however You need me; for Jesus' sake. Amen.

Albert L. Neibacher

John 10:14–18

Everyone's Christ

There is neither Jew nor Greek, slave nor free, male nor female, for you are all one in Christ Jesus. *Galatians 3:28*

God loves everyone. Jesus is here for everybody. We are inclined to say, "That's obvious!" It should have been obvious to the first disciples. But it wasn't at times. At first, converts did come from everywhere: east, from Mesopotamia; west, from Rome; north, from Asia Minor; south, from Ethiopia. Then a change came. In the West the Christian faith won its greatest success.

We in America are inheritors of it, but the universality of the Gospel is sometimes obscured by us. Often we want Him to be *our* Jesus. If we are shocked to see Him pictured as an oriental Jesus, it is because we have made Him a western Jesus. If we feel resentment when reminded that He was a Jew, it is because we have made Him a Gentile Jesus. If we resist supporting missions abroad on the grounds that we should not export our religion to other lands, we deny the Christ made manifest to all.

All are invited to Christ's feast. The sole condition for admittance is that we confess our need. He is everyone's Christ because He came to give what everyone needs: forgiveness and power for life.

O God, You made Yourself known to both local shepherds and distant Wise Men. Grant that all the kingdoms of the world become the kingdom of Your Son; for Jesus' sake. Amen

August Bernthal

John 1:1–14

God among Us

The Word became flesh and made His dwelling among us. … full of grace and truth. *John 1:14*

"The Word became flesh" immediately evokes images of the Christmas story and a tiny babe wrapped in swaddling clothes. "And made His dwelling among us" reflects the great tabernacle in the midst of the tents of the children of Israel as they moved from oasis to oasis in the Sinai Desert.

God's house among our houses! We see it each day in cities and towns. On a quiet street a humble clapboard church shares a place with the homes of working families. An ancient brick church stands between towering skyscrapers. A cathedral thrusts its spire heavenward. Each gives its silent testimony to God who dwells among us in Word and sacraments. He lives among ordinary people going about their ordinary lives. Jesus, the Word made flesh, is part of birth and death, part of the lives of businesspeople, farmers, homemakers, students, and children. He listens to our prayers, rejoices in our laughter, and shares our tears.

The churches stand in the heart of our cities, in town squares, on suburban streets, and on country lanes. Each church building testifies to the God who through His Son, our Lord and Savior Jesus Christ, dwells in our midst, sharing the lives of His people.

Be with us, Lord Jesus, and bless us with Your grace and truth as we come and go. Amen.

Alston S. Kirk

Luke 24:15–32

Our Traveling Companion

My Presence will go with you, and I will give you rest. *Exodus 33:14*

We have walked the pathway of our life through almost another full year of time. As we continue in the days and weeks ahead, we have the promise of our traveling companion that He will go with us into the future. As God promised to be with Moses in his work of leading God's people, so He will go with us wherever the pathway of our life may lead us.

Our God is the holy triune God, the God of whom we have been speaking in these devotions. He is the almighty one, the forgiving Lord, the all-knowing Father, the ever-present God, the protector and keeper of all His children. We have this great and gracious God as our daily companion. As we walk in faith and trust in our Lord, we can walk fearlessly and confidently through life.

Our God not only goes with us but He also gives us the promise that He will support us. He daily forgives us all our sins for Jesus' sake. Through His Word, He guides our footsteps upon the ways that will lead to the accomplishment of our calling in life. Through His Word, He directs us safely over all stony paths and leads us to heaven. This is the life we lead when we walk with God.

O God, walk with me and talk to me along life's way; in Jesus' name. Amen.

Edgar C. Rakow

Job 33

My Life

Now this is what the LORD Almighty says, "Give careful thought to your ways." *Haggai 1:5*

I am alive. And great is the possession of life, the first and most precious gift of God. To feel the sunshine warm on my skin or the coolness of the rain; to glory in a sunset or the smile of a loved one; to revel in the exercise of my body or to relax in utter weariness; to eat and drink and talk and laugh and even to cry— all this is life. All this is God's gift to me.

Let me now consider my ways. What am I doing with my life? Are my years well spent or a waste? Am I thankful for life— or thoughtless? Does my life reflect the glory of the Creator?

But even more important, am I living all the possible dimensions of life? I share with all humanity an origin in the dust, and to that dust I shall return. But there is more to living than that. "I have come," said Jesus, "that they may have life, and have it to the full" (John 10:10). The gift of eternal life, which Christ came to give, begins here and now. It adds to life's meaning and purpose and courage and hope and peace. "I no longer live, but Christ lives in me. The life I live in the body I live by faith in the Son of God" (Galatians 2:20). Only then am I really alive. Great is the possession of this life!

Thank You, Lord Jesus, that new life is ours. Empower us by Your Word and sacraments to live always for You; for Your sake. Amen.

Walter E. Kraemer

Philippians 1:3–11

The Master Painter

We know that in all things God works for the good of those who love Him. *Romans 8:28*

It is intriguing to observe an artist at work. After sketching the outline of her subject on the canvas she sets to work on the painting proper. A dash of color here is followed by a bold stroke there. Bright and somber colors are intermingled to furnish shading and contrast. We cannot understand why the artist chooses this tint or that hue or why the strokes of her brush are sometimes heavy and sometimes light, but in the completed work every line and dash of color is full of meaning and purpose.

Our life is a canvas that God is preparing for the art gallery of heaven. Each day the master painter adds details until the picture is complete at life's end. The radiant colors are the joys and pleasures of life. The darker hues represent trials and suffering. Here and there some bold strokes from the master's brush seem to mar the picture. A dash of somber color seems meaningless. But in the end, under the divine artist's touch, there emerges an exquisite portrait.

In life "all things," whether joy or sorrow, "work for good," marvelously intermingled for our blessing as God's children.

Dear Lord, we thank You that all our experiences work together to bring us to our eternal home above. Amen.

Julius W. Acker

Ephesians 4:17–32

Love Is from God

God has poured out His love into our hearts by the Holy Spirit, whom He has given us. *Romans 5:5*

Let's not mess it up. Too many have the wrong idea about what forgiveness is. It is not excusing sin or "sweeping it under the rug." It is not tolerance of abusive or sinful behavior, nor is it a matter of time healing all wounds.

God tells us, " 'In your anger do not sin': Do not let the sun go down while you are still angry" (Ephesians 4:26). At times we have reason to be angry and to feel hurt. Then, with the Spirit's help, love takes over. Let the anger go and stop holding things over others or against them. From this point on, God calls us to be "kind and compassionate to one another" (Ephesians 4:32). As we forgive, we will have more concern for others than for what they did to us.

Is this possible? On our own, no way! But God pours out His love into the hearts of all who believe in His Son, enabling us to love others.

A man once asked Corrie ten Boom for her forgiveness because of what he had done to her and her sister in a German prison camp. As he extended his hand, she prayed, "Jesus, I can raise my hand toward him, but You must supply the love." Jesus did that for her, as He will for all of us.

Jesus, lover of my soul, help me to love others, even when it is hard to do so. Amen.

Barry J. Keurulainen

Hebrews 11:4

Lasting Impressions

Blessed are the dead who die in the Lord. … their deeds will follow them. *Revelation 14:13*

Many years ago a beautiful fern grew in a deep vale, nodding in the breeze. One day it fell and sank away. Years later a geologist went out with his hammer in the interest of his science. He struck a rock, and there in the seam lay the form of a fern—every leaf, every fiber, the most delicate traceries of the leaves imprinted in the sides of the cleft. It was the fern that ages before grew and dropped into the indistinguishable mass of vegetation. It perished, but its memorial was preserved, and today we have its legacy.

So it is with the stories of all beautiful lives that have served God and humankind and have vanished from the earth. Only a few names of the good and the useful in every age are preserved. The great multitude are forgotten. Earth keeps scant record of its benefactors. But there is a place where every kindness, be it ever so small, done in the name of Christ, is recorded and remembered. Nothing is lost; nothing is forgotten. The memorials are preserved in other lives, and someday every touch and trace and influence and impression will be revealed. The acts of worthy lives are cut deep in the eternal rock, where they shall be visible forever.

Your every act will in some shape or form affect the life and manner of others. Be it ever so insignificant, it nevertheless makes lasting impressions.

Dear Jesus, give me a humble and willing spirit to labor for You wherever You place me. Let me be faithful to You wherever You place me. Let me be faithful in imprinting Your image on other lives. Amen.

Alfred W. Koehler

Revelation 5:6–14

An Explosion of Praise

Worthy is the Lamb, who was slain to receive power and wealth and wisdom and strength and honor and glory and praise. *Revelation 5:12*

It isn't too often that people seem able to really get excited about something. It doesn't seem fashionable to demonstrate one's obvious delight and sing for joy.

Our text shows that this is not the way it is in heaven. While on earth we, the heirs and beneficiaries of God's grace in Christ, often worship God in a subdued manner. Heaven itself undergoes an explosion of praise and thanksgiving centering in Jesus Christ.

Since Christ was slain and by His blood ransomed all people for God, heaven is ringing with praise to Him for gaining followers "from every tribe and language and people and nation" and for making them "a kingdom and priests to serve our God" (Revelation 5:9–10).

Let the redeemed people of God accord the Savior glory and honor also here on earth, for He has broken the power of sin over them and has set them free to serve the living God. Let them sing: "Hosanna to the Son of David! Blessed is He who comes in the name of the Lord! Hosanna in the highest" (Matthew 21:9). Saints above and saints below have every reason to join in the celebration of our Lord's glorious victory.

Dearest Jesus, we rejoice, give thanks, and sing to You, for You alone are worthy. Amen.

Willis L. Wright

Ephesians 4:1–13

Our Birthday Gifts

We have different gifts, according to the grace given us.
Romans 12:6

Birthdays are synonymous with the giving and receiving of gifts. Few of us long remember or perhaps even retain those gifts, but we are usually ready for a new round of them.

Not always remembered either are those gifts we received early on from our heavenly Father. With what marvelous talents and abilities He already endowed us as He formed us in our mother's womb! And Paul in our text reminds us that a further giving took place at the time of our rebirth by Holy Baptism, when we received the Holy Spirit with His varying gifts. Reception into God's family is always marked by gifts distributed according to His grace in Jesus Christ.

A commentary on the use of God's gifts to us is provided by the story of the small boy who scraped together enough coins to buy a fine pair of gloves for his mother's birthday. Weeks later he noticed his mother's still chapped hands and asked why she wasn't wearing the gloves. She said she was so thankful for them that she was saving them. His noteworthy response: "But, Mom, you thank me best when you wear them!" How very true also of the special gifts God has given to us!

Help us, O Lord, to thank You best for our gifts by using them in the service of our Lord Jesus; for His sake. Amen.

Raymond L. Hartwig

Ephesians 2:1–10

Professional Challenge

Joseph collected all the food produced in those seven years of abundance in Egypt and stored it in the cities. *Genesis 41:48*

Joseph's early experiences were exciting, difficult, and at times unpleasant. Then, suddenly he became Egypt's prime minister. All this didn't happen casually. When Pharaoh designated him to be overseer, Joseph was 30 years of age. He brought considerable experience to his new job. Recall that period when he was in charge of Potiphar's household as well as later when he was supervisor of all the prisoners in jail. No question, Joseph had leadership qualities plus experience that promised success to this new undertaking. Indeed, he was an astute administrator with the public-relations ability to gain the people's confidence and trust so that during the years of plenty it was possible to lay in store much food in the cities throughout Egypt.

The lesson for us all, especially for graduates, is that in our professional life almost no one begins at the top. Success is not the result of chance or of "the breaks," but rather of solid preparation. The Christian views his life, including certain abilities and talents, as a gift from God. Life is a challenge to do our very best day by day to the Savior's glory.

Through Joseph's life, and especially Your own, Lord Jesus, You have given us inspiration to be faithful. Amen.

Raymond C. Hohenstein

Ephesians 5:21–33

An Invitation

On the third day a wedding took place at Cana in Galilee.
John 2:1

Wedding plans soon follow the excitement of an engagement. Invitations are sent well in advance to family members and friends, asking them to join the celebration. How meaningful when our Lord Jesus is also expressly invited to be one of the wedding guests!

The Lord is invited when the couple chooses to exchange their vows in God's house. The Lord is invited when the marriage service, as well as the marriage itself, is begun "in the name of the Father and of the Son and of the Holy Spirit." The Lord is invited when the couple in prayer asks the blessing of God on the union of husband and wife.

The presence of our Lord at a wedding brings an added element of joy to the celebration. How wonderful for the wedding couple to know of God's interest in their marriage. How gracious of God to supply His blessing to the marriage. And how good of God to model His love and forgiveness as both the example and the power for a husband and wife to live in love and forgiveness with each other.

Father, bless all husbands and wives and every family with Your love and forgiveness; in Jesus' name we pray. Amen.

Charles A. and Jeanette L. Groth

1 Peter 3:1–7

An Adventure of Faith

You are joint heirs of the grace of life. *1 Peter 3:7 RSV*

The richest people to enter the estate of holy matrimony are those whom God in the Scriptures calls His heirs. To be a son or daughter of the eternal, almighty God is to be rich indeed. When two people to whom God has said, "You are Mine," say this to each other, they are entering upon a great adventure of faith. And Christian marriage is just that—an adventure of faith.

Heirs of the grace of life can in Christian marriage find life's richest values together. You will find deepest happiness not in pleasing yourselves but in pleasing each other to please God. In pleasing God you will discover that you are pleasing each other.

Your chief purpose in marriage as heirs of God is to help each other get to heaven. This is the final aim and end of your adventure of faith. Your daily experiences are to be weighed in the balances of the eternal glory awaiting you. Your prayers for each other will include petitions for steadfastness in your faith in Christ so together you may receive the crown of glory won for you by Christ on the cross and certified to you by His resurrection.

Dear Lord, pour out a rich measure of Your Holy Spirit on all who are newly married so they may encourage each other to love and live for You; for Jesus' sake. Amen.

M. L. Koehneke

John 14:1–7

Our Father's House

In My Father's house are many rooms; if it were not so, I would have told you. *John 14:2*

During our lifetime we will have occupied any number of homes. Each of these major changes in our life can be a special time of reflection.

As we settle in and make this house our home, we ask God that His presence may cover us with His abundant grace. God has promised to abide with us if we abide in His Word. When God is present, our home becomes a holy place, as Jacob declared, "This is none other than the house of God; this is the gate of heaven" (Genesis 28:17). While we refer to our new home as "our house," it is really our "Father's house," for here we serve God and day by day forgive one another even as God has forgiven us.

There are many requests we make of God as we occupy our new home. We ask that He may bless our life together, grant us many joys, assist us in our work, comfort us in sorrow, and always deepen us in our faith in Jesus Christ, the Son of God, who once left His home above that here on earth He might give His life for our salvation.

Our new home, as solidly constructed as it may be, is not our final home. We are only temporary residents on earth, anticipating our permanent home above. Our home here and now is a forecourt of our heavenly home.

Dear Lord, bless our home here with Your presence as we look forward to our heavenly home with You; in Your name. Amen.

Unidentified

Luke 18:15–17

A Child, God's Gift

A woman giving birth to a child has pain because her time has come; but when the baby is born she forgets the anguish because of her joy that a child is born into the world. *John 16:21*

It is with joy and thanksgiving that parents receive a new son or daughter into the family. They are filled with gratitude because the mother who was sustained through the months of pregnancy and the hours of labor and childbirth now has the joy of holding their baby in her arms. They are thankful too for the help of doctors and nurses, through whom God has ministered His kindness and love.

Children are precious gifts from God, entrusted to the care of parents in His behalf. Aware of their privilege and responsibility, fathers and mothers implore God for the help they need to bring up their child in the Christian faith. Therefore they bring that child as soon as possible to Holy Baptism in the name of the triune God because it is their conviction that little children, no less than others, are saved from sin by Jesus Christ and that through the Sacrament of Baptism they are brought to this faith.

At the birth of a baby, parents ask God to bless their child with good health. It is their petition that this child will grow up in the love of God and bring joy into their hearts and home. As God has been the dwellingplace of His people in all generations, so He will guard and guide the person newly come into the world and made His own by water and the Word.

Gracious God, Father, Son, and Holy Spirit, we thank You for the gift of our child. Bless us all; for Jesus' sake. Amen.

Unidentified

Romans 6:1–10

Baptized into Your Name

I tell you the truth, no one can enter the kingdom of God unless he is born of water and the Spirit. *John 3:5*

Children learn to recognize their names at an early age. Once they learn to write, one of their first joys is to print their name. Their last name identifies them as members of a particular family. No matter what difficulty the last name may pose in writing or pronunciation, they are quick to master it.

Adults are also sensitive about their name. They wince and are quick to correct if someone mispronounces it. It is that important.

At our Baptism, we are given a name that identifies us as a member of the Christian family. Washed free from all our sins by the marvelous Sacrament of Baptism, we are given full rights as sons and daughters of the Most High God. We are now heirs of God, joint heirs with Christ. Forgiveness of sins, eternal life, the protection of angels, and the assurance that our prayers are heard are but a few of the marvelous gifts we are given through our Baptism. Through daily repentance our old nature, inherited from Adam, is drowned, and new life comes forth. Marked with the sign of the cross, the symbol of Christ's death, we are His through all eternity.

Almighty God, thanks and praise to You for washing us free of our sins in Baptism and for making us Your children forever. In Jesus' name we pray. Amen.

James Freese

John 2:1–11

A Wedding Anniversary

[Jesus] thus revealed His glory, and His disciples put their faith in Him. *John 2:11*

The miracle Jesus performed at the marriage in Cana reminds you of the many wonders of His love that you experience in your lives. It is as St. Paul has written: "My God will meet all your needs according to His glorious riches in Christ Jesus" (Philippians 4:19).

God provides for all the needs of your married life. The blessings you are reminded of today—health and strength, home and family, children and relatives, good friends and faithful neighbors—all are the gifts of God in Christ. You are especially thankful for all spiritual blessings: for peace with God through the reconciling work of Jesus Christ. This peace you are finding to be the basis of your marriage because Christ's love for you sustains the love you have for one another as husband and wife.

The miracle of Jesus drew this response: "His disciples put their faith in Him." By the power He demonstrated in turning water into wine He showed Himself to be the Son of God. In faith the disciples accepted Him as such. Similarly, all that Christ has done for you—all that He means to you in your married life—prompts you to trust in Him.

Dear Father, thank You for all the blessings You have given us in our life together. As You continue to pour out Your blessings on us, keep our eyes open to Your goodness and our hearts thankful for each other and to You; for Jesus' sake. Amen.

Unidentified

Revelation 21:1–4

The Wonders of Heaven

God Himself will be with them and be their God. He will wipe away every tear from their eyes. *Revelation 21:3–4*

Heaven will be wonderful! We will have no tears, death, sorrow, crying, or pain. We will be without sin. We will see Jesus as He really is. In His presence we will live forever.

God promises to answer all the unanswered questions of life. In heaven we will completely understand how in everything God worked for our good. The pieces of the puzzle of life will be put together for us, and we will praise God for all His dealings with us. This is true: No eye has seen nor any ear heard the wonderful things God has prepared for those who love Him.

What boggles the mind more than anything else is that sinners like us are going to heaven. But our Savior assures us that "whoever believes in Him shall not perish, but have eternal life" (John 3:16).

It is incredible that God has given us the gift of eternal life in heaven. We do not deserve it. We never will. Only by God's undeserved love, His amazing grace, have we come to faith and received heaven as our home. Now as strangers on earth we joyfully live for Him before we live with Him in our heavenly home.

Lord, I believe that for me to live is Christ and to die is gain. I thank You for opening the door of heaven for me; in Jesus' name. Amen.

Andrew Simcak Jr.

Index

Abortion 69, 119, 183, 302, 352

Abundant Life 3, 86, 134, 194, 254, 363

Advocate 302

Alcohol 146, 208

Angels 44, 355

Anger 162, 317, 365

Baptism 263, 373, 374

Bible 35, 133, 193, 291, 320, 326

Body 104, 146, 230, 268, 279, 321

Calling 108, 168, 182

Caring 23, 64, 93, 139, 156, 253, 289, 317, 345

Children 57, 87, 92, 183, 246, 270, 288, 339, 373

Christian Life 40, 117, 124, 149, 157, 215, 278, 341, 348

Church 32, 46, 53, 158, 172, 228, 249, 265, 305, 361

Citizenship 45, 135, 184, 310

Commandments 84

Commissioned 24, 199, 206, 290, 318

Commitment 108, 115

Communication 148, 169, 260

Conflict 50, 225, 232, 246, 267, 323

Conformity 7

Congregation 80, 93, 130, 132, 227, 269, 319, 356

Conscience 63

Contentment 27, 153, 293, 335

Courage 5, 192, 255

Creation 34, 82, 104, 181, 209, 277

Cursing 285

Decisions 35, 266, 336

Devil 89, 272

Discipleship 226, 241, 271

Divorce 295

Doubt 33, 217

Earth 167

Encouragement 151

Enemies 240, 281

Envy 27, 202

Eternity 42, 189, 195, 308

Euthanasia 69

Failure 28, 171, 220

Faith 12, 37, 81, 113, 137, 217, 221, 222

False Beliefs 77, 284, 291

Family 85, 155

Fate 61, 210, 292

Father 39, 187

Feelings 12

Focus 60, 95

Forgiveness 22, 75, 123, 209, 232, 266, 282, 306, 322, 365

Friendship 8, 68, 141, 197

Future 5, 98

Gambling 293

Goal 42, 237, 308, 322, 343

God 4, 39, 53, 61, 187, 252, 362

God's Gifts 13, 76, 110, 174, 175, 252, 258, 297, 318, 368

Good Deeds 37, 114, 128, 177, 219, 282, 331, 338, 366

Gospel 31, 59, 94, 178, 191, 306

Graduation 369

Growth, Christian 180, 221, 231, 320

Guilt 13, 74, 102

Heaven 41, 152, 353, 367, 376

Holy Spirit 25, 76

Holy Communion 354

Home 106, 351, 372

Homosexuality 211

Hospitality 344

Jesus 54, 68, 88, 96, 194, 229, 360

Joy 212, 223, 257

Judgment Day 20, 136, 300, 332

Law 306

Leisure 107, 159, 261

Love 4, 15, 43, 47, 65, 134, 204, 224, 239

Marriage 78, 176, 190, 218, 295, 309, 370, 371, 375

Meditation 131, 242, 264, 273

Mentor(s) 26, 38, 120, 186, 316

Mind 13, 214, 279

Ministry 200

Miracles 103

Mission 17, 52

Morality 330

Motivation 11, 79, 83, 91, 121, 179, 185, 303, 324

Neighbor 58, 65

New Life 145, 166, 313

Obedience 301

Offering 160, 234, 256, 328

Opportunity 125, 129, 262, 276

Opposition 164, 304

Parents 358

Plans 126, 140, 147, 161, 182, 203, 210, 245, 280, 350, 357, 364

Possessions 62, 153, 244, 258, 335, 342

Praise 116, 285, 347, 367

Prayer 25, 49, 66, 70, 109, 126, 138, 143, 163,

197, 201, 207, 224, 248, 259, 281, 289, 294, 310, 315, 316, 325, 329, 334, 340

Preaching 144

Pride 202

Priorities 14, 133, 189, 196, 307, 353

Purpose 10, 56, 105, 359

Responsibility 71

Sacrament 235

Salvation 311

Self-Worth 111, 216

Sex 29, 113, 176, 230, 274, 330

Sin 7, 123, 218, 243

Single Adults 99

Standards 21, 84, 154, 238, 287

Stewardship 48, 55, 83, 167, 349

Stress 19, 264

Submission 112

Success 72, 171, 185, 220

Talents 139, 216, 286, 300, 307, 356

Teaching 57, 270

Teacher 186

Thanksgiving 48, 90, 97, 127, 223, 265

Time 6, 20, 118, 170, 195, 273, 296, 307

Today 236, 296

Trinity 284

Troubles 235, 250, 299

Values 7, 41, 188, 205, 251, 272, 298, 314

Virtue 36, 51, 100, 113, 173, 275, 337

Vocation 9, 16, 65, 198, 233, 247

Vounteerism 30, 142, 331

*Witness 17, 73, 87, 101, 122, 150, 171, 213, 227,
        283, 304, 346*

Word of God 67, 144, 235, 294

World 292

Worry 327

Worship 11, 18, 165, 179, 242, 312, 333